Praise for

"One of the best across-the-[ ] community strategic understanding in modern Marxist theory. A must read for anyone serious about the coming systemic transformation."
—**GAR ALPEROVITZ**, author, *What Then Must We Do? Straight Talk About the Next American Revolution*

"Lebowitz reminds us of the continued power of the socialist dream. Attentive to developments in international socialism as well as pressing issues of climate change, the essays in this collection impress the urgency of the collective struggle to bring the capitalist nightmare to an end."
—**JODI DEAN**, author, *The Communist Horizon*

"Does our 21st-century world generate a socialist imperative? Michael Lebowitz thinks that it does. . . . With lucidity and acuity, he moves from the nightmare of capitalism to the dream of socialism and explores its specific contours, bringing into play insights gleaned from historical experiences of the USSR, Yugoslavia, Cuba, Vietnam, and Venezuela and charting a viable path forward for our times."
—**HELENA SHEEHAN**, Professor Emerita, Dublin City University

"This is a must read for everyone struggling for a better world. Once again, Michael Lebowitz complements frontline struggles against the nightmare of capitalism with an audacious and grounded vision of a socialist alternative. Together with our struggles, *The Socialist Imperative* will be an important part of making that vision a reality."
—**STEVE WILLIAMS**, National Coordinator for LeftRoots

"Karl Marx once asked who educates the educator? His answer was 'revolutionizing practice.' Michael Lebowitz exemplifies such revolutionizing practice in today's struggle for a Socialism for the 21st Century, in which he has already played such an outsized role. His new work, *The Socialist Imperative*, constituting his most expansive vision yet, and a companion work to his *The Socialist Alternative*, is an informed, inspiring, and, for me, altogether indispensable guide to the necessary socialist transition of our time."—**JOHN BELLAMY FOSTER**, editor of *Monthly Review*; professor of sociology, University of Oregon

THE SOCIALIST IMPERATIVE

From Gotha *to Now*

by MICHAEL A. LEBOWITZ

MONTHLY REVIEW PRESS

New York

Copyright © 2015 by Michael A. Lebowitz
All Rights Reserved

Library of Congress Cataloging-in-Publication Data
available from publisher.

Typeset in Minion Pro 11/14

Monthly Review Press
146 West 29th Street, Suite 6W
New York, New York 10001

www.monthlyreview.org

5 4 3 2 1

Contents

*In memory of Hugo Chávez Frias, who understood
that it is necessary to reinvent socialism and struggled to do so.
We look in the same direction.*

Handwritten notes in top margin:

sources of
wealth –
labor & nature
degraded, destroyed
&
deformed

capital – vampire
Labor – host
+
Nature

Foreword

"Change the system, not the climate!" More and more, this demand has emerged in response to the overwhelming signs of environmental destruction around us. It reflects a growing understanding of the incompatibility of capitalism and life. However, many people concerned about what is happening to the planet think that regulations that check the destructiveness of current patterns are sufficient. Measures that try to limit carbon emissions by offering big carrots and small sticks, that propose taxes to encourage rational economic actors to choose less harmful options, that offer subsidies for forms of power generation deemed less harmful to the environment—all these efforts to patch up the problems that have emerged remain the first choice of those who look upon themselves as realists, living in the real world.

The idea that we can regulate abuses within capitalism is not unique to environmental issues. We see the same pattern when it comes to financial crises. New regulations, new limits, new forms of oversight are seen as a solution to abuse and excess. They are proposed as ways to encourage good behavior on the part of the agents who have created the situation. From this perspective, bad capitalists rather than capitalism itself are identified as the source of all evils. Indeed, a "bad" neoliberal capitalism is viewed as the enemy, which implies that all can be resolved by a "good" capitalism.

Failure to understand the system, to grasp the nature of capital and capitalism, underlies all such utopian illusions. It is a failure to recognize that the logic of capital is its tendency to expand without limits and in the process, as Marx argued, destroy human beings and nature, the original sources of wealth. Once we realize this and act without illusions, we see clearly that the condition for building a society that can produce enriched human beings and enriched nature must be, as it always has been, ending capitalism.

This is the socialist imperative—end capitalism and build a society of associated producers oriented to the full development of human potential, an association that (in the words of the *Communist Manifesto*) understands that the free development of all is the condition for the free development of each. In this respect, the socialist imperative is not new. However, the clash between capital's tendency to expand without limits and the existence of the limits given by the natural world has now brought humanity to the point where the need to act upon the socialist imperative is immediate.

What are we waiting for? There are many reasons why people do not move to put an end to capital. One, to which Marx pointed, is that capital tends to produce a working class that sees capital's logic as self-evident natural laws, that is, as common sense. Another is the belief that there simply is no alternative to capitalism, an idea strengthened by the experience of attempts to build socialism in the last century, including their ultimate retreat to capitalism. Both have contributed to the death of our dreams; and, without the dream of an alternative, there will be no struggle to end capitalism.

To restore the dream, we have to learn from previous experiences. Accordingly, essays included in this volume explore party-building efforts in nineteenth-century Germany (and the commentaries of Marx and Engels on the Gotha Program), "real socialism" in the Soviet Union, market-self-management in Yugoslavia, the emergence of the concept of the "elementary triangle of socialism" in Venezuela, and Vietnam's experience with a market economy "with a socialist orientation." Though learning from experience is important, we must make our own paths. This is the theme in the section "Struggling to Build Socialism Now" (chapters 7 through 11), where we consider the working class as a revolutionary subject, the concept of democracy in relation to building socialism, the moral economy of the working class, the state in socialism, and the struggle to end capitalism.

As will be seen in the headnote introducing each chapter, these essays, with the exception of the opening and closing ones, written especially for this volume, originated from around the world— some from talks in Yugoslavia, Serbia, India, Greece, Cuba, and Canada, and others prepared for publication or implementation in Turkey, Iran, and Venezuela. Despite the differences in origins and particular topics, there is a recurring theme: a focus upon Marx's key link of human development and practice, the importance of building the capacity and strength of the working class through spaces and practices like workers' councils and communal councils, and what happens when you do not.

Repetition of key points, quotations, and passages in a collection of essays and talks centered about a particular theme is not unusual. In reviewing the text as a whole, I concluded that such parts were both necessary to develop particular arguments and also that their appearance in different combinations reveals different aspects of those parts. Accordingly, I have retained most of these and ask the indulgence of the reader for whom familiarity breeds contempt. Similarly, characteristic of such a collection is the accumulation of many debts as the result of encouragement, criticism, and comments in relation to these essays (and linked work). Among those to whom I owe thanks are Greg Albo, John Bellamy Foster, Patrick Bond, Bill Burgess, Al Campbell, Fred Fuentes, Sam Gindin, Robin Hahnel, Marta Harnecker (as always), Marty Hart-Landsberg, Fred Magdoff, John Milios, Leo Panitch, John Riddell, and assorted comrades in various countries who may prefer not to be named. Special thanks go to Michael Yates, for his excellent work and support as editor and guide at Monthly Review Press, in addition to continuing his own individual contributions.

Development of the vision of an alternative to capital and commitment to make that vision real—this is the socialist imperative. By struggling to realize the socialist dream, we can change circumstances and ourselves; we can make ourselves fit to create a new world of rich human beings and enriched nature. The need to combine that vision and the purposeful will to achieve it has never been greater than now, as capitalism's destruction of human beings and nature and the prospect of barbarism increasingly haunt us. We need that combination to sustain our struggles and build the dream. In the words of the revolutionary Hindi poet, Maheshwar (translation thanks to Kavita Krishnan, upon whom I draw in the concluding essay), "*With tomorrow's songs on our lips, our fight today continues.*"

—22 JANUARY 2015

Building Socialism:
Ideas and Experiences

1. The Capitalist Nightmare and the Socialist Dream

In this essay, I revisit themes from earlier books with new insights and a new urgency as the result of my belated consideration of the ecological dimension to which I have given lip service in the past.

In the beginning is the dream, the promise of a society that permits the full development of human potential, a society in which we relate to each other as human beings and where the mere recognition of the need of another is sufficient to induce our deed. In the beginning is the vision of a society where the products of our past activity serve our own need for development and where in working together we develop our capacities, our needs, our human wealth.

Vampires and Zombies

Capitalism is not that dream. Rather, as David McNally has illustrated, it is a world haunted by vampires and zombies—the vampire that lives by sucking living labor and not letting go "while there remains a single muscle, sinew or drop of blood to be exploited," the zombies whose life-energies have been absorbed into capital and who stagger hungrily through the shopping malls.[1]

Like the vampire, capital has a never-ending "thirst for the living blood of labour" because that is the source of its growth, and growth is at the very core of its nature.[2] Capital, Marx understood, constantly drives to go beyond its quantitative barrier: "The goal-determining activity of capital can only be that of growing wealthier, i.e. of magnification, of increasing itself."[3] Capital, indeed, has "one sole driving force, the drive to valorize itself, to create surplus value" and "vampire-like, lives only by sucking living labour, and lives the more, the more labour it sucks."[4]

At the heart of capitalist relations is the process in which a worker relinquishes control over her productive activity and the property rights in the product of that activity to the capitalist and receives in return a wage. That transaction gives the capitalist the power to compel the performance of surplus labor in the process of production; the sale of labor-power, in short, is the condition for capitalist exploitation—a process facilitated by the capitalist's ability to increase the amount of work performed by workers (extensively or intensively) and to reduce the wage component (either by driving down wages or by increasing productivity relative to wages). As with the metabolism of the vampire, which converts the blood of its victims into its eternal life, capital consumes human beings and nature (the elements of the labor process) and transforms these through its particular metabolism into products containing surplus value, the source of its life-blood.[5]

Yet, capital cannot survive simply by exploitation within the sphere of production. It must sell the commodities produced under its reign to secure money, its true life-blood. Once it succeeds (in this "second act") in making the surplus value contained in commodities *real*, it can use a portion of the proceeds (surplus value in its form as money) to expand. The accumulation of capital is the result of its "constant drive to go beyond its quantitative limit: an endless process," its search for eternal life.[6]

Capital's Barriers

There is more, however, to the advance of capital than merely quantitative growth. Capital's never-ending hunger brings it constantly up against obstacles to its growth and, as it drives beyond those barriers, it develops qualitatively. Consider some of the barriers that capital has encountered in the sphere of production. The resistance of workers to the extension of the workday and to the driving down of wages compelled capital to find ways to change the mode of production it inherited in order to grow upon the basis of increased productivity. Capital succeeded by introducing a new form of organization based upon new divisions of labor. Capital's dependence upon the training of skilled workers under the system of manufacture emerged, however, as another barrier; accordingly, capital introduced machines, allowing it to go beyond this "regulating principle of social production." Thus "the barriers placed in the way of domination by this same regulating principle" fell.[7] Similarly, on the basis of the labor-intensive mode of production it inherited, capital's ability to grow without limit was checked by the pace of natural population growth: "The demand for wage-labor therefore grew rapidly with every accumulation of capital, while the supply only followed slowly behind."[8]

For these reasons, capital went beyond these particular barriers to the extraction of surplus labor by developing a "specifically capitalist mode of production," one characterized by machinery and the factory system. To the extent, though, that the machine builders themselves were "a class of workers who, owing to the semi-artistic nature of their employment, could increase their numbers only gradually, and not by leaps and bounds," capital's advance was still checked.[9] With the development of production of machines by machines, however, capital now created for itself "an adequate technical foundation."[10] The story of capital, in short, is one of qualitative as well as quantitative change—the result of its continuing ability to leap over all barriers to its growth. With the development of a specifically capitalist mode of production, capital acquired "an elasticity, a capacity for sudden extension by leaps and bounds, which comes up against no barriers but those presented by the availability of raw materials and the extent of sales outlets."[11]

What are those barriers presented by the availability of raw materials? One that Marx stressed was that the output of natural products could *not* grow by leaps and bounds. Given that the growth and production of plant and animal products are "subject to certain organic laws involving naturally determined periods of time," they cannot be suddenly increased. Accordingly, in periods of expansion, "the demand for these raw materials grows more rapidly than their supply, and their price therefore rises."[12] And the result of this relative underproduction of raw materials, as with all barriers to the growth of capital, is reflected in a fall in the rate of profit: "The general law [is] that, with other things being equal, the rate of profit varies inversely as the value of the raw material." [13]

Yet even here, capital contains within it the means by which it can transcend this barrier: "Raw materials are supplied from a greater distance," "their production is expanded," and "all kinds of surrogates are now employed that were previously unused."[14] Marx was clear that capital refuses to accept any limits posed by organic conditions to its growth:

> Hence exploration of all of nature in order to discover new, useful qualities in things; . . . new (artificial) preparation of natural objects, by which they are given new use values. The exploration of the earth in all directions, to discover new things of use as well as new useful qualities of the old; such as new qualities of them as raw materials etc; the development of the natural sciences, hence, to their highest point. . . . is likewise a condition of production founded on capital.[15]

This tendency of capital to drive beyond immediate barriers posed by organic requirements can be seen clearly in Marx's discussion of the original "metabolic rift," which John Bellamy

Foster has done so much to bring to our attention.[16] Drawing upon Justus von Liebig's groundbreaking analysis of how urbanization prevented "the return to the soil of its constituent elements consumed by man in the form of food and clothing" and thereby hindered "the operation of the eternal natural condition for the lasting fertility of the soil," Marx described this development as the disturbance of "the metabolic interaction between man and the earth."[17] There has been, he argued, "a squandering of the vitality of the soil"—the result of "an irreparable rift in the interdependent process of social metabolism, a metabolism prescribed by the natural laws of life itself."[18]

Capital found several ways to navigate past this particular obstacle. As Foster has detailed, the exhaustion of the soil as the result of "the blind desire for profit" led first to the necessary "manuring of English fields with guano" and then to the development of synthetic phosphates, which could restore nitrogen content to the soil.[19] Further, consider inventions such as the cotton gin, which "increased the production of cotton," "colonization of foreign lands, which are thereby converted into settlements for growing the raw material of the mother country," "a new and international division of labour"— all ways in which capital went beyond the barrier posed by "the availability of raw materials."[20]

And then there are the barriers presented by "the extent of sales outlets." Here it is obvious that capital produces its own barriers, that "the *true barrier* to capitalist production is *capital itself.*"[21] All the successes of capital that allow it to drive up the rate of exploitation in the sphere of production come back to haunt it when it comes to realizing the surplus value contained in commodities: "The more productivity develops, the more it comes into conflict with the narrow basis on which the relations of consumption rest." Accordingly, since the commodities must be sold within this "framework of antagonistic conditions of distribution," there is a "contradiction between the conditions in which this surplus-value was produced and the conditions in which it was realized."[22] And the result is "constant tension between the restricted dimensions of consumption on the capitalist basis, and a production that is constantly striving to overcome these immanent barriers."[23]

Thus capital must find ways to expand consumption, without at the same time engaging in self-denial with respect to its thirst for surplus labor: "A precondition of production based on capital is therefore the production of a *constantly widening sphere of circulation*."[24] To satisfy this requirement, capital is driven to find ways for "the production of new consumption," and it pursues this by: (1) "quantitative expansion of existing consumption," (2) "creation of new needs by propagating existing ones in a wide circle," and (3) "production of *new* needs and discovery and creation of new use values."[25]

Nothing must stop capital. Thus capital "drives beyond natural barriers and prejudices ... as well as all traditional, confined, complacent, encrusted satisfactions of personal needs." Capital's tendency to grow without limit is present in the sphere of circulation as well as in production. "The tendency to create the *world market* is directly given in the concept of capital itself. Every limit appears as a barrier to be overcome."[26] And, as capital drives forward "to tear down every spatial barrier" to exchange and to "conquer the whole earth for its market," it also strives "to annihilate this space with time, i.e. to reduce to a minimum the time spent in motion from one place to another."[27]

Capital's success in creating the world market and global capitalism, however, does not allow it to escape the contradiction between the production of surplus value and its realization. It cannot escape the recurring tendency for economic crises that are the result of "*overproduction*, the fundamental contradiction of developed capital."[28] Marx was clear on this point: "The bourgeois mode of production contains within itself a barrier to the free development of the productive forces, a barrier which comes to the surface in crises and, in particular, in *overproduction*—the basic phenomenon in crises."[29]

But crises "are never more than momentary, violent solutions for the existing contradictions, violent eruptions that reestablish the disturbed balance for the time being."[30] What was significant about a crisis is that it reveals the existence of a barrier to capital. It does not, however, in itself portend an end to capitalism.

The Undead

Consider what our discussion of capital's barriers reveals. Over and over, Marx talks about barriers: in the sphere of production, in the sphere of circulation, in capital as a whole. And, over and over again, he demonstrates that capital can drive beyond each barrier to its growth; indeed it goes beyond all barriers. In doing so, too, it develops qualitatively. Barriers, contradictions, are not impasses; rather, they are a source of movement, change, and development. A barrier is not a limit. Rather, a barrier is a limit that can be *negated*, that can be surpassed. As Hegel explained the concept in his *Science of Logic*, "By the very fact that something has been determined as barrier, it has already been surpassed."[31] Indeed, the surpassing of barriers is the way in which a thing develops: "The plant passes over the barrier of existing as a seed, and over the barrier of existing as blossom, fruit or leaf."[32]

As we have seen, Marx embraced this concept of the barrier. "Capital," he explained, "is the endless and limitless drive to go beyond its limiting barrier. Every boundary is and has to be a barrier for it."[33] In that tendency to drive beyond every barrier, capital posits Growth as the third term in the sequence: Growth-Barrier-Growth. Although its barriers are constantly overcome, they are just as constantly posited, "and inasmuch as it [capital] both posits a barrier *specific* to itself, and on the other side equally drives over and beyond *every* barrier, it is the living contradiction."[34]

This process of creating barriers, transcending them, and creating them anew is endless. It is an infinite process. Indeed, it was in the course of exploring the relationship between Ought and Barrier that Hegel investigated the manner in which the concept of the Finite passes into the concept of Infinity: "The Finite (containing both Ought and Barrier) thus is self-contradictory; it cancels itself and passes away. . . . [But] the finite in perishing has not perished; so far it has only become another finite, which, however, in turn perishes in the sense of passing over into another finite, and so on, perhaps ad infinitum."[35]

Does capital's ability to drive over and beyond all barriers, then, mean that it is *infinite*, that eternal life is its fate? For capital to be other than infinite, for it to be finite, it must be incapable of surpassing a particular barrier. One barrier must, in fact, be its Limit. If it does have a Limit, then capital is finite and must perish. As Hegel put it, "its perishing is not merely contingent, so that it could be without perishing. It is rather the very being of finite things, that they contain the seeds of perishing as their own Being-in-Self and the hour of their birth is the hour of their death."[36]

Is capital a finite thing? If it has only barriers, it will always find a way to renew itself. Although repeatedly facing crises, these will be temporary, mere obstacles that, in their transcendence, allow capital to develop qualitatively. However much we struggle against capitalism, dead labor will continue to nourish itself by drawing upon living labor unless capital has a Limit.

Capital's Waste Products: Workers

The standard assertion by Marxists is that capitalism contains the seeds of its own destruction. Capital, we are taught, is finite because it contains a Limit—the working class, created, united, and expanded by capital in the course of its development. As the *Communist Manifesto* famously declared, what capital produces, "above all, is its own grave-diggers. Its fall and the victory of the proletariat are equally inevitable."[37]

Yet, who are those real subjects assigned the historic mission of ending capitalism? The working class does not spring full-grown from Marx's forehead as the pristine embodiment of the idea of capital's finiteness. The working class in capitalism is a product of capital. As in every process of production, every process of human activity, there are two results, joint products. These are the change in the object of labor and the change in the laborer herself. Consider the second product, the human product. To understand Marx's rage against capitalism, it is essential to recognize explicitly that, for him, workers are not only exploited under capitalist relations of production. They are also *deformed*. The social metabolism of capital does not only convert natural materials and human beings into surplus value. It also produces a particular kind of worker, a crippled human being. This is one of its waste products.

In capitalism the worker exists to satisfy the need of capital to grow. Within the capitalist workplace, people are subjected to "the powerful will of a being outside them, who subjects their activity to his purpose."[38] Marx described the result of this subordination to that alien power. In *Capital*, he stressed the mutilation, the impoverishment, the "crippling of body and mind" of the worker "bound hand and foot for life to a single specialized operation" that occurs in the division of labor characteristic of the capitalist process of manufacturing. But did capital's development of machinery rescue workers from this fate? No, he said, it *completes* the "separation of the intellectual faculties of the production process from manual labour." It completes, in short, the crippling of body and mind.[39]

In this situation, Marx explained, head and hand become separate and hostile, and "every atom of freedom, both in bodily and in intellectual activity" is lost. While capital develops productive forces to achieve its preconceived goal (the growth of profits and capital), "all means for the development of production undergo a dialectical inversion." The result, Marx indicated, is that "they distort the worker into a fragment of a man," and they degrade him and "alienate from him the intellectual potentialities of the labour process."[40]

These are the human products of capital, which exist alongside the commodities containing the labor extracted from workers. Think of what this means in terms of the worker's capacities. "Labour-power, or labour capacity," Marx indicated, is "the aggregate of those mental and physical capabilities existing in the physical form, the living personality, of a human being, capabilities which he sets in motion whenever he produces a use-value of any kind."[41] In the "dialectical inversion" characteristic of capitalism, the mental and physical capacities of individual producers are degraded.

For workers subject to the capitalist inversion, producing is a process of a "complete emptying-out," "total alienation," the "sacrifice of the human end-in-itself to an entirely external end."[42] Indeed, the world of wealth faces the worker "as an alien world dominating him." And that alien world dominates the worker more and more because capital constantly creates new needs to consume as the result of its requirement to realize the surplus value contained in commodities. Upon this creation of new needs, Marx noted, "the contemporary power of capital rests." Every new need for capitalist commodities is a new link in the golden chain that links workers to capital.[43]

How else but with money, the true need that capitalism creates, can we fill the vacuum? We compensate for that "emptying-out" by filling the void with things. We are driven to consume. In short, the joint product of capitalist production that Marx identified in *Capital* is the fragmented, crippled human being whose enjoyment consists in possessing and consuming things. More and more things. In addition to zombie-laborers, the mindless workers subjected to "the powerful will of a being outside them" to produce surplus value, capital produces the zombie-consumers whose appetites can never be satisfied.

Capital's Waste Products: Nature

This is only one side of capital's waste products. In addition, Marx described how capitalism tends to destroy the natural environment. We already have seen that while capital's tendency to grow by leaps and bounds comes up against a barrier insofar as plant and animal products are "subject to certain organic laws involving naturally determined periods of time," capital constantly drives beyond that barrier. However, if we consider this interaction from the *other* side, the side of nature, we can see that the "irreparable" metabolic rift that Marx described is neither a short-term disturbance nor unique to agriculture. Indeed, the "squandering of the vitality of the soil" is a paradigm for the way in which the "metabolism prescribed by the natural laws of life itself" is violated under capitalist relations of production.

Nature has its own metabolic process through which it converts various inputs and transforms these into the basis for its reproduction. In his discussion of the production of wheat, for example, Marx identified a "vegetative or physiological process" involving the seeds and "various chemical ingredients supplied by the manure, salts contained in the soil, water, air, light." Through this process, inorganic components are "assimilated by the organic components and transformed into organic material." Their form is changed in this metabolic process, from inorganic to organic through what Marx called "the expenditure of nature."[44] Also part of the "universal metabolism of nature" is the further transformation of organic components, their deterioration and dying through their "consumption by elemental forces."[45] In this way, the conditions for rebirth (for example, the "vitality of the soil") are themselves products of this metabolic process. "The seed becomes the unfolded plant, the blossom fades, and so forth": birth, death, renewal are moments characteristic of the "metabolism prescribed by the natural laws of life itself."[46]

This universal metabolism of nature, however, must be distinguished from the relation in which a human being "mediates, regulates and controls the metabolism between himself and nature."[47] That labor process involves the "appropriation of what exists in nature for the requirements of man. It is the universal condition for the metabolic interaction between man and nature." This "ever-lasting nature-imposed condition of human existence," Marx pointed out, is "independent of every form of that existence, or rather it is common to all forms of society in which human beings live."[48]

Nevertheless, though it is a useful abstraction, in the real world there is no general labor process. The "metabolic interaction between man and nature" always occurs "within and through a specific form of society."[49] That is, "purposeful activity," which begins with a preconceived goal, always occurs within specific social relations of production. Under capitalist relations of production, that preconceived goal is the growth of capital, and the particular metabolic process that occurs is one in which human labor and nature are converted into surplus value, the basis for that growth.

Accordingly, rather than a process that begins with "man and his labour on one side, nature and its materials on the other," in capitalist relations the starting point is capital, and "the labour process is a process between things the capitalist has purchased, things which belong to him."[50] Nature, "the universal material for labour," the "original larder" for human existence, consequently becomes a means not for human existence but for capital's existence.[51] And that has an obvious implication, because "the entire spirit of capitalist production—which is oriented towards the most immediate monetary profit—stands in contradiction to agriculture, which has to concern itself with the whole gamut of permanent conditions of life required by the chain of human generations."[52]

As the result of the logic of capital, "capitalist production, therefore, only develops the technique and the degree of combination of the social process of production by simultaneously undermining the original sources of all wealth—the soil and the worker." In the same way as it affects workers, the actions of capital diminish the capacities of nature: "All progress in increasing the fertility of the soil for a given time is a progress towards ruining the more long-lasting sources of that fertility."[53]

Yet there is nothing inherent in agricultural production that leads to the "squandering of the vitality of the soil" that Marx described. On the contrary, Marx pointed out that a society can bequeath the earth "in an improved state to succeeding generations."[54] But this requires an understanding that "agriculture forms a mode of production *sui generis*, because the organic process is involved, in addition to the mechanical and chemical process, and the natural reproduction process is merely controlled and guided"; the same is true, too, in the case of fishing, hunting, and forestry.[55] Maintenance and improvement of the vitality of the soil and of other sectors dependent upon organic conditions requires the recognition of the necessity for the "systematic restoration as a regulative law of social production."[56]

Capital, however, is propelled not by recognition of the organic requirements for production and reproduction but by preoccupation with its need to grow. With every increase in capitalist production, there are growing demands upon the natural environment, and the tendency to exhaust nature's larder and to generate unabsorbed and unutilizable waste is not at all limited to the metabolic rift that Marx described with respect to capitalist agriculture. Thus, Marx indicated that "extractive industry (mining is the most important) is likewise an industry *sui generis*, because no reproduction process whatever takes place in it, at least not one under our control or known to us," and, he noted as examples, "the exhaustion of forests, coal and iron mines, and so on."[57]

Except insofar as its growing demands upon nature are reflected in rising costs and falling profits, capital has no interest in the contradiction between its logic and the "natural laws of life itself." As we have seen, faced with barriers to its growth, capital seeks a way to get beyond each particular barrier to posit growth once more. In short, the contradiction between its drive for infinite growth and a finite, limited earth is not a concern because for capital there is always another source of growth to be found. Like the vampire, it seeks the last possible drop of blood and does not worry about keeping its host alive.

Accordingly, since capital does not worry about "simultaneously undermining the original sources of all wealth—the soil and the worker," sooner or later it destroys both.[58] Marx's comment with respect to capital's drive to drain every ounce of energy from the worker describes capital's relation to the natural world precisely: "*Après moi le deluge!* is the watchword of every capitalist and every capitalist nation. Capital therefore takes no account of the health and the length of life of the worker, unless society forces it to do so."[59]

Capital's Waste Products: Society

Can the society produced by capital succeed in putting an end to capital's destruction of human beings and nature? That is, can it be a limit to capital? Or, at best, does it force upon capital particular barriers, such as restrictions on the workday or specific environmental controls, that capital can drive beyond? What is the society produced by capital, and what can it do?

To paraphrase Margaret Thatcher, in the world of workers that capital produces, there is no such thing as society. Rather, there are individual owners of labor-power and their families. Self-interest drives them, and their bond is "based not upon the association of man with man, but on the separation of man from man."[60]

Capital produces this separation insofar as its relation to workers takes the form of individual commodity transactions. Separate owners of labor-power compete every day with each other as sellers. They compete to sell their capacities to particular capitalist purchasers and, given that capital in reality exists as many capitals, tend to identify their own interest with the success of the particular capitals that employ them rather than with the workers employed by other capitalists. Their separation, as Engels explained, "makes nothing else possible for them but restriction to their immediate, everyday interests, to the wish for a good wage for good work"; and it "restricts the workers to seeing their interest in that of their employers, thus making every single section of workers into an auxiliary army for the class employing them."[61]

That separation is not simply the result of capital's form of existence as separate and competing capitals. In its drive to maximize its growth, capital constantly searches for cheaper sources of labor and often finds these where workers for historical reasons are accustomed to lower standards of necessity. The effect is to increase the intensity of competition among workers where they are unable to bridge the separation among them; for example, because of divisions of race, religion, sex, age, nationality or simply distance. The result of this separation is that capital gains at the expense of workers. Marx was well aware of this because of the antagonism at the time between English and Irish workers. Indeed, discussing that hostility, he identified it as "the *secret of the impotence of the English working class*."[62]

Where there is not competition and hostility, there is indifference. Insofar as these separate owners accept the norms of commodity exchange, what matters is the best possible return in their exchange transaction with capital: the more they provide, the greater the equivalent to which they consider themselves entitled. And those who provide less are entitled to less. As owners of labor-power, they are indifferent to the needs of those who fail to find a buyer for their own property or those with problematic health or large families. Despite "the all-around dependence of the producers on one another," a characteristic of capital's society is "the total isolation of their private interests from one another," a "connection of mutually indifferent persons."[63] Thus an inherent one-sidedness that takes the form of indifference to inequality and to the needs of others in the community flows from the individual ownership of labor-power.

Like other owners, these producers may see it in their mutual interest to form cartel-like arrangements to preserve and enhance the value of their property. They may form trade unions to reduce competition among themselves and to strengthen their market position. They may engage in political action (as in the case of the Ten Hours' Bill, if "private settlement between the working men and the capitalists" cannot achieve their goals), and they even may struggle to transform the power of the state "now used against them, into their own agency."[64]

But will these producers put an end to capital? As long as they view themselves as commodity-sellers, they do not understand capital as the result of previous exploitation. When you focus upon commodity exchange, you "consider each act of exchange by itself, apart from any connection with the act of exchange preceding it and that following it."[65] The fairness of the particular exchange becomes the focus.[66] But where, then, does the capital come from that faces the worker? By considering workers as a whole, Marx demonstrated that the capitalist relation is "the constant appropriation by the capitalist, without equivalent, of a portion of the labour of others." Only by considering capitalist production as a whole "in the uninterrupted flow of its renewal" can we understand where the capital that faces the worker in each individual transaction comes from.[67]

Capital is the workers' own product turned against them. However, in their everyday experience, the very nature of capital is mystified: "All the productive forces of social labour appear attributable to it, and not to labour as such, as a power springing forth from its own womb." Fixed capital, machinery, technology, and science all necessarily appear only as capital: "The accumulation of knowledge and of skill, of the general productive forces of the social brain . . . appears as an attribute of capital."[68] The message transmitted to workers is that capital is everything, and they are nothing.

Precisely because capital appears *necessary*, in the normal course of things capital can rely upon the workers' dependence upon capital. Increasingly, capital tends to produce the working class it *needs*, workers who treat capitalism as common sense. As Marx explained in *Capital*:

> The advance of capitalist production develops a working class which by education, tradition and habit looks upon the requirements of that mode of production as self-evident natural laws. The organization of the capitalist process of production, once it is fully developed, breaks down all resistance.[69]

This is strong and unequivocal language; and Marx added that capital's generation of a reserve army of the unemployed "sets the seal on the domination of the capitalist over the worker." With the constant generation of a relative surplus population of workers, wages are "confined within limits satisfactory to capitalist exploitation, and lastly, the social dependence of the worker on the capitalist, which is indispensable, is secured." The capitalist can then rely upon the workers' "dependence on capital, which springs from the conditions of production themselves, and is guaranteed in perpetuity by them."[70]

Guaranteed in perpetuity! How could we ever think that the society that capital produces could kill the monster? Capital wastes human beings, nature, and society. The story told in *Capital* is that of eternal life for the vampire. That is the nightmare.

Inverting the Capitalist Inversion

Yet, *Capital* also contains within it the *dream*, the "inverse situation, in which objective wealth is there to satisfy the worker's own need for development."[71] It is the dream of a society in which human development is the guiding principle, one that grasps the key link of human development and practice. What kinds of workers, environment, and society are produced in that inverse situation? We can glimpse Marx's answer, his vision of a socialist alternative, by understanding how capitalism inverts everything.

Characteristic of capitalist relations of production is that "it is not the worker who makes use of means of production, but the means of production that make use of the worker." Referring to this same inversion, Marx noted that "it is not the worker who employs the conditions of his work, but rather the reverse, the conditions of work employ the worker."[72] Thus subjects become objects, means become ends in "this inversion, indeed this distortion, which is peculiar to and characteristic of capitalist production, of the relation between dead labour and living labour, between value and the force that creates value."[73] Within the capitalist system, Marx concluded, "all means for the development of production undergo a dialectical inversion so that they become means of domination and exploitation of the producers."[74]

Inversion, inversion, inversion! Marx envisioned a society in which the means for development of production are *not* means of domination and exploitation. In the society of associated producers, the capitalist inversion itself is inverted; "this distortion, which is peculiar to and characteristic of capitalist production" is ended. Rather than the crippling and fragmentation of the producers, in the socialist society the producers are able to develop their capabilities; here, the joint product of their productive activity is "the rich individuality which is as all-sided in its production as in its consumption."[75]

Consider the development of capacities implied by that "inverse situation." In capitalist production, we see that workers are subordinated to "a plan drawn up by the capitalist" and subordinated to his authority—i.e., to "the powerful will of a being outside them, who subjects their activity to his purpose."[76] As a result, Marx argued, the worker is placed in a "state of complete indifference, externality and alienation" in relation to his own labor and "actually treats the social character of his work, its combination with the work of others for a common goal, as a power that is alien to him."[77] But invert that inversion! In the *inverted* process, workers develop the capacity to work with others according to their *own* plan, one in which the "worker's own need for development" rather than the expansion of values prevails. In that "inverse situation" workers develop their capacities: "When the worker co-operates in a planned way with others, he strips off the fetters of his individuality, and develops the capabilities of his species."[78]

Further, in the inverse situation the despotism of the capitalist workplace comes to an end, and the process of production loses its "antithetical character."[79] As the cooperative factories, which Marx described as the "first examples of the emergence of a new form," demonstrated, "the present pauperising and despotic system of the *subordination of labour* to capital can be superseded by the republican and beneficent system of *the association of free and equal producers*."[80] In this "new form," the collective worker calls "his own muscles into play under the control of his own brain" and enjoys his activity "as the free play of his own physical and mental powers."[81]

In particular, in this society of associated producers, workers put an end to the separation of thinking and doing. In contrast to that "dialectical inversion" peculiar to capitalist production that cripples the body and mind of the worker and alienates her from "the intellectual potentialities of the labour process," the new society ends "the enslaving subordination of the individual to the division of labour, and therewith also the antithesis between mental and physical labour."[82] There is "no doubt," Marx indicated in *Capital*, "that those revolutionary ferments whose goal is the abolition of the old division of labour stand in diametrical contradiction with the capitalist form of production."[83]

How to end that "enslaving subordination of the individual to the division of labour"? One way was by introducing education into the workplace. This was a method not only of "adding to the efficiency of production, but as the only method of producing fully developed human beings." Marx also argued that variation in productive activity was important: "The partially developed individual must be replaced by the totally developed individual, for whom the different social functions are different modes of activity he takes up in turn."[84]

In the inverse situation, workers democratically decide upon a plan, work together to achieve its realization, solve problems that emerge, and shift from activity to activity. This constant succession of acts expands their capacities—that "ensemble of actual potentialities, innate or acquired, to carry out any act whatever and whatever its level."[85] This is the realization of the worker's own need for development—the "development of the rich individuality which is as all-sided in its production as in its consumption." The inversion of the capitalist inversion is the necessary condition for the emergence of the "*rich human being* and rich *human* need. The *rich* human being," Marx wrote, is the human being "in whom his own realisation exists as an inner necessity, as *need*." Real wealth, the development of human capacity, is possible with the negation of the capitalist negation.[86]

With an end to the capitalist crippling of producers, Marx projected in his *Critique of the Gotha Program* that "the productive forces have also increased with the all-around development of the individual, and all the springs of co-operative wealth flow more abundantly."[87] However, ending the capitalist fetter does not translate into the boundless production of things. The worker's own need for development goes well beyond productivity in the sphere of production. For this "all-around development," it is necessary to invert the capitalist inversion with respect to nature and society as well.

In contrast to capital's treatment of human beings and nature as means to its growth, in Marx's vision of the inverse situation, the metabolic process begins with "man and his labour on one side, nature and its materials on the other" and concludes by simultaneously *enhancing* "the original sources of all wealth—the soil and the worker." As we have seen, Marx definitely believed that capital's destructive effects upon both human beings and nature could be negated and reversed. Just as he envisioned the all-round development of the producers and the development of the "rich human being," so also did he see the potential for successive generations to inherit the earth "in an improved state." Indeed, Marx proposed that "the earth continuously improves, so long as it is treated correctly."[88] To achieve this, the "metabolic interaction between man and the earth" must be guided by an understanding of the need for "systematic restoration as a regulative law of social production."[89]

There are several conditions for "a genuinely rational agriculture" and for forest management "in the common interest."[90] One certainly is a scientific understanding of the "metabolism prescribed by the natural laws of life itself." As John Bellamy Foster has detailed, Marx closely studied Liebig and contemporary natural scientists as the basis for his understanding of the importance of recognizing organic laws.[91] Based on Marx's grasp of this scientific work, especially focused on agriculture and soil fertility, he stressed the "regulative law" of "systematic restoration" as the "inalienable condition for the existence and reproduction of the chain of human generations."[92] We need to begin, in short, by recognizing "the whole gamut of permanent conditions of life required by the chain of human generations."[93]

Further, collective human practice (for example, "a conscious and rational treatment of the land") informed by this understanding of the "ever-lasting nature-imposed condition of human existence" is essential. Through this "metabolic interaction between man and the earth," both human beings and nature are transformed. This is always true as the result of this interaction, but, as we have seen, the type of human being and nature that develops depends upon the specific character of the relations of production. In the inverse situation based upon the worker's own need for development, the society of associated producers, the products of this interaction are rich human beings and a rich nature.

There is a necessary condition for that correct treatment that permits nature to be passed on in "an improved state," namely, social ownership. "From the standpoint of a higher socio-economic formation," Marx proposed, private ownership of portions of the earth would appear just as absurd as slavery: "Even an entire society, a nation, or all simultaneously existing societies taken together, are not the owners of the earth. They are simply its possessors, its beneficiaries, and have to bequeath it in an improved state to succeeding generations, as *boni patres familias*."[94]

The necessary condition for the "conscious and rational treatment of the land" that permits "the existence and reproduction of the chain of human generations" is that the land is "permanent communal property."[95]

The imperative is obvious. If there is to be an end to the crippling of human beings and the destruction of our world—"the original sources of all wealth—the soil and the worker"—it is essential to put an end to capitalism. Only by creating the conditions in which people can develop their capacities by cooperating with others according to their own plan and ensuring that the earth "continuously improves" through "permanent communal property" can we end the nightmare of capitalism before it puts an end to us.

The Socialist Dream

Negating the capitalist negation with respect to human beings and nature is a necessary condition for the realization of the socialist dream, that "inverse situation, in which objective wealth is there to satisfy the worker's own need for development." But it is not a sufficient condition. Can we talk about either cooperative planning or communal property without a community?

Consider the implications of worker management and of social ownership of nature's larder in the absence of a conscious community. As we have seen, the society inherited from capital is one in which the producers are separate, self-interested, indifferent to inequality and the needs of others, despite "the all-around dependence of the producers on one another." Neither rich human beings nor an enriched nature are possible without inverting that society.

Certainly, with the negation of the capitalist inversion in the sphere of production, one cannot speak of a "connection of mutually indifferent persons" or of "the total isolation of their private interests from one another" within individual workplaces. Once capital's particular "distortion" in the workplace comes to an end, producers have the opportunity to develop their capacities by cooperating in a planned way with each other. Left to itself, however, the conscious connection and solidarity of these associated producers extends only to the boundaries of the particular workplace. Self-interest, a collective self-interest, binds the group, and outside are competitors, suppliers, and customers.

In this situation, society remains based not upon "the association of man with man, but on the separation of man from man." Outside of individual islands of cooperation, the premise is that we are *separate*. In this respect, much like what Marx wrote in 1843, what links people is "natural necessity, needs and private interest, the preservation of their property and their egoistic selves."[96] Thus, even though he hailed the production cooperatives of his time as "the first examples of the emergence of a new form" because they demonstrated that workers do not need capitalists, Marx nevertheless argued that they were "based upon individual and antagonistic interests." In the battle of competition, the associated workers had "become their own capitalists," using the means of production to "valorize their own labour." Marx argued that those cooperatives, in fact, were reproducing "all the defects of the existing system."[97]

Separation and self-interest similarly infected the market self-management experiment in Yugoslavia. Although the system was composed of socially owned enterprises controlled by workers' councils, the self-orientation of producers, as manifested by their focus upon maximizing income per worker in their enterprise, generated indifference and inequality both in relation to producers in other enterprises and in relation to society in general. There was growing inequality between workers in firms in the same industry, between workers in different industries, between workers in different regions, and between urban and rural workers. Rather than social ownership of the means of production, there was group property with differential access to particular means of production. And, insofar as the central goal of the producers was to maximize their income, to this end they yielded the de facto power to think and decide to the managers and experts and did not develop their own capacities.[98]

Separation/self-interest is not only a barrier to the development of rich human beings in the sphere of production. This combination also stands in the way of that "genuinely rational" treatment of nature that ensures that "the earth continuously improves." Ending capital's relentless destruction of nature as it pursues its growth is a necessary condition for the development of an enriched nature. But, as suggested above, it is not a sufficient condition. Is the "systematic restoration" that is the "inalienable condition for the existence and reproduction of the chain of human generations" possible in the absence of a conscious community that focuses upon the needs of the whole?

Consider the combination of "communal ownership" and separation/self-interest. If each individual, each workplace, each locality, indeed each nation—and "all simultaneously existing societies"—acts in its own interest with respect to the use of nature's commons, who is looking after the commons to ensure that we "bequeath it in an improved state to succeeding generations"? Add to that the inequality within and between societies as the result of our inherited differential access to the products of the social brain and the social hand, and there is real potential for a *tragedy* of the commons.

As Elinor Ostrom and others who have worked on the question of common property have explained, however, the problem is not common property itself. Rather, the absence of a community determined and able to monitor the utilization of the commons turns it into "open-access property," and that is what produces the tragedy of the commons. Open access means that parts of the whole, despite "the all-around dependence" of the parts upon each other, may act as if their private interests are isolated from one another.[99] Excess grazing, fishing, hunting, land-clearing, chemical-fertilizing, mineral-extracting, carbon-emitting, water-using—excess relative to "the whole gamut of permanent conditions of life required by the chain of human generations"— are among the probable results of separation/self-interest and the absence of community. And the probability of such harmful results increases in proportion to the existence of significant inequality and indifference to that inequality.

Separation/self-interest is an infection. And it does not automatically disappear with the creation of the "cooperative society based on common ownership of the means of production." For example, in discussing the defects of the new society as it emerges from capitalism, Marx stressed the limitations of the idea that individual producers are entitled to an equivalent in exchange for the labor they perform. This concept, which some call "the socialist principle," he declared, is *"a right of inequality."* As discussed in chapter 2, this concept does not consider the needs of others; rather, consistent with "the total isolation of their private interests from one another," individual owners of labor-power treat "unequal individual endowment and thus productive capacity as natural privileges," with "everything else being ignored." Do we build a society oriented to the worker's own need for development this way?

Of course, the source of inequality in a society that has emerged from capitalism goes well beyond personal endowment. Far more significant are the *inherited* sources of inequality—differential access to the means of production, both those supplied by nature and those that are the result of previous activity of the social hand and the social brain. In the "co-operative society based on common ownership of the means of production," no individuals, groups, societies, or nations have a higher claim than others upon nature and the results of past social labor. Precisely because advantages are treated as property, as "natural privileges," by those who are their possessors, immediate and inherited inequalities become the basis for inequity and injustice. And, insofar as others contest that "right of inequality," the stage is set for struggles in which no one is thinking about society as a whole, in which no one is guarding the commons.

Inequality is the elephant in the room. No understanding of Marx's vision of that inverse situation oriented to full human development is possible unless we directly recognize the existence of inequality and explore its implications. Though inequality and difference are inevitable, they exist only "in and through a particular society." Since the meaning of parts depends upon the particular whole of which they are a part, inequality has a different meaning in a society where separation/self-interest prevails with its corollary of property and exclusion, compared to one which begins from the concept of community and where solidarity is the bond between people.

In the first case, those producers who are privileged seek to maintain and increase their advantages, whereas those who lack them are inclined to struggle to emulate the higher standards. In the process, the separation among the producers is reproduced, demands upon the commons are limitless, and there is no basis for the development of solidarity. In the second case, producers who are privileged by their individual and inherited endowments recognize their unity as members of the human family and act upon this basis to ensure the being of others within this family. Characteristic of this relation is the conscious *reduction* of differentials. Unlike the society based upon separation/self-interest where "the development of the human capacities on the one side is based on the restriction of development on the other," this society recognizes that human development is indivisible. It places upon its banner the words of the *Communist Manifesto*: "The free development of each is the condition for the free development of all."[100]

Central, therefore, to this socialist dream is solidarity. In the solidarian society, inequality can be a stimulus for the development of human potential. Rather than a situation in which people relate as owners, the solidarian society is a "gift economy," one in which those who give are rewarded not by the anticipation of what they may receive at some point in return but rather by the way in which they "construct themselves as certain kinds of people, and build and maintain certain relationships of debt and care."[101] Through such activity, we develop our own capacities. As Marx proposed in 1844, by producing consciously to satisfy your needs, I look upon my activity as having worth: "I would have directly *confirmed* and *realised* my true nature, my *human* nature, my *communal* nature."[102]

In short, in the process of producing consciously for others, people are transformed. In the course of their activity, there is a joint product—the rich human being "in whom his own realisation exists as an inner necessity, as *need*." In that process, our needs change. Instead of filling the void left by alienated production with *things*, our activity itself becomes "life's prime want" because activity and enjoyment become one. This relation, in which we produce consciously for others and do so to the best of our ability, not only advances the needs of others and ourselves for full human development but also, by reducing the tendency for consumerism, is the necessary condition "for the existence and reproduction of the chain of human generations."

Marx called these social relations among the producers "communality" and explained that "communal production, communality, is presupposed as the basis of production. The labour of the individual is posited from the outset as social labour."[103] Thus, the "communal character," the "*social character*," of our activity is presupposed; and characteristic of these productive relations is an exchange not of exchange values (which are a manifestation of private property) but of "activities, determined by communal needs and communal purposes."[104]

The concept of a community was central for Marx, and it is one we must not forget if we are to struggle to realize the socialist dream. Daly and Cobb identify some of the elements of a community in their challenge to the logic of capital: "(1) There is extensive participation by its members in the decisions by which its life is governed, (2) the society as a whole takes responsibility for the members, and (3) this responsibility includes respect for the diverse individuality of these members."[105] Through the concept of a community, we can focus specifically on what is necessary for rich human beings and an enriched nature.

Begin from a presupposed communal society, and social production that is "directly social," which is "the offspring of association," follows. Begin with the communal character of our activity, and the product of our activity is "a communal, general product from the outset." Begin with communality, and "instead of a division of labour, . . . there would take place an organization of labour."[106] There is, in other words, the association of free producers that Marx described in *Capital* as "working with the means of production held in common, and expending their many different forms of labour-power in full self-awareness as one single social labour force."[107] Similarly, the distribution of products follows: the exchange of our activities "would from the outset include the participation of the individual in the communal world of products." [108]

Social ownership of the means of production, social production organized by workers, for the purpose of social needs—three sides all premised upon the relations of production of associated producers, communality. In this organic system of production, distribution, and consumption, which Hugo Chávez called "the elementary triangle of socialism," each side is necessary for the reproduction of those relations of production, and each side is necessary for the realization of the socialist dream.[109]

Here, then, is the vision of a society of "free individuality based on the universal development of individuals and on the subordination of their communal, social productivity as their social wealth." Through this interaction of "individuals who are associated on the basis of common appropriation and control of the means of production," rich human beings produce and reproduce themselves and a society based upon trust and solidarity.[110]

The socialist dream will not be realized overnight, and previous efforts, heroic in many cases, to make it real have failed. But the dream remains, and so does the capitalist nightmare. As Marx indicated in *The Eighteenth Brumaire of Louis Bonaparte*, in the struggle to realize that dream, we must be prepared to criticize those previous efforts and to "deride with unmerciful thoroughness the inadequacies, weaknesses, and paltriness of their first attempts."

Capital, as we know, has driven beyond all barriers placed before it and seems to "draw new strength from the earth and rise again, more gigantic, before them." Capital, in short, appears infinite and all-powerful. Accordingly, it is not surprising if we occasionally despair about the possibility of putting an end to capital, of acting as its gravediggers. That is, "until a situation is created which makes all turning back impossible, and the conditions themselves cry out: *Hic Rhodus, hic salta!*" Leap now![111]

When we consider the capitalist nightmare and the destruction of human beings and nature occurring at this very time, we understand that such a situation has been created, one which "makes all turning back impossible." Very simply, if we are to have any dreams, we must end capitalism now, by all means possible. *Hic Rhodus, hic salta!*

2. Understanding the *Critique of the Gotha Programme*

This chapter was prepared for a Turkish collection of essays on Marxist classics in which authors were asked to explore, among other things, the historical conditions behind a particular work, its importance for Marxist ideology and struggle and its consequences.[1] This is its first appearance in English. However, I did send a copy to David Laibman, editor of Science & Society, *in the hope of finally convincing him of an interpretation I knew he rejected. I was spectacularly unsuccessful, as his immediate response was to write an editorial published in July 2014 of* Science & Society *titled "Quotology, Stages, and the Posthumous Anarchization of Marx" in which he pointed to this (then-unavailable) essay as a demonstration that "anarchism and romantic idealism have resurfaced." My reply, "Build it 'from the outset': An infantile disorder?" appears in* Science & Society *of July 2015. Aside from the theoretical interpretation that so irritated Laibman, the essay calls attention to the combining of economic and political demands in the unity document that was crucial in bringing about in Germany the largest and most successful socialist party in the world. It also reveals problems in the immediate response of Marx and Engels to this "real movement."*

The *Critique of the Gotha Programme* is not like other writings of Marx. It is not a completed work prepared for publication like the *Communist Manifesto* or the *Civil War in France*. It is also not a work such as the *Grundrisse,* which, although not intended for publication, is the result of a sustained process of reasoning. Very simply, the *Critique* was, as Marx described it, "critical marginal notes."

And that has several implications. As with all marginal notes, the content is dictated largely by the document that is the object of criticism; both the order and the chain of reasoning are externally determined. Further, while some remarks may be obvious on their face (as, for example, when we can easily demonstrate that a point in the document in question is idiocy), in other cases, the points made may reflect an underlying analysis that is not fully apparent on the surface. The failure to reconstruct the inner argument, which may be present elsewhere, may lead, then, to significant misinterpretation.

Finally, in the case of the criticism of a particular document, it is important to understand both the document in question and the relation of the critic to that document. We need to situate the *Critique of the Gotha Programme* both historically and theoretically.

THE HISTORY
"Real Movement"

"Every step of real movement is more important than a dozen programmes."[2] So wrote Marx in May 1875 to a German friend in relation to the draft program prepared for the Unity Congress of two German parties scheduled for the city of Gotha later that month.[3]

If "real movement" refers to the development of a powerful socialist party, indeed the most important in the world and a model for elsewhere, there certainly was "real movement" in Germany in the latter part of the nineteenth and early twentieth centuries. In 1863, two new working-class parties were created, the General German Workers League (ADAV) and the Union of German

Workers Leagues (VDAV), and there is a direct link between these and the Socialist Workers Party of Germany (SAPD) created at Gotha, which would rename itself the Social Democratic Party of Germany (SPD) in 1890.

The ADAV was founded by Ferdinand Lassalle (a flamboyant leader much influenced by Marx's early writing and apt to plagiarize it) in response to overtures from workers, and it focused upon capitalists as the enemy of workers. The VDAV (or Verband), based on local associations (many related to workers education) with over 20,000 members, allied itself with liberal reformers especially in the south of Germany. The political orientation of the two definitely differed at the outset: whereas ADAV did not stress trade union activity and looked instead to the development of workers' cooperatives (with the financial support of the Prussian government of Bismarck), VDAV stressed a general program of liberal reform including support for workers.

Yet the two moved closer together in political policies. First, Wilhelm Liebknecht, an associate of Marx, left the ADAV in 1865 and became a leader, along with August Bebel, of VDAV. Second, VDAV associated itself in 1868 with the program of the First International led by Marx and lost in the process 5,000 of its members who rejected this program. With the creation in 1869 at Eisenach of the Social Democratic Workers Party (SDAP), a united working-class party initiated by 66 members of ADAV and 114 of the Verband led by Liebknecht and Bebel, the two players who would meet at Gotha were formed—the "Eisenachers" (SDAP) and the "Lassalleans" (ADAV).

As of 1871, ADAV had 14,000 members while SDAP had 10,000, and in the 1874 elections ADAV received 180,000 votes to 170,000 for the SDAP. But the Eisenachers were growing, especially among the working class, in this period because of their support for trade unions and strike activity that involved 200,000 workers between 1871 and 1873. In contrast, the general union created by ADAV fell from a high of 25,000 members in 1870 to 5,000 in 1874. In the context of general state persecution of socialist organizations, particularly the ADAV, by Bismarck, the "Lassalleans" now offered to merge with the Eisenachers, something they had resisted until that point. Negotiations became serious in mid-February 1875 with the meeting of a joint commission at Gotha; and in May 1875, 130 delegates, 60 percent of whom came from the Lassalleans, formed the Socialist Workers Party of Germany (SAPD) and adopted the Gotha Program on behalf of 25,000 members.

Within a year of its formation, the new party had 38,000 members and 291 local associations, and it proceeded to obtain close to a half-million votes and to elect twelve deputies in the 1877 elections. And, despite the impact of the Anti-Socialist Laws introduced by Bismarck in 1878 and lasting until 1890, the party increased its votes by 1890 to one million (19.75 percent of the vote) and then approximately to three million by 1903. Without question, the party created at Gotha, which became the largest party in Germany, was a great success.

"A Thoroughly Objectionable Program"

But that outcome wasn't at all what Marx and Engels anticipated. Although they knew that unification discussions were occurring, they were "astonished" to read a draft of the Gotha Program in the newspapers. How was it, they wondered, that no one had sent them any information about all this! "I cannot forgive" Liebknecht, Engels wrote to Bebel, "for not having told us a *single word* about the whole business." We are blamed abroad, he complained, for everything our party does—even though we hardly interfere. But "this programme marks a turning point." If adopted, we "could *never* recognise a *new* party established on that basis."[4] Very simply, Marx wrote in his letter to Bracke, the program is "altogether deplorable." True, "the mere fact of unification is enough to satisfy the workers," but "this momentary success" has been bought at too high a price. And, momentary is all it will be, Engels predicted to Bebel: "I am, moreover, convinced that a union on *this* basis would not last a year."

What was it in the draft that so enraged Marx and Engels, aside from the fact that its content had been hidden from them by their own followers? In particular, their letters stressed the extent to which the program drew upon the theoretical perspective of Lassalle. Engels, for example, emphasized the presence of classic Lassallean precepts such as support for state aid to producer cooperatives, evocation of the "iron law of wages," and the call for a "free state," all points developed at length in Marx's subsequent *Critique* of the program. How could our party give credibility to the Lassalleans in this way! Union should have been made dependent on the extent to which they were willing to drop their sectarian slogans and their state aid, that is, a condition of union should be that they drop their focus upon "the universal panacea of state aid."

In short, rather than accepting the Lassallean positions, Engels argued that it was the party's duty to ensure that the Lassalleans would not be able to "restore, at our party's expense, their shattered reputation in the general working-class opinion." Marx made the same point: the Lassalleans were in dire straits. If it were impossible to agree upon an advanced program, it would have been far better to have "come to an agreement for action against the common foe" and to prepare the basis for the program by a considerable period of common activity rather than to surrender "unconditionally to men who are themselves in need of help."

Yet it was *not* only the Lassalleans who were the problem. It was also "our party" that concerned Marx and Engels (and for neither the first nor last time, as their correspondence over the years reveals). In particular, they blamed Liebknecht not only for the concessions he made but also for "the muddle-headed and convoluted clichés in the programme." As Engels commented to Bebel sixteen years later, these were "quintessential Liebknecht; they have been a bone of contention between us for years and the chap's besotted with them. Theoretically he has always been muddle-headed and our clear-cut style is still an abomination to him today."[5]

By taking the Lassallean positions as its own, Engels warned, the party would disarm itself theoretically: it "will never again be able to come out wholeheartedly against the Lassallean maxims which for a time it inscribed on its own banner." But there was an even greater prospective problem: "What have the others conceded? That a host of somewhat muddled and *purely democratic demands* should figure in the programme." Consider, then, what would happen when the union of the two parties failed: "Should the Lassalleans again declare themselves to be the sole and most genuine workers' party and our people to be bourgeois, the programme would be there to prove it. All the socialist measures in it are *theirs,* and *our* party has introduced nothing save the demands of that petit-bourgeois democracy." Indeed, of "the seven political demands" in the program, "there is not one that is not *bourgeois*-democratic."[6]

In addition to the Lassallean phrases and slogans that "should not have been accepted under any condition," there also were what Engels called months later "a series of vulgar democratic demands, drawn up in the spirit and style of the People's Party" (Liebknecht's old party).[7] How could those committed to the program of the First International ever accept this particular combination, a document that was even worse than the limited Eisenach program? True, Engels admitted, "less importance attaches to the official program of a party than to what it does. But a *new* programme is after all a banner planted in public, and the outside world judges the party by it."[8] Consider "what the workers of other countries will think of this programme." That was Marx's concern as well: with this program, one sets up "benchmarks for all the world to see, whereby it may gauge how far the party has progressed."[9]

Accordingly, it was necessary to *denounce* the program. "It is my duty," Marx announced, "to refuse recognition, even by maintaining a diplomatic silence, to a programme which, I am convinced, is altogether deplorable as well as demoralising for the party." For this reason, he warned that "after the Unity Congress is over, Engels and I will publish a short statement to the effect that we

entirely disassociate ourselves from the said programme of principles and have nothing to do with it."

But no such statement was written. Indeed, not until years later
when the party decided to replace the document adopted at Gotha
were the criticisms of Marx and Engels revealed publicly. Not until
the eve of the Party Congress at Erfurt in 1891, where the new
document drafted largely by Karl Kautsky (the Erfurt Program)
would replace the Gotha Program, did Engels publish Marx's
"critical marginal notes" on the latter program. And the reason for
not denouncing it at the time was obvious: the Unity Congress at
Gotha was a great success, a step of real movement.

As Engels explained to Bebel five months after the Gotha
Congress, this "excessively disjointed, muddled, inconsequential,
illogical and discreditable" program would have exposed "our
whole party to the most dreadful ridicule, but for the fact that "the
jackasses on the bourgeois papers have taken this programme per-
fectly seriously, reading into it what isn't there and interpreting it
communistically." Further, "the workers are apparently doing the
same." The official program, in short, did not hold back the real
movement in Germany. "So long as our opponents as well as the
workers continue to read our views into that program, we are justi-
fied in saying nothing about it."[10]

However unhappy they were, Marx and Engels were wise to
conform ultimately to the judgement of militants familiar with
concrete conditions in Germany. Marx and Engels had been
wrong, Liebknecht argued in 1891 at the Erfurt Congress, with
respect to the potential for the party unified on the basis of the
Gotha Program. Yes, of course, that program was theoretically
incorrect in many key respects, but it was what was needed at
the time in order to survive. Indeed, he declared that "theory and
practice are two different things" and that "as unconditionally as
I trust Marx's judgement in theory, so in practice I go my own
way."[11] Twenty years later Bebel recalled that "it was no easy thing
to reach agreement with the two old men in London. What on our
part was a clever calculation and an adroit tactic was seen by them

as weakness and irresponsible complacency. In the end the main point was achieved: the unification."[12]

Can a general theory (however correct it is) be applied without reference to specific concrete circumstances? As Lenin understood, "The categorical requirement of Marxist theory in investigating any social question is that it be examined within *definite* historical limits, and if it refers to a particular country (e.g., the national programme for a given country), that account be taken of the specific features distinguishing that country from others in the same historical epoch."[13] It is essential to consider Marx's *Critique of the Gotha Programme* both as a general theory and in relation to the specific features characterizing Germany in this period.

THE DOCUMENTS
The Gotha Program

Two points immediately strike one when looking at the program adopted by the party at its congress at Gotha. First, how *short* it is. Marx's *Critique* far exceeds in length the program itself. Almost every sentence in the draft document became the occasion for an extended analysis and exposition of Marx's own theory. Second, the Gotha Program appears less problematic in reading than one would anticipate from the letters of Marx and Engels and Marx's "marginal notes" on the draft. One reason is the importance of taking into account the specific features characteristic of Germany in this historical epoch. A second is that the Program as passed is not precisely the same as the draft to which Marx and Engels responded.

There are three basic sections of the Program that united the two competing parties at Gotha: (1) general theoretical principles, (2) specific directions for the Socialist Workers Party, and (3) what Marx called "the democratic section"—the particular democratic demands made by the party under current conditions. Consider the key elements of the general analysis. The first section asserts that labor is the source of all wealth and that the whole product of labor should belong to all members of society, to each according to his reasonable needs. Further, it describes the misery of workers as the result of the monopoly of ownership of the means of production by the capitalist class and accordingly calls for the transformation of those means of production into the common property of society. This, the program states, must be the work of the working class itself.

Given this general perspective, what was the responsibility of the Socialist Workers Party? On the domestic front, it needed to struggle to build a new, "free state" and a socialist society and to abolish the system of wage labor and all exploitation. Internationally, the program states that while working initially within national boundaries the party is fully conscious of the international character of the labor movement and resolves to meet all the obligations this places upon workers to bring about the brotherhood of mankind. Further, as a step toward building socialism, the Socialist Workers Party demands that the state support the development of productive cooperatives, in industry and agriculture, under the democratic control of the working people.

Finally, among the immediate democratic demands made upon the autocratic German state, the party called for universal suffrage, the secret ballot, the replacement of the standing army by the popular militia, the right of the people to vote directly on the question of war, universal and popular education through the state, a single progressive income tax in place of indirect taxes, an end to all restrictions on the right of association and freedom of thought and expression, the shortening of the workday, and an end to child labor.

When you look at these elements of the Gotha Program, it is not at all surprising that the press of the time was "interpreting it communistically" and that the workers were "apparently doing the same." Although that reaction likely would have occurred without any of the changes made to the draft program, some of the criticisms made by Marx and Engels had a major impact upon the document passed at Gotha.

Consider, for example, the very first paragraph of the Program. The draft included the point that the proceeds of labor belong "undiminished" to all members of society. In his *Critique*, Marx wrote at length about the necessity that those "proceeds," more appropriately "the product of labour," *cannot* be distributed undiminished because there are necessary "deductions" to that product, which he then detailed. The word "undiminished," however, disappeared from the final document. Similarly, the draft stated that those proceeds belong with equal right to all members of society. "To those who do not work as well," Marx asked. The final document made it clear that this applied "where there is a general obligation to work." Finally, Marx asked, what is meant by "equal right" in this draft? The final document expanded on this point, setting out the goal that the "product of labour" belongs to all members of society, "by equal right, to each according to his reasonable needs." Those changes were obviously a direct response to Marx's criticism of the Program.

Or take the criticism by Marx and Engels of the weak internationalism (certainly weaker than both the Program and actions of the Eisenachers) contained in the draft. "To what does the German workers' party reduce its internationalism," Marx asked. "To the consciousness that the result of its [nation-based] efforts will be '*the international brotherhood of peoples.*'" "Not a word, therefore, *about the international functions* of the German working class!" We see there, the theorist of the First International stressed, the continuation of the perspective of Lassalle, who "conceived the workers' movement from the narrowest national standpoint . . . and that after the work of the International!"

The same point about the inadequacy of the draft was made by Engels: "The principle that the workers' movement is an international one is, to all intents and purposes, utterly denied in respect of the present." The "very least" that could have been said, Engels complained, is that "*though first of all* the German workers' party is acting within the limits set by its political frontiers . . . it is nevertheless conscious of its solidarity with the workers of all other countries and will, as before, always be ready to meet the obligations that solidarity entails."[14] Here, too, the draft was amended at the Gotha Congress. This section now indicated that the party, "although for the time being confining its activity within national bounds, is fully conscious of the international character of the labour movement, and is resolved to meet all the obligations which this lays upon the labourer, in order to bring the brotherhood of all mankind to a full realization." Again, can there be any doubt at all that the criticisms made by Marx and Engels were accepted in this case?

Although there were other changes in response to Marx's "critical marginal notes"—for example, "promotion" of the means of production into the common property of the society was replaced by their "conversion" or "transformation" and a "normal" workday by "the shortening of the workday"—the Program definitely retained the Lassallean theory in the form of its references, in particular to the "iron law of wages" and state aid to cooperatives. Given the greater numerical strength of the Lassalleans at Gotha, it is not surprising that the platform would not reject their theoretical perspective.

Was there a realistic alternative to the Gotha Program for a workers' party under the concrete conditions of Germany in this period? Consider the program of the Social Democratic Workers Party (SDAP) adopted in Eisenacher five years earlier.[15] It opened by calling for "the establishment of the free people's state"—"pure nonsense" according to Engels and not significantly different from the concept of the "free state" that Marx denounced in his marginal notes. In the first principle that followed, party members were called upon to recognize that "the current political and social conditions are extremely unjust, and therefore to be fought with the utmost energy." Hardly a ringing denunciation of capitalism, and anyone familiar with Marx's *Critique* can guess what he might have said about "unjust" or about the reference to "equal rights and obligations" contained in the next principle.

Surely, this reveals something about the consciousness of the German working class at this time and allows us to consider what the Eisenachers brought to the bargaining table on economic issues. Rather than unconditional surrender, much of the Gotha Program was already endorsed by the Eisenachers. For example, the third principle of their program opens by stating that "the economic dependency of the worker on the capitalists constitutes the basis of slavery in all its forms"; although the Gotha Program echoed this point, proposing that the "dependence of the working class" on the capitalist class is "the cause of misery and servitude in all its forms," Marx denounced the latter for ignoring the landlord class and attributed this to Lassalle's politics. Similarly, the Eisenacher program called for the abolition of the wage system, for workers to receive "the full proceeds" of their labor and even "state support of the cooperative system and state loans for free producers cooperatives subject to democratic guarantees." These were all points in the Gotha Program.

What the Eisenacher program *lacked*, however, were the specific declarations of Gotha that "labour is the source of all wealth," that the means of production must be converted into the common property of society, that all exploitation must be ended, and that the labor of society must be cooperatively regulated. Small wonder that Engels could complain that "all the socialist measures" in the Gotha Program came from the Lassalleans! When it came to an economic program on behalf of the German working class, the Lassalleans definitely were more advanced.

Certainly, neither party came close to the theoretical sophistication of Marx and Engels. But recall Lenin's point: "The categorical requirement of Marxist theory" is the importance of considering "*definite* historical limits, and if it refers to a particular country [e.g., the national program for a given country] that account be taken of the specific features distinguishing that country from others in the same historical epoch." By considering the democratic demands contained in the Eisenacher program—demands made upon a state that Marx described in the *Critique* as "nothing but a police-guarded military despotism, embellished with parliamentary forms"—we can gain some understanding of the concrete conditions under which the new party would be formed at Gotha.

Think about such Eisenacher demands as the replacement of standing armies by a people's militia, direct legislation by the people, "universal, equal, direct and secret" male suffrage for election to all representative bodies (with adequate pay for elected deputies), free education in all public educational institutions, abolition of all privileges attached to class and property, abolition of all laws aimed against the press, associations, and trade unions. Were these demands compatible with that autocratic state, that "police-guarded military despotism"? Not only did the presence of such demands reveal the perspective that the interests of the working class transcend purely economic demands but the fourth principle of the Eisenach Program explicitly recognized the *inseparability* of the "social question" from the political one. "Political freedom," it declared, "represents the most essential precondition for the economic liberation of the labouring class." This was, in short, a call to struggle to win the "battle of democracy" and to use the state to abolish the wage system.

Despite the criticisms of Marx and Engels, who called these "a series of vulgar democratic demands," these demands were incorporated in the Gotha Program, although *not* with the clause that political freedom was a "precondition" for economic liberation. Further, with significant additions such as the demands for abolition of all laws that place women at a disadvantage compared with men in legal matters, free medical care, and abolition of capital punishment, these democratic demands *also* were incorporated in the Erfurt Program of 1891. Justifying such demands, the latter program argued that "without political rights, the working class cannot carry on its economic struggles and develop its economic organization. It cannot bring about the transfer of the means of production into the possession of the community without having first obtained political power."[16]

The banner raised by the Unity Congress at Gotha, a banner that would wave for another sixteen years without change, was thus a particular combination of the Lassallean and the Eisenacher tendencies. More than a simple addition, by articulating the socialist economic position of the former and the political demands of the latter, it marked a theoretical union that was an advance. Combined with the acceptance of the organizational structure of the Eisenachers and the practice of German workers, it produced a political advance as well.

Given this outcome, what makes the scathing attacks of Marx and Engels on the Program important today? To find out, we need to consider the *Critique of the Gotha Program* both in its immediacy as a furious reaction and also as a theoretical contribution that transcends the immediate.

The Critique *as Exorcism*

The last five or so years had not been kind to Marx politically. In particular, the First International in which he had such great hopes had disintegrated by 1873. So much of Marx's energy had gone into attempting to make the First International a coherent and theoretically advanced international organization: he had written its inaugural address and its rules, had been at the core of its General Council in London, had prepared instructions for delegates at its international congresses, and had issued statements on behalf of the International. But now, after the fall of the Paris Commune, the intense internal battles with supporters of the anarchist Bakunin (who had much more influence than Marx anticipated), the resulting decision in 1872 at the Hague Congress to shift the General Council to New York, and the development of antagonism among many previous supporters (including in England), the International was gone, and Marx's political influence was significantly reduced.[17]

Yet there was still Germany. Marx had served as corresponding secretary for Germany and had close relationships with some German activists, including Wilhelm Liebknecht. In the German working class, there was hope. As Engels had written in his 1874 preface to *The Peasant War in Germany*:

The German workers have two important advantages over
those of the rest of Europe. First, they belong to the most theoretical people of Europe; and they have retained that sense
of theory which the so-called "educated" classes of Germany
have almost completely lost. . . . Without a sense of theory
among the workers, this scientific socialism would never have
entered their flesh and blood as much as is the case. What
an immeasurable advantage this is may be seen, on the one
hand, from the indifference towards all theory, which is one
of the main reasons why the English working class movement
crawls along so slowly in spite of the splendid organization
of the individual unions; on the other hand, from the mis-
chief and confusion wrought by Proudhonism, in its original
form, among the French and Belgians, and in the form further
caricatured by Bakunin, among the Spaniards and Italians. . . .
For the first time since the workers movement has existed,
the struggle is being contacted pursuant to its three sides—
the theoretical, the political and the practical-economic
(resistance to the capitalists)—in harmony and in its inter-
connections, and in a systematic way. It is precisely in this as
it were concentric attack that the strength and invincibility of
the German movement lies.[18]

Slightly more than six months later Marx and Engels were
enraged to read that "thoroughly objectionable program," the draft
of the Gotha Program. Accordingly, Marx set out in his *Critique
of the Gotha Program* to attack the two devils he saw within it: the
petit-bourgeois perspective of the Eisenachers and the sectarian-
ism of the Lassalleans.

Let us look at Marx's comments upon the "democratic" demands
contained in the draft. In response to the call to end child labor,
Marx responded that "a general prohibition of child labour is
incompatible with the existence of large-scale industry and hence
an empty pious wish." Indeed, he continued, "its realisation—if
it were possible—would be reactionary." Why? Because "an early

combination of productive labour with education is one of the most potent means for the transformation of present-day society."

Similarly, with respect to the demand for "universal and equal popular education by the state," Marx wrote, can we imagine that in "present-day society . . . education can be equal for all classes"? This demand, he argued, is "entirely objectionable": rather than "appointing the state as the educator of the people," we see that "the state has need, on the contrary, of a very stern education by the people." And the same perspective comes through with respect to the demand for ensuring "freedom of conscience," which Marx saw as another bourgeois demand. Rather than the toleration of "all possible kinds of religious freedom on conscience," the workers' party should indicate "that for its part it endeavours to liberate the conscience from the witchery of religion."

Indeed, the political demands of the program, Marx insisted, "contain nothing beyond the old democratic litany familiar to all: universal suffrage, direct legislation, popular rights, a people's militia, etc. They are a mere echo of the bourgeois People's Party, of the League of Peace and Freedom." That same deficiency permeated the economic positions in the draft: he described concepts such as "equal right" and "fair distribution" as "obsolete verbal rubbish," "ideological nonsense about right and other trash so common among the democrats and French Socialists." Demonstrating that his focus was the international movement rather than Germany itself, Marx pointed out that many of the demands in the program had already been achieved elsewhere (for example, Switzerland and the United States) without transforming society. Marx, in other words, made few concessions here to "the specific features distinguishing that country [Germany] from others in the same historical epoch."

There was also the presence of "the Lassallean articles of faith," in particular the "iron law of wages" and the path to the Promised Land of socialism through the creation of producers' cooperatives with state support. It certainly is true that what Lassalle called "the iron and cruel law that controls the working wage" in his "Open

Letter" to workers in 1863 was pure Malthusianism.[19] Any increase in the daily wage above "the subsistence level necessary for a given people to exist and propagate in the manner in which it is accustomed" necessarily leads, Lassalle argued, to increased workers' marriages, workers' propagation, and a rise in the workers' population. Thus the average wage was restricted to "the barest means necessary for a given people to exist and propagate."

Who could deny this Lassalle asked. If someone "speaks to you about improving the condition of the working class" but does not acknowledge this law, "you must tell him from the start that he either wants to deceive you or else is miserably schooled in the science of national economy." And, if he does acknowledge this iron law of wages, "then you should go on to ask him: how he proposes to eliminate it." Certainly, trade union struggles to raise wages could not eliminate that law. For Lassalle, the message was clear. You have to abolish the wage system together with the iron law of wages.

But Marx *did* deny this "iron law." His discussion in volume one of *Capital* on the "General Theory of Capital Accumulation" is a devastating critique of the Malthusian population theory as applied to wages. Throughout *Capital* and his 1865 talk to the General Council on "Value, Price and Profits," he stressed the possibility that real wages could rise and the importance of trade union struggles. As a result, Marx argued in the *Critique* that his theoretical analysis of wages had "gained more and more ground in our party" in the period after the death of Lassalle in 1864. What did it mean, then, to incorporate such a position in the new party program?

To accept the concept of the "iron law" of wages, Marx insisted, was "a monstrous attack on the understanding that has spread among the mass of our party." The essential point is *not* that workers are doomed to obtain physiological subsistence. Rather, it is critical to focus upon the nature of the social relation between the capitalist and the wage-laborer. "The system of wage labour is a system of slavery, and indeed of a slavery which becomes more severe in proportion as the social productive forces of labour develop, whether the worker receives better or worse payment." Therefore, to place the obsolete notion of the "iron law of wages" in the party program was like inscribing on the banner of a slave rebellion: "Slavery must be abolished because the feeding of slaves in the system of slavery cannot exceed a certain low maximum!" This misses the entire point. It was, Marx declared, a "truly outrageous retrogression" and proof of the lack of conscience of "the representatives of our party . . . in drawing up this compromise" program.

In the Lassallean framework, if the system of wage-labor must be abolished because of the iron law of wages, how is this to be done? The answer for Lassalle was that workers should join together in producer cooperatives to become their own employers. In this way they would capture the profits that capitalists secure, and this would be a step toward socialism. To do this on an adequate scale, however, would require state credit and, indeed, for the state to function as a silent partner of these new institutions. "It is worthy of Lassalle's imagination," Marx commented, "that with state loans one can build a new society just as well as a new railway!"

Lassalle's imagination in this case had its source in his mystical Hegelian conception of the state. The function of the state, he believed, is the development of freedom. "The object of the State," he argued in 1862, is to "bring the destiny of man . . . into actual *existence*; it is the *training and development* of the human race to freedom."[20] And that process would be advanced by "the working man's idea of the State," by the "moral idea of the State according to the working class"—presumably what the request for state aid to cooperatives represented. This idea of growing into socialism through state aid, then, was the proposal that became part of the Gotha Program. In fact, "Lassallean state aid in its starkest form," as Engels pointed out to Bebel, was the "*one and only social demand*," put forward in the draft program, one that contained "absolutely no mention of the organisation of the working class as a class through the medium of trade unions."[21]

Still, it wasn't the reference to cooperatives as such that concerned Marx and Engels. After all, in the Inaugural Address of
the First International, Marx had described the cooperative factories as a great "victory" of the political economy of the working
class. Through the "dwarfish forms" inherent in the private efforts
of individual workers, though, Marx pointed out (in his 1866
"instructions" to delegates to the Congress of the International)
that the cooperative system would "never transform capitalis-
tic society." Accordingly, it would be necessary to transfer "the
state power, from capitalists and landlords to the producers
themselves."[22] And that would never happen by relying upon the
existing state to support producer cooperatives. Indeed, Marx
pointed out in the *Critique* that the desire of workers to "revo-
lutionise the present conditions of production . . . has nothing in
common with the foundation of co-operative societies with state
aid." The reason is obvious: the red thread in Marx's theory is the
concept of *revolutionary practice*—"the simultaneous changing of
circumstances and human activity or self change."[23] It is through
their struggles that workers make themselves fit to create the new
society. That is precisely why Marx could add in the *Critique* that
cooperatives "are of value *only* insofar as they are the independent
creations of the workers and not protégés either of the governments or of the bourgeois."

By yielding to "the Lassallean sect's servile belief in the state,"
Marx argued that the Eisenachers had taken "a retrograde step
from the standpoint of a class movement to that of a sectarian movement." But despite all their efforts, "the two old men in
London" were not able to convince their comrades to purge this
Lassallean article of faith from the program. "Our party could
hardly demean itself further," wrote Engels.[24]

Nevertheless, the party not only survived this humiliation but
thrived. The Lassallean ideas in the Program succumbed to those
of Marx and Engels over time as the result of workers' struggles
and the political and economic organizing of the party. Very
simply, the "iron law of wages" and dependence upon the state

to support producers' cooperatives reflected a movement as yet undeveloped, and they disappeared from the Erfurt Program. The real exorcism, in short, occurred through "real movement." Even if Marx had been successful in his attempt to remove them by argument, however, the *Critique of the Gotha Program* would not be viewed as one of the classics of Marxism. Its particular significance results from another element.

The Critique *as Contribution*

The special theoretical contribution of the *Critique* revolves in particular around the question of socialism/communism—Marx uses the terms interchangeably in the document—and the nature of the state in post-capitalist society.[25] Although Marx wrote elsewhere about aspects of the new society, extended passages in these marginal notes have provided important insight into his view of the characteristics of socialism (communism). Those passages are isolated glimpses, however, and underlying them is a theoretical conception that needs to be brought to the surface if we are to grasp their inner connections. This means, among other things, the need to consider other, more fully reasoned works and also to reorder those passages.

Marx's entry point into this discussion flows from his criticism of the draft's references to the concepts of "right," justice, and fairness and of their relation to the state. Consistent with his materialist conception since *The German Ideology,* and summarized in the "Preface" to the *Critique of Political Economy*, he asked, What do we mean by "fair"? Does this conception rest in midair? "Are economic relations regulated by legal conceptions, or do not, on the contrary, legal relations arise out of economic ones?" We need to recognize, he insisted, the importance of seeking the secret to the dominant conceptions of right and justice of a society in its economic relations: "Right can never be higher than the economic structure of society and its cultural development conditioned thereby."

But what is the economic structure of post-capitalist society? What are the relations of production that characterize that society? Marx answered that it depends. We need to distinguish "a communist society... as it has *developed* on its own foundations" from one "just as it *emerges* from capitalist society; which is thus in every respect, economically, morally, and intellectually, still stamped with the birthmarks of the old society from whose womb it emerges."

What does it mean to speak of a society that "has developed on its own foundations"? Very simply, Marx was describing here a "completed" system, one that produces its own premises, one that is dependent upon results it itself has created (its own foundations). As he noted in the *Grundrisse* about capitalism, "In the completed bourgeois system, every economic relation presupposes every other in its bourgeois economic form, and everything posited is thus also a presupposition; this is the case with every organic system."[26] That is, it is a system that contains within itself the conditions for its own reproduction, one which, as he explained in volume 1 of *Capital*, when viewed "as a connected whole, and in the constant flux of its incessant renewal," is understood as "a process of reproduction."[27]

In a communist society "as it has *developed* on its own foundations," the conditions are present for the full development of human potential; in the words of *Capital*, "objective wealth is there to satisfy the worker's own need for development."[28] This is the society of "rich individuality" that Marx described in the *Grundrisse*, a society of associated producers in which each individual is able to develop his full potential, that is, the "absolute working out of his creative potentialities," the "complete working out of the human content," the "development of all human powers as such the end in itself."[29] This is the "being" of the new society, an organic system that produces its own premises, one where, as Marx noted in the *Critique*, "the enslaving subordination of the individual to the division of labour, and therewith also the antithesis between mental and physical labour, have vanished," and "the productive forces have also increased with the all-around development of the individual, and all the springs of co-operative wealth flow more abundantly."

However, as Marx explained in the *Grundrisse*, "The new forces of production and relations of production do not develop out of nothing, nor drop from the sky." We need to distinguish the "Being" of the system from its "Becoming."[30] When the new system first comes on the scene, it *never* produces all its premises; rather, it necessarily begins by inheriting premises from the old—"historic" premises and presuppositions produced outside the system. The process of becoming an organic system is one of *transcending* those historic premises: "Its development to its totality consists precisely in subordinating all elements of society to itself, or in creating out of it the organs which it still lacks. This is historically how it becomes a totality."[31] The economic, moral, and intellectual "birthmarks of the old society from whose womb it emerges" are among the historic premises that must be suspended in this process of development of the new society.

The new system is, therefore, defective as it emerges from capitalist society. "But these defects are inevitable in the first phase of communist society as it is when it has just emerged after prolonged birth pangs from capitalist society." To understand those defects, we need to begin by considering how this society differs from the capitalist society it has replaced. The premise and result of capitalist relations is "the fact that the material conditions of production are in the hands of non-workers in the form of property in capital and land, while the masses are only owners of the personal condition of production, of labour power." Separating communist society from capitalism, then, is the transformation of those material means of production into the common property of society.

Is there more to the immediate change than that the proletariat will "centralise all instruments of production in the hands of the State," as indicated in the *Communist Manifesto*? The *Critique* refers to a society in which "the instruments of labour are common property and the total labour is co-operatively regulated." Is the latter clause essential or is it there only because it was present in the original Gotha draft upon which Marx is commenting? If "the co-operative society based on common ownership of the means of production" implies "co-operative regulation of the total labour," then clearly we cannot talk about any market or spontaneous process of distributing the labor of the society. Rather than the indirectly social labor characteristic of a society based upon commodity exchange, with cooperative regulation of society's labor, the premise (as indicated in the *Grundrisse*) must be that "the labour of the individual is posited from the outset as social labour."[32] And that is precisely what Marx states in the *Critique*: "In contrast to capitalist society, individual labour no longer exists in an indirect fashion but directly as a component part of the total labour."

The rupture of the property rights of capitalists can be achieved much more rapidly than putting into place a process of cooperative regulation and planning of the allocation of the total labor of society. If the latter has not yet been realized, this would be a "defect" characteristic of the communist society as it emerges from capitalist society, one that must be subordinated if the new society is to develop. But certainly not the only defect. Even *if* cooperative regulation of labor is present in some form, Marx described a particular defect inevitably characteristic of this birthmarked society—a relation of distribution in which "the same amount of labour which he [the individual producer] has given to society in one form, he receives back in another."

In this particular distribution relation, the individual producer is entitled to means of consumption that contain an equivalent quantity of labor to that which he contributed to the total social labor. In short, "the same principle prevails as in the exchange of commodity equivalents: a given amount of labour in one form is exchanged for an equal amount of labour in another form." The producer has a right to an equivalent. *But why is there this particular concept of right and entitlement?* After all, relations of distribution don't drop from the sky.

Indeed, Marx insisted that it is "a mistake to make a fuss about so-called *distribution* and put the principal stress on it. Any distribution whatever of the means of consumption is only a consequence of the distribution of the conditions of production themselves. The latter distribution, however, is a feature of the mode of production itself." Recall, then, Marx's description of the characteristics of capitalism: "The material conditions of production are in the hands of non-workers in the form of property in capital and land, while the masses are only owners of the personal condition of production, of labour power." *Transformation of the means of production into social property still leaves the individual producers as "owners of the personal condition of production, of labour power."*

As the new society emerges from capitalism, there is a continuation of "bourgeois right"; the right of property has not yet been "crossed in its entirety." Underlying the idea of exchange of equivalents between the individual producer and society is *ownership*, the private ownership of labor-power. Two owners of property, the owner of labor-power and society as owner of articles of consumption, face each other and engage in an exchange, a *quid pro quo*, I give you this in return for that. Rather than dropping from the sky, this relation of distribution has real roots—a relation of production characterized by the combination of individual owners of labor-power. Here was one of the errors of the Gotha Program: it took over "from the bourgeois economists the consideration of distribution as independent of the mode of production and hence the presentation of socialism as turning principally on distribution."

Rather than repeating this "mistake"—"to make a fuss about so-called *distribution* and put the principal stress upon it"—we need to recognize that particular relations of distribution are the product of particular relations of production. Change the relations of production, the economic structure of the society, and you change the basis of the relations of distribution. Change the relation of production and you change the dominant conception of "right."

Necessarily characteristic of the relations of production of this new society "just as it *emerges* from capitalist society" is that the individual producer enters into productive relations with others as the owner of his own capacity. What are the potential implications of such a relation inherited from capitalism? Consider this thought-experiment: As an owner, the producer wants as much as possible for his property in an exchange with society. He therefore looks upon his labor as a means to obtain articles of consumption, and if he does not get what he considers his entitlement, the equivalent, he offers less labor. Alienated labor to obtain alien products and, indeed, alienation from other members of society. There exists, as Marx described the exchange relation in the *Grundrisse,* a "connection of mutually indifferent persons." In this exchange between owners, there is "the total isolation of their private interests from one another."[33]

Further, how do these owners of the personal condition of production look upon the socially owned material conditions of production? Can we envision any conditions in which alienated producers who relate as owners of their labor-power might waste means of production or even steal them as a means of securing more articles of consumption? Can we exclude, for example, the possibility that, flowing from this particular relation, "the worker actually treats the social character of his work, its combination with the work of others for a common goal, as a power alien to him; the conditions in which this combination are realized are for him the property of another, and he would be completely indifferent to the wastage of this property if he were not himself constrained to economize on it"?[34]

Marx did not explore all the implications of such alienation in the *Critique,* although the elements for this thought-experiment are present in his theoretical work. The *Critique* was meant only as marginal notes on the draft program and not as a full development of his ideas on post-capitalist society. However, he did identify one aspect of this particular defect of the new society, which is "in every respect, economically, morally, and intellectually, still stamped with the birthmarks of the old society from whose womb it emerges." *Inequality!* The individual owner of labor-power in this relation considers "unequal individual endowment and thus productive capacity as natural privileges." His claim as owner to an equivalent, thus, was *"a right of inequality"*; it is his right as an owner, given the economic structure of the society.

Insofar as the individual producer relates to others only as owner, nothing else matters. Not the differing needs of producers, for example, that "one worker is married, another is not; one has more children than another, and so on and so forth," nor indeed any characteristic of people other than as performers of labor. Insofar as they relate as owners, they do not care about others in this "connection of mutually indifferent persons." Marx understood this as a deformed, one-sided perspective that entirely ignores producers as human beings, as members of society. Years earlier, Marx had described the bourgeois economists as one-sided because they look at the producer "only as a *worker* [and do] not consider him when he is not working as a human being." He returned to the same point in the *Critique*, pointing out that in the focus upon the right to equivalents the producers are considered "from one *definite* side only, for instance, in the present case, are regarded *only as workers* and nothing more is seen in them, everything else being ignored."[35]

What are the implications of this self-interest of the private owners of labor-power that is inherited from capitalist society? Clearly, alienation (of labor, products, other human beings) and inequality reflects this defect of the new society as it emerges from capitalism. But it is more than just a defect: it is also an *infection*. The producers in this society do not exist only as private owners of labor-power. They are also common owners of the means of production and people engaged in cooperative activity. And, insofar as they exist in the latter relation, the tendency is toward equality (as *they are equal* as owners of the means of production) and for a connection of people who are not "mutually indifferent."

Thus there are *two* tendencies that are in struggle. The inherited defect of private ownership of labor-power must be subordinated if the new society is to move forward, and if this infection is not to dissolve the cooperative society based upon the common ownership of the means of production.[36] Consequently, the development of the new system "consists precisely in subordinating all elements of society to itself, or in creating out of it the organs which it still lacks. This is historically how it becomes a totality."

How does the new society subordinate its defects and create the new organs that it still lacks? Although Marx did not address this question explicitly in the *Critique*, an answer can be found there nevertheless. Consider his discussion of the deductions from the total product of labor once there is the common ownership of the means of production. Before distribution of the total social product to individual producers for consumption goods, Marx noted the need for deductions for reasons such as replacement and expansion of means of production.[37] Then, he turned first to "*the general costs of administration not belonging to production,*" presumably costs associated with state administration. "This part," Marx indicated, "will, from the outset, be very considerably restricted in comparison with present-day society, and it diminishes in proportion as the new society develops."

There is an obvious way to understand Marx's point about these reduced deductions. His comment must be put in the context of what he learned four years earlier from the Paris Commune. Why are those costs restricted? Very simply, it is because the state immediately ceases to be "a public force organized for social enslavement"; "*from the outset,*" state functions are "wrested from an authority usurping pre-eminence over society itself, and restored to the responsible agents of society."[38] The success of the struggle would have meant that in place of the old centralized government, "all France would have been organized into self-working and self-governing communes." And the result would be "state functions reduced to a few functions for general national purposes."[39] "As the new society develops," the state would be converted more and more (in the words of the *Critique*) "from an organ superimposed upon society into one completely subordinate to it."

New organs, those self-working and self-governing communes, thus must be created in place of the "systematic and hierarchic division of labour" in which state administration and governing are treated as "mysteries, transcendent functions only to be trusted to the hands of a trained caste—state parasites, richly paid sycophants and sinecurists." In place of the old state, public functions in the Commune became *"real workmen's* functions."[40] In this way, the experience of the Commune revealed "the political form at last discovered under which to work out the economical emancipation of Labour."[41] That political form characterized by "self-working and self-governing communes" was a particular type of state—the workers' state, the dictatorship of the proletariat. Do you want to know what the dictatorship of the proletariat looks like, asked Engels at the time of the Erfurt Program. He answered, "Look at the Paris Commune. That was the Dictatorship of the Proletariat."[42] The Paris Commune demonstrated that the "revolutionary transformation" of capitalist into communist society requires what the *Critique* described as *"the revolutionary dictatorship of the proletariat"* to carry it forward.

This is one side of the transformation implied by the *Critique's* discussion of the deductions from the total social product. *"Secondly,"* there was *"that which is intended for the common satisfaction of needs, such as schools, health services, etc."* In contrast to the last deduction, Marx indicated that "from the outset this part grows considerably in comparison with present-day society, and it grows in proportion as the new society develops." In short, the new society moves immediately to expand its provision of use-values for common satisfaction of needs. Thus, for the society to develop its own premises, more and more of its output is deducted from what individuals may claim on the basis of their private ownership of labor-power; more and more "what the producer is deprived of in his capacity as a private individual benefits him directly or indirectly in his capacity as a member of society." As the new society develops, our claim upon the output of society increasingly is *as a member of society.* The measure of the development of the new society is the expansion of the commons.

This emerging relation of distribution, however, cannot rest in midair. No distribution relation does. It requires a change in the relation among the producers, from one in which they interact as individual owners of labor-power to one in which they function consciously as members of a community. To subordinate the bourgeois right based upon individual ownership, the associated producers must create new organs that ensure conscious cooperation of "activities, determined by communal needs and purposes." As described in the *Grundrisse*, in this relation of associated producers "a communal production, communality, is presupposed as the basis of production." And this new relation of production determines the relation of distribution: "Its presupposed communal character would determine the distribution of products. The communal character of production would make the product into a communal, general product from the outset." [43]

The relation of distribution is not changed by exhortation. Rather, it changes as the new society involves producers directly in a conscious process of planning as "determined by communal needs and purposes." Through such communal organs, the result is "an organization of labour whose consequence would be the participation of the individual in communal consumption." "In proportion as the new society develops," it learns to "distribute its time in a purposeful way, in order to achieve a production adequate to its overall needs." As Marx noted in the *Grundrisse*, "Economy of time, along with the planned distribution of labour time among the various branches of production, remains the first economic law on the basis of communal production." [44] *Planning by the associated producers* is at the core of this economic structure, one in which "the instruments of labour are common property and the total labour is co-operatively regulated."

This is how the new society develops upon its own foundations, by creating new organs for cooperatively planning the distribution of society's labor in order to satisfy "the worker's own need for development" and by doing so not through a state standing over and above society but rather through democratic institutions "completely subordinate" to society—through those "self-working and self-governing communes."[45] By creating the conditions through which people are able to develop all their potential—that all-sided "rich individuality"—through their activity, the new society develops productive forces specific to a society of associated producers, just as the productive forces created under capitalist relations are specific to that society; and the result, as the *Critique* indicates, is that "the productive forces have also increased with the all-round development of the individual, and all the springs of co-operative wealth flow more abundantly." With the development of this new economic structure, society can inscribe on its banners: "From each according to his ability, to each according to his needs!"

The Misuse of the Critique of the Gotha Programme

We build the new society by "subordinating all elements of society to itself, or in creating out of it the organs which it still lacks." We build communist society upon its own foundations by developing new communal relations of production that subordinate the private ownership of labor-power and by creating a new state that is society's "own living forces instead of as forces controlling and subduing it."[46] This process begins "from the outset" and advances until such time as the society of associated producers spontaneously generates its own premises and thus rests upon its own foundations. This was Marx's vision in his *Critique of the Gotha Program.*

Unfortunately, the standard interpretation of the *Critique of the Gotha Programme* offers a different picture.[47] Rather than a continuous struggle to go beyond the defects inherited from capitalist society, the standard interpretation introduces a division of post-capitalist society into two distinct "stages"—each with its own strikingly different relation of distribution—and argues the necessity to build upon those defects. Whereas the higher stage of "communism" would be characterized by distribution in accordance with need, the "two-stagers" argue that in the lower stage of "socialism" the principle of distribution is necessarily one in which each individual producer receives in accordance with his contribution.

Upon what do these two principles of distribution rest and why are they different? It is not because there is a difference in the productive relations among the associated producers. Indeed, there is no discussion at all of relations of production! The standard story simply assumes that the relations of production are equivalent to state ownership of the means of production and that, since the latter is presumably unchanging in both stages, the source of the difference between the stages must be *something else*. That something else, we are told, is the level of the development of society's productive forces. This singular focus upon productive forces, however, is not to be found in the *Critique*. Aside from Marx's reference to wage slavery in capitalism becoming more severe as capitalist productive forces increase, the only other mention of productive forces refers to their growth "with the all-around development of the individual."

What, then, is the source of this focus upon the level of productive forces? Very simply, it is Marx's statement in the *Critique* that *"Right can never be higher than the economic structure of society and the cultural development conditioned thereby."* That statement, we have seen, refers to the nature of the relations of production of the society. But not for the two-stagers! For them, "the economic structure of society" is the level of productive forces rather than its relations of production. Their whole argument rests upon this premise. Once you magically conjure away the relations of production of the new society and leave only the level of productive forces seemingly visible, then the story is told: to move from one stage to another, you must increase the productive forces. The task assigned to the socialist stage is to create "an enormous development of productive forces" that makes possible the higher stage of communism, the society of abundance in which there can be distribution in accordance with need.[48] Develop the productive forces, develop the productive forces! That, we are told, is Marx and the prophets.

Here, then, is a potential theoretical basis for the justification in practice for anything that may be deemed to increase productive forces, be it gulags, state repression of workers' organizations, support for capitalist institutions, insistence upon a centralized state over and above society, or all of the above. The goal, after all, is "communism," that state of abundance that will allow every individual to take from the total social product in accordance with his needs. Since this is the designated route to the Promised Land, then surely anyone who denies the primacy of productive forces is by definition confused, petit bourgeois, or even counterrevolutionary.

Until that Promised Land has been reached, however, society in the "socialist stage" requires the enforcement of the distribution rule of "an equal amount of products for an equal amount of labour," which is presumably "the socialist principle." Why? The answer is that "right" can never be higher than the level of productive forces, and workers will not work efficiently and productively unless they receive what they deem to be their equivalent. The implicit premise of the standard interpretation is that workers are alienated (from their labor, their products, and each other) and that this inherited defect can only be removed by that enormous development of productive forces that makes all products free. And, if productivity is low, it must be because of "serious infractions of the socialist principle of distribution according to work," in the words of Gorbachev.[49]

No need, then, to consider whether continuation of alienation may have anything to do with the nature of relations within the workplace or a state ruling over the producers. No need to consider if abundance can ever be reached if alienated labor leads to constantly growing needs to possess alien products. On the contrary, the two-stagers insist upon the need to rely upon the "socialist principle" for the foreseeable future, that is, to build upon the self-interest of the producers.

One would search in vain for any such suggestion from Marx that it is possible to get to that future stage of abundance by trying to build upon a defect inherited from capitalism. His discussion of the growing deduction for satisfaction of common needs points in precisely the opposite direction. As Che observed in his *Man and Socialism in Cuba* (and as the twentieth century demonstrated), relying upon the material self-interest of producers, the "socialist principle," is a dead end:

> The pipe dream that socialism can be achieved with the help of the dull instruments left to us by capitalism (the commodity as the economic cell, individual material interest as the lever, etc.) can lead into a blind alley. And you wind up there after having travelled a long distance with many crossroads, and it is hard to figure out just where you took the wrong turn.[50]

So why does this sparse interpretation of Marx's *Critique of the Gotha Program* continue to dominate? First, it supports the position of those who occupy positions in states standing over and above society (or who consciously justify that occupation); it deflects attention from the pressing need from the outset to change the relations of production in workplaces and communities and to transform the state into what Marx called the revolutionary dictatorship of the proletariat—that state of self-working and self-governing communes fostering the revolutionary practice through which people change themselves as they change circumstances.

But there is a second reason for the staying power of this caricature of Marx's theoretical conception. Those who enforce it rely upon authority, that of Lenin. For there can be no doubt that the division of post-capitalism into two stages and the insistence upon enforcement of "the socialist principle" emanated from Lenin's interpretation of the *Critique* in his *State and Revolution*. Writing in a revolutionary period during a war in which Russia was under attack by a more developed neighbor and when supporters of capitalism were deriding the utopian demagoguery of the Bolsheviks for wanting to introduce Communism, Lenin stressed that only the first stage was on the immediate agenda and that an enormous development of productive forces was needed before the higher stage was possible. Although there was far more to *State and Revolution*, the standard interpretation of Marx's *Critique* has taken only what is usable in the present.

This is not the occasion to examine what Lenin wrote at the time. However, we need to keep in mind his understanding that "the categorical requirement of Marxist theory in investigating any social question is that it be examined within *definite* historical limits, and if it refers to a particular country (e.g., the national program for a given country), that account be taken of the specific features distinguishing that country from others in the same historical epoch."

If we want to understand Marx's theoretical contribution in his *Critique of the Gotha Program*, there is no alternative to reading Marx. Read Marx's "marginal notes," and read the theoretical bases for them.

3. Transcending the Crisis of Socialist Economy

In preparing this collection, I came across the following artifact, a 1985 paper presented at the annual Roundtable of Socialism in the World at Cavtat, Yugoslavia. This state-sponsored conference was unique in bringing together representatives of Communist governments, non-aligned states, Eurocommunist parties, Yugoslav intellectuals, and assorted Western leftists (among them editors of Monthly Review, New Left Review, *and* Studies in Political Economy*). Papers were prepared on the conference theme for the year, and debate in plenary sessions was lively and often triggered by Western critiques of "real socialism."*

I have reproduced the talk as presented with minor changes, such as using the term "real socialism" in place of "actually existing socialism," the more familiar usage at the time, and with the elimination of the technical aspects (equations and symbols) of the simple model contained in the original. The paper points to important aspects of both "real socialism" and the "market-self-management" of Yugoslavia, identifying both positive characteristics and dynamics that would contribute soon after to their demise; however, the deficiencies of the paper reflect the time and place of its presentation.

For one, given the culture of the conference, I attempted to be subtle in order to open up questions for discussion rather than to engage in a direct critique of the two models. Clearly, I wasn't subtle enough, as I was asked gently by a Yugoslav comrade if I would agree to waive presentation of the paper in the plenary as it had been discussed already in one of the workshops. Was this, I asked, because my stress upon the inherent tendency to generate unemployment in the Yugoslav model would encourage the Soviets, etc., to attack that model? Yes, I was told. Although I rejected that request, the concerns of my hosts were not realized as the plenary discussion in question revolved around Harry Magdoff's paper on the economic laws of socialism and a presentation by a Czech participant.

The second problem in the paper was that my own analysis of the two experiences was deficient. Missing in particular was sufficient consideration of class relations and class dynamics. It was not until I analyzed the reproduction of "real socialism" as a system in Contradictions of "Real Socialism" *(2012) that I was able to proceed further, and these insights are reflected in chapter 4. Finally, although the paper did stress the inherent problems associated with private ownership of labor-power, I was still drawing upon the terminology of distinct "stages," which I subsequently rejected, as shown in chapter 2.*

At this point in the history of early socialism, it is apparent that barriers have emerged that challenge the further development of socialism. No longer is it opponents alone who speak of crisis within socialist economy. Now discussion of shortages of raw materials and labor, declining rates of growth, inefficiency of investment, lagging productivity of labor, and unemployment can be found in the literature of socialist economies themselves. It is appropriate, then, to turn our attention to these questions at a gathering with the theme of "Socialism on the Threshold of the 21st Century."

Let us consider two distinct models characteristic of existing socialism: (1) the model that roughly corresponds to the experience of the USSR and other Soviet-bloc countries; and (2) the model that roughly corresponds to the Yugoslavian experience. We may designate these as "real socialism" (RS) and "market-self-management"(MSM), respectively. In one short paper, we cannot provide a full discussion of either experience; however, it is nevertheless possible even with overly generalized models to pose some questions about the efficiency of the two systems with respect to the alternative conditions of labor abundance and labor scarcity.

Real Socialism (RS)

Characteristic of RS is the central role of the state in directing the economy and expanding the production of means of production. In the centrally planned variant, initiative rests with the planners and the political leadership, and the essential thrust is for growth. Whether we assume the political leadership acts in this manner for reasons of "altruism" or whether particular interests and privileges underlie their actions is not of our immediate concern; the central issue is that the initiative, the thrust, the "responsibility" for looking after the general interest is absorbed by a relatively small body concentrated in the upper echelons of the party.

In this situation, the overwhelming characteristic has been the reproduction of shortages, a phenomenon once advanced as a law of socialism by Stalin in his distinction between capitalism and socialism—"Purchasing power continually outstrips the growth of production and pushes it ahead."— What emerges is a shortage economy; it emanates in the attempt to grow beyond existing potentials, which are themselves constricted by the absorption of initiative by the center.[1]

It has been, in part, an attempt to solve this problem emanating from the monopoly of initiative that has marked various reform measures within RS. In the reform variant (for example, Hungary) substantial initiative with respect to investment decisions passed to firm managers as part of an attempt to more efficiently realize the goals of the center. Yet, the pattern of shortages did not thereby disappear. Investment hunger and an expansion drive on the part

of individual enterprise managers became the basis of the reproduction of shortages. Each manager bargained and struggled with
the center for resources to permit an increase in the level of output
and the size of his enterprise. Yet, in itself, this impulse would
not be sufficient to generate shortages. What is critical is that the
center retained its responsibility for looking after the general interest; and central decisions, "helping out" firms operating at a loss,
have produced a "soft budget constraint" for firms, thereby gener-
ating an expansion drive undertaken without fear of failure.[2]

Underlying the decisions of the leadership in both centrally
planned and reform variants of RS is an important aspect of RS,
namely the commitment of the leadership to providing for full
employment. It is seen as a unique characteristic of socialism
that no worker be subject to the fear of unemployment present
in capitalism. In addition to contributing to the reproduction of
shortages, the stress on full employment has had significant implications. Effectively, workers in RS possess "job rights" in that it
is extremely difficult to dismiss them or to alter their jobs in a
way that reduces work satisfaction against their wills. Workers
thus have an undisputed right of access to means of production.
(Whether this is a right of access to *particular* means of production or to means of production in general remains unresolved.)
In contrast to the experience in the USSR before 1956, they are
able to shift jobs in response to the existence of higher wages or
jobs more appropriate to their training. Though they themselves
possess little if any initiative in the production process, workers in
RS expect that the political leadership will protect their job rights
and will direct the economy such that their real consumption will
rise over time. These expectations, in turn, act as constraints upon
the leadership and are operative in affecting its growth orientation.

Market-Self-Management (MSM)

In the model of market-self-management, initiative rests with
self-managing collectives of producers. I stress here the "model,"

since there are concrete historical circumstances in Yugoslavia that involve departures from a pure model. To such collectives go the responsibilities for organizing the labor process, for permitting the satisfaction of the immediate needs of the producers, and for ensuring expanded reproduction of the means of production. In this sense, MSM shifts initiative and responsibility to the workers and is an important advance in the development of a socialist economy, that is, the realization of an economy controlled by the associated producers themselves.

The self-managed collective has as its central thrust the maximization of the income of its members, in the short run by the distribution of net revenue as personal income and in the long run by investment that increases productivity. Thus the central decision in each enterprise is the division between personal income and accumulation, and the ability to make that decision is seen as critical in the process of workers taking charge. The role of the state here is substantially reduced, although political authorities may, through influence on bank policies, create a soft budget constraint for enterprises that can affect the decision to invest or distribute personal income.

In contrast to RS, in MSM there is not a commitment to a full employment policy; rather, the commitment is to permitting workers in the existing enterprises to "rule over expanded reproduction." Nevertheless, a pattern of "job rights" exists as well here, in that "worker solidarity" militates against dismissals and layoffs of co-workers in the event of reduced demand. Precisely because full employment is not the focus, the experience of MSM differs considerably from that of RS under conditions of labor abundance.

"Extensive" and "Intensive" Development

Consider these two models under the conditions of labor abundance and labor scarcity. The historical experience of socialist economies has been that they have emerged in economies with substantial pools of underemployed labor in the countryside. The absorption of those pools of labor has been, therefore, characteristic of the construction of developed socialist economies. RS accomplishes this absorption through the pattern of what has come to be known as "extensive" development: the creation of new means of production (new factories, etc.) combined with new labor drawn from the countryside.

What this extensive development represents is the expansion of a relation characterized by state-owned means of production and workers who possess job rights, which in effect are a form of property right in the means of production. The process here is one of *expanded reproduction* of the state property/worker relation; its counterpart in capitalism is expanded reproduction of capitalist relations, where the additions of labor are drawn from pre-capitalist relations whose non-reproduction is a condition for the expanded reproduction of capitalist relations. The predominant form of extensive development is the creation of new workplaces.

The process of extensive development means increases in production and productivity for the economy as a whole (given that productivity in the state sector is higher than in pre-socialist sectors); it thereby permits increases in real consumption. Yet these increases depend upon the continued existence of labor pools— labor abundance—that it ultimately absorbs.[3] The particular growth path characteristic of extensive development, then, is no longer possible. The expectations of the population for continuing increases of real consumption, expectations based upon previous experience, now are threatened. A crisis emerges within RS.

The crisis is not the result of the inevitable absorption of labor reserves, however. The emergence of labor shortage produces a crisis for RS because it cannot shift to "intensive" development, a focus upon increasing productivity in existing enterprises, without encroaching upon existing job rights. That is, there are major difficulties in introducing new techniques of production and thereby altering the work process. Efforts to introduce new technology in existing enterprises have met with worker resistance; further, managers also have been reluctant because of the potential effect on meeting production plans (and thus bonuses) and the potential effect upon the displacement of workers.[4] Rather than seeking out new technology in existing enterprises, the tendency has been that of "dodging away from it the way the devil does from incense" (Brezhnev).

RS has attempted to resolve this difficulty by introducing new techniques in *new* factories and then bidding away workers. Priority continues to be assigned to newly constructed plants for the introduction of new machinery and technology. Construction of new plants, in contrast to machinery and equipment, in the USSR accounts for a very substantial portion of new investment, roughly 60 percent in 1966–73 compared to 23 percent in the United States in the same period. And backlogs of unfinished construction projects grow. The result, too, of this approach is that it does not solve but increases the problem of labor shortages.

Thus RS faces a crisis that is reflected in declining output/capital ratios, lagging productivity gains (increasing less than capital per worker), and declining growth rates. In the USSR this in part reflects major investments under way in Siberia, but the difficulty of following the intensive growth path in existing centers exacerbates the situation. Under these circumstances, RS searches for ways to transcend the crisis. But how?

There are two directions, each oriented toward intensive development. Both involve an alteration in the existing relation of workers to the means of production. One direction emphasizes an increase in "worker discipline," which effectively means an increase in the authority of managers over workers, an intensification of labor, and a loss of "job rights," especially with regard to job content. Whether this is done by administrative means or by the introduction of "slack" within the economy to remove a "sellers' market" for labor (that is, the creation of unemployment, as advocated by Kornai), the effect is to move away from what workers have regarded as one of the important contributions of RS.[5]

The other direction would be to build upon those job rights that exist, that particular relation to the means of production, by establishing greater rights and incentives for workers in the production process and thereby increasing the initiative of the producers. In short, progress in a *socialist* direction moves in the direction of a "self-management" model.

In contrast to RS, the MSM model is admirably suited to the process of intensive development. Since collectives are oriented toward maximizing the income of their members, the enterprises have a direct interest in the introduction of new, improved techniques that increase productivity, and along with it, income per worker. There is thus a tendency for investment to be machine-intensive. Under conditions of labor shortage, MSM allows for growing output by increasing productivity. We can conclude that once expanded reproduction of the state property/worker relation has developed to the point where further additions from pre-socialist relations are less possible—that is, once the possibilities for quantitative expansion of the relation are reduced—then transcending the labor barrier would occur much more easily under self-management. In this sense, we may suggest that the future development of RS may be increasingly in the direction of self-management.

On the other hand, the performance of MSM in the situation of labor *abundance* is quite different. There is no tendency in MSM as such to absorb the preexisting labor pools. Precisely because each collective is oriented to maximizing income per collective member and investment tends to be machine-intensive, new jobs created in existing enterprises are minimal. Therefore, insofar as movements from those labor pools occurs, for example, from the countryside, the result is unemployment.

The inappropriateness of a "pure" MSM economy under conditions of labor abundance can be illustrated with a simple model. Assume a two-sector economy consisting of (1) one MSM firm, in order to abstract from the phenomena of competition among many self-managing firms, in the same way that Marx first considered "capital in general"; and (2) a pre-socialist (indeed, pre-capitalist) sector within the countryside that is characterized by abundant labor. The goal of the MSM sector is to increase income per member of that sector. Workers in this sector begin by identifying as their goal a given level of personal income per person and also a certain level of investment for the purpose of increasing productivity, the basis of future increases in personal income.

In this manner, the MSM sector acts to secure growing personal income based on increasing productivity; it thus is successful in pursuing intensive development. Yet nothing in the normal functioning of the MSM sector will permit it to absorb labor from the pre-capitalist countryside; such absorption is, indeed, contrary to the natural tendencies of MSM. On the other hand, rising income in the MSM sector, including those portions of it within the countryside itself, encourages movements of labor (new generations) to the MSM sector. It follows that inherent in this "pure" MSM model is growing unemployment within the economy as a whole.

How, then, can employment be provided for these increments to the available labor supply in this particular two-sector economy? Those unemployed in this economy are clearly separated from the means of production. Since the absorption of the unemployed will not come spontaneously from the MSM sector and since we assume for our model that such a situation of unemployment will be regarded as contrary to a socialist society, the economy clearly requires yet another sector, a state sector, that will attempt to maximize not income per employed member of the MSM sector but, rather, employment itself.

To maximize employment, the state must secure a surplus for the construction of new means of production and must combine these with the additions to the labor force; that is, it must proceed with extensive development. Further, if we assume that the new workplaces, once established, are self-managed, then it is apparent that this state sector will be the means by which expanded reproduction of the MSM relation occurs. That is, it is essential to distinguish between expanded reproduction of means of production—which remains largely in the hands of the collective—and expanded reproduction of the self-management relation.

To secure this surplus for extensive development the state sector must *tax* the MSM sector. What might we say, however, about a tendency on the part of members of the MSM sector to *oppose* such a tax, even calling it extraction of a surplus by a "Stalinist" state? Such a tendency is inherent in the very nature of this MSM sector, with its thrust to maximize income per member, because any taxation of its resources reduces its ability to realize its goals. But consider the implication of the *absence* of such a tax: the implication is that the existing means of production are the property of workers only in the MSM sector rather than the property of all citizens within the society. In short, the tendency is for means of production to be viewed as "group property," the basis for the income of an exclusive subset of the society, rather than as social property.

The acceptance of continued high levels of unemployment would be precisely the effect of a group property tendency: the unemployed would have no claim on existing means of production either directly in production or indirectly through potential surpluses. If group property is the tendency for MSM as a whole, it should not be surprising to find it functioning when we consider many self-managing enterprises, where substantial differences in income between enterprises may be found according to the nature of *their* means of production. In fact, complaints about the group property tendencies of particular collectives may be seen as inappropriate, insofar as the general tendency is part of the essential nature of MSM. (One might as justifiably complain about the profit-maximizing behavior of particular capitalists.) *Rather than as an aberration, group property behavior should be understood as a manifestation of the inherent characteristics of MSM.*

We conclude that a necessary condition for a socialist economy where we have MSM and abundant labor is the existence of a state sector that operates according to principles and goals apparently *contrary* to MSM, one that is oriented toward increasing employment—that is, "socializing" the means of production via its taxation—and doing so as long as there remain pools of labor that have yet to be absorbed within the MSM sector. This state sector is not contrary to self-management; rather, it is the means for expanded reproduction of the MSM relation and continues as such until the MSM sector is universal. Further, it should be emphasized that this is not necessarily an argument for expanding the state in Yugoslavia; it may be read as a limitation and direction of the state role to this one question—expanded reproduction of the self-management relation.

Our consideration of the two models of existing socialism leads us to conclude that although MSM more closely corresponds to the goal of a society of associated producers, aspects of RS—in particular, the role of the state as a means for the expanded reproduction of the relation and the associated commitment to full employment—are essential elements that must be incorporated. Yet does the argument only apply under the particular conditions of labor abundance?

The Barrier of a Group Property Tendency

If group property is indeed the inherent tendency of self-management, is the necessity for a "mixed economy," that is, one with a state sector, removed when the MSM relation is universal and thus all citizens are members of the "group"? What is the case under conditions of labor shortage? Although the effects of the group property tendency are clearly mitigated, they necessarily remain both at the level of MSM as a whole and at the level of many MSM's enterprises. As long as the goal of members of the MSM firm is maximizing their income, the tendency will be increased productivity, more machine-intensive activity, *and* the failure to create sufficient jobs for new generations of workers. The tendency, though mitigated, remains; by this logic, so also must a role for the state.

Is there no basis, then, for transcending the tendency toward group property? We must first understand its source in a self-managed economy.[6] We should consider the extent to which the basis of the group property tendency within the MSM economy is inherent in the "lower phase of communist society"—and is manifested in the principle of distribution according to contribution. As long as the relation of producers is one in which they expect and demand a *quid quo pro* in return for their productive activity, which means that they view their labor-power as their *own*, as their property, and merely as a means to secure their requirements, the tendencies toward group property are necessarily reproduced. They may be administratively suppressed under some conditions but they do not disappear.

The maximization of income for a given expenditure of labor, or alternatively, the minimization of labor for a given set of use-values, flows from the relation among producers as owners. It may take a group rather than an individual form insofar as production is carried out by collectives. but the result is the same. That is why the choice of technique is biased toward machine-intensive investment within MSM and why particular producers consider themselves to be exclusively entitled to the "results of their activity." The tendency toward the treatment of means of production as group property is inherent in the conception of labor-power as property, in the self-orientation of producers.

Yet other tendencies present in the MSM economy point in the direction of the *transcendence* of the group property tendency. They are best described under the heading of "solidarity." Solidarity is present when the members of a collective do not lay off or dismiss other members of the collective at a period when demand for output declines; this tendency, which is counter to the general thrust of the MSM firm, involves the recognition of the needs of one's co-workers. Solidarity is similarly present in the recognition of the necessity to provide employment for new increments to the labor force; this is the recognition that the needs of others must be satisfied. In particular cases, though, this may take the negative form of nepotism, the creation of jobs for the children of collective members.

Similarly, the recognition that basic socially determined needs should be satisfied for producers in backward regions and less advanced sectors, and that resources should be directed to permit those producers to increase their productivity, is an essential element in the emergence of solidarity among producers. In short, the encroachment of the principle of distribution in accordance with need implies a process of dissolution of labor-power as property and its corollary of a tendency toward group property, the specific barrier of the MSM economy.

Precisely because the tendencies for solidarity and the recognition of interdependence of all members of society are not entirely spontaneous, or the *only* tendencies present within the MSM economy, the transcendence of the barrier in MSM requires the conscious nurturing of the future of the movement, the elaboration of the interests of producers as a whole. This consideration points to the necessary role of subjective forces.

All the exhortation in the world, however, would not by itself suffice to realize a transition from the "lower phase" to the "higher phase" of communist society. The specific barrier of the MSM economy generates a *crisis,* one whose manifestations are unemployment, growing gaps between the incomes of producers in differing regions and sectors, disintegration and "dissolidarity" within society. Crises can be opportunities. We can anticipate that there will be many such crises, and that in these crises not only the specific barrier of MSM but also the means to transcend it will come to the fore. We can anticipate that this process will be severe and protracted, but as we consider the question of Socialism on the Eve of the 21st Century, it is in this direction that the potential for a further socialist evolution exists.

4. Contested Reproduction and the Contradictions of Socialism

In late April 2013 I had the opportunity to speak at a conference in Ljubljana on primitive accumulation organized by the Workers and Punks University. I was also fortunate enough to be present for the May Day announcement of the Initiative for Democratic Socialism, which has since gone on to representation in the Slovenian parliament through the United Left Coalition. From there, in subsequent weeks I proceeded to speak on struggles based upon moral economy (explored in chapter 9) in Zagreb sponsored by the Centre for Workers Studies and then to Belgrade where I gave the following talk organized by the Centre for Political Emancipation. This last gave me an opportunity to do two things: (1) introduce my analysis of "real socialism" as developed in my recent book, Contradictions of "Real Socialism": The Conductor and the Conducted; *and (2) extend that analysis to interrogate the experience of market self-management in the former Yugoslavia. The latter was the real challenge, because although I had written several essays related to that experience, with which a number of young scholar-militants in the former Yugoslavia were familiar, I had not before even thought about how this new understanding applied to the Yugoslav experience.[1]*

Some Explanations about the Fall of "Real Socialism"

Why did "real socialism" and, in particular, the Soviet Union fall? Let me note a few explanations that have been offered. With respect to the Soviet Union, one very interesting explanation is that it's all the fault of Gorbachev. And not simply the errors of Gorbachev but the treachery. Those who offer this explanation rely in particular upon a document that is sometimes described as his "confession." This document begins :

> My ambition was to liquidate communism, the dictatorship over all the people. Supporting me and urging me on in this mission was my wife, who was of this opinion long before I was. I knew that I could only do this if I was the leading functionary. In this my wife urged me to climb to the top post. While I actually became acquainted with the West, my mind was made up forever. I decided that I must destroy the whole apparatus of the CPSU and the USSR. Also, I must do this in all of the other socialist countries. My ideal is the path of social democracy. Only this system shall benefit all the people. This quest I decided I must fulfill.

Now, one of the most interesting things about this document is that it is virtually untraceable. It is said to come from an interview in Turkey but the actual source is unverifiable and, indeed, appears to have occurred with different interviewers.[2] I suggest this document is not credible at all. So why mention it? Simply because there are people who believe it and cite it as authority. I discovered this to my surprise a few years ago at a conference in Beijing on the fall of the Soviet Union where it was repeatedly quoted by members of Russian and Bulgarian communist parties and also, interestingly, by some Chinese scholars within the state structure who were clearly warning against Chinese Gorbachevs. The inference in this is that all was well with "real socialism," but that it's important to watch out for the liquidators and saboteurs.

A second explanation prevalent among economists and reformers inside and outside real socialism was that the Soviet Union was a victim of its own success. It had succeeded in building up the productive forces with particular methods of central planning (using administrative-command methods) to the point where the old methods of organizing the economy no longer were appropriate for the more complex, industrialized economy. Now those old methods had become a fetter on the development of productive forces and the result was crisis. Accordingly, it was necessary to change the relations of production and to move away from central planning to focus on individual enterprises. The call was for a profound restructuring (perestroika) and the creation of a new economic mechanism. The problem, it was asserted, is that it took far too long to make these changes in the economy, which had already gone into crisis.

Another argument stressing the failure to make necessary reforms emphasized that the problem was the legacies of the past. For example, the orientation of workers to egalitarianism and equality was described by one former Yugoslav sociologist, Josip Županov, as an "egalitarian syndrome" that was "a relic of traditional societies"—indeed, their "vicious legacy"—and thus a barrier to the development of a modern society. An orientation toward equality was often described as a legacy of traditional peasant culture and was thus distinctly "non-proletarian." As one Soviet labor economist, Efim Manevich, declared, "Marxism-Leninism decisively sweeps away the petit-bourgeois theory of leveling distribution and consumption," and that such ideas are "alien to the proletariat."[3] Here was another argument about the necessity to move vigorously to a market economy.

Yet another Marxist-sounding explanation for the failure of "real socialism" was that it was *premature*, that the level of productive forces was too low and that therefore it was inappropriate to introduce socialist relations of production. It was first essential to build up the productive forces, presumably under capitalist relations. This was a very familiar argument among Mensheviks who were critical of the Soviet Revolution, but it is also significant that I heard it a few years ago in meetings at the Party School (the Ho Chi Minh Political Academy) and with leading party intellectuals in Vietnam.

Then there was the argument made in 1950 in Yugoslavia by Boris Kidric, and supported by many others in the party leadership, that described real socialism as a state socialism that "unavoidably leads to an increase in strengthening of privileged bureaucracy as a social parasite, to a suppression . . . of socialist democracy and to a general degeneration of the system into . . . state capitalism."[4] This was the argument that "real socialism" did not have socialist relations of production and that you cannot build socialism without worker management, a position subsequently endorsed by President Chávez of Venezuela. The implicit premise of this position is that the failure to develop new socialist relations of production is the source of the failure of "real socialism."

Contested Reproduction in "Real Socialism"

Though in principle I agree that characteristic of real socialism was the absence of socialist relations of production, this is insufficient to explain the course of real socialism as consolidated in the period of the 1950s through the 1980s. In contrast to many approaches that look upon "real socialism" as a particular system, I argued in *Contradictions of "Real Socialism": The Conductor and the Conducted* that we need to consider it as a concrete phenomenon that contained within it several different productive relations. That is, it is essential to recognize the existence of contested reproduction between differing logics. Therefore I stress the importance of focusing upon class struggle.

Consistent with Marx's methodology, from my examination of particular concrete phenomena like the shortage economy and the apparent behavior of actors within real socialism, I distilled a simple concept from which to develop logically the inner connections of the system and an understanding of the concrete whole. That logical starting point was the vanguard party, which is central to an understanding of vanguard relations of production, the dominant relation between the vanguard party and the working class in real socialism. I identified in the book three tenets or doctrines characteristic of the logic of the vanguard party:

1. *The goal of system change*: an absolute commitment to replacing capitalism with socialism and to building a communist society, which has as its premise the appropriate development of productive forces.
2. *The need for a political instrument*: this goal requires a political party with the mission and responsibility of organizing, guiding, and orienting the working class, all working people, and social organizations.
3. *The necessary character of the vanguard party*: the struggle to defeat the enemies of the working class requires a disciplined, centralized, and united revolutionary party—*our* party.

Consider these three points. The goal of system change distinguishes the concept of the vanguard party from a body of self-interested bureaucrats or would-be capitalists. It begins from a clear rejection of capitalism and the belief in the necessity of socialism. Given that essential goal, the question is: What is to be done? Characteristic for the supporters of the vanguard party is the conviction that the achievement of this goal will not happen spontaneously; it requires leadership. The orchestra needs a conductor. And since the conductor alone can see the whole picture and has the whole score before him, there is no place for spontaneity and improvisation. Discipline and hierarchy are essential. Within the workplace and community, it is only appropriate that all parts, all instruments, follow a predetermined plan determined by the vanguard party. Socialism in this perspective is a gift to those below by those above, who are the only ones who know how to create socialism.

But, characteristic of "real socialism" was not simply the logic of the vanguard, a logic we can observe in many would-be conductors. Also key was that the working class *accepted* the leadership of the vanguard party. And it did so insofar as it was able to achieve some desired goals from the relation. Within "real socialism" there was a social contract (described by Boris Kagarlitsky as an obligatory or asymmetrical social contract), and an essential part of that contract for workers was protection and security from unemployment, the maintenance of their job rights (which meant that jobs could not be changed in a way that workers regarded as reducing their individual welfare), a short length and low intensity of the workday, the expectation of rising income over time, subsidized necessities, and relative egalitarianism. In return for these benefits, workers accepted the rule of the vanguard party and their own powerlessness and subordination in every aspect of society.

Implicit in the logic of the vanguard was the necessity that the vanguard control the state, that the means of production be the property of the state, and that the state control the direction of the economy through central planning. These are not abstract characteristics. In every dialectical presentation, all later moments are implicit in the starting point. Hence, in real socialism, these institutions embodied the hierarchy inherent in this conception of the vanguard. Thus there was a vanguard form of the state, a vanguard form of state ownership, a vanguard form of planning, and a specifically vanguard mode of production. Further, there were specific tendencies, laws of motion, inherent in this relation. Given the job rights ensured in the social contract, for example, expanded reproduction by intensive development, that is, introducing new machines and techniques in existing productive centers, was difficult. Development tended to take the form of building new centers of production and then attracting workers to these with better working conditions, wages, and benefits. Inherent in this emphasis upon extensive development was the tendency, sooner or later, to create resource and labor shortages and thus a potential crisis.

Yet this was the immediate source of neither the crisis of real socialism nor its dysfunctional and irrational character. There is nothing in the vanguard relation as such that can explain such perverse phenomena as heavy chandeliers, thick paper produced by the paper industry, incomplete buildings because construction enterprises were credited with more value added in the early stages of production than later, and the practice of "gold-plating," where, for example, a clothing factory used material for a coat lining that cost twice as much as the cloth for the outside, thereby substantially increasing the value of the coats produced. Similarly, consider the mad rush known as "storming" at the end of plan periods in order to obtain bonuses, a wasteful practice that produced useless and dangerous products such as vacuum cleaners that electrocute you. Or the hoarding of productive materials and labor by individual enterprises and the distorted reports on productive capacity sent upward from enterprises to the planning authorities. These patterns are not at all consistent with the goals and practices of the vanguard.

Rather, these tendencies emanated from a source *outside* the social contract between vanguard and working class. In particular, they were the result of the bonus-maximizing behavior of the enterprise managers, who embody a logic different from that of the vanguard. The logic of the vanguard focuses upon the whole, upon the interconnection and harmony of the parts. It is the logic of the orchestra conductor, which the vanguard views as essential to ensure harmonious cooperation. In contrast, for the managers there is no focus upon the whole; their logic emphasizes maximization for each individual unit. The implicit argument is that by acting in accordance with individual self-interest, each unit is led as if by an invisible hand to act in the interest of the whole.

For the managers, it was rational to understate the productive potential of their enterprises in order to obtain lower quotas, which enhanced the potential for achieving bonuses, even though this deprived the planners of accurate information on the economy. It was rational to stockpile inventories of resources and excess labor even though this produced shortages, and it was rational to produce inputs that might be inaccessible because of shortages even though this introduced irrational duplication in the economy.

Further, it was rational to interpret quotas in such a way as to increase recorded output, as in "gold-plated" products for which the quotas were stated in value terms and the heavy chandeliers for which weight was the criterion for achieving bonuses. The sum of individual rational decisions obviously does not necessarily yield social rationality.

What was that alternative logic? Although these managers didn't own the means of production, didn't have the power to compel workers to perform surplus labor, and didn't own commodities (as a result of the labor process) that could be exchanged to realize surplus value, they did contain within them the *logic of capital*— just as merchant and money-lending capitalists did before capital was successful in seizing possession of production.

Although the constraints placed upon the managers by the regulations of the vanguard prevented them from functioning as capitalists, the drive, impulse, the *logic* of these managers is a different matter. If these income-maximizing managers, these constrained capitalists, struggled to remove the constraints placed upon them—for example, specific output targets, designated suppliers and customers, the appropriation of enterprise profits, the inability to discipline or fire workers, or to introduce freely new methods of production, what was this drive if not the logic of capital? Expressing that logic is the mantra—*Free capital!*

Thus, two different logics—the logic of the vanguard and the logic of capital. And the result of their interaction is what we observe in looking at the phenomena characteristic of "real socialism." As Preobrazhensky pointed out in the 1920s, when there is contested reproduction between differing sets of productive relations, the interaction of the systems can generate crises, inefficiencies, and irrationality that wouldn't be found in either system in its purity. This is the unarticulated story of "real socialism," that its particular characteristics were the result of neither the logic of the vanguard nor the logic of capital. Rather, it was the particular combination of the two that yielded the dysfunction and deformation identified with "real socialism." Two systems and two logics do not simply exist side by side. They *interact*. They interpenetrate. And they deform each other.

In the book, I explore the effect of contested reproduction in "real socialism." The combination of the behavior of managers attempting to income-maximize in their own enterprises under the constraints of the plan and the efforts of the planners to compel the managers to produce as much as possible (and to dismiss what they saw as the "bogus difficulties" the managers invented) produced the particular pattern of shortages characteristic of "real socialism." Yet this was only one aspect of the relation: there was more than just a struggle of opposites. As well as the serious dysfunctions (indeed, the crisis) in the economy as a whole, which result from the struggle between these two logics, each side was deformed as they interpenetrated. On the one side we see managers who in practice preferred to seek out and lobby allies in ministries and planning bodies rather than take their chances on the market. On the other side there were planners and ministers who (much like Hegel's Lord in his *Phenomenology*) recognized their dependence upon the managers for the success of the plan within their particular jurisdiction and accordingly ignored the perverse effects of managerial behavior on the economy as a whole.

We see here a definite tendency for the line between the two opposites to become blurred in practice—that is, a tendency for an identity of opposites to emerge. On the one hand, managers who focus upon lobbying those above for support; on the other hand, planners who support the actions of self-oriented managers. Though the coming together of these opposites can provide mutual security for a time and can generate an apparent stabilization within "real socialism," this unity is only apparent. What prevailed was the now hidden, now open *struggle* between the two logics—a struggle over property, that is, the ownership of the means of production.

To whom did the bundle of property rights over the means of production belong within "real socialism"? We need to distinguish between juridical ownership and real ownership, between juridical power and real power over the means of production. Who had the right to direct people, to use and distribute the surplus product and residual income, and the right to control the means of production (including the power to delegate that control)? Under vanguard relations of production, the vanguard party has all the attributes of the owner of the means of production with the exception of the ability to sell, bequeath, or alienate that property. Demonstrating its ownership as well was the vanguard's ability under the social contract to grant job rights to workers, rights that ensured their link in practice to specific means of production.

The vanguard as vanguard, though, did not *possess* the means of production. Following Charles Bettelheim, we note that specific units of production, in fact, are possessed by those who have the technical capacity to direct and utilize the means of production in a labor process. As long as the proprietor of the means of production is able to control those who possess, that possession cannot be transformed into property. In the case of "real socialism," the more that the vanguard brings the means of production under its control and coordinates *a priori* the different units of production through the central plan, the more those who possess the means of production are subordinated to the vanguard as proprietor.

However, if those who possess the means of production are able to *escape* control under the plan and to make their own decisions about the use of the means of production they possess, then this is a process of the transfer of real (as opposed to juridical) property rights. The agents of possession then become agents of property. If it is effective, the central plan prevents enterprises from transforming their possession into property. According to Bettelheim, the state acts as owner "on the one hand when state property effectively enables the governmental authorities to 'reappropriate' all or part of what each enterprise possesses; on the other hand, when the state effectively *dominates* the use that the enterprises make of their means of production and products."[5] Within "real socialism," then, the struggle over property takes the form of a struggle between plan and market, and replacement of the plan by the market represented a transfer of property rights to the enterprise managers.

In the end, the logic of capital defeated the logic of the vanguard in "real socialism." There were several reasons. In part, it was due to the failure to make the shift to an intensive development path under the existing structure and the very clear signs that the Soviet Union economy was deteriorating in the absence of such a shift (as Gosplan predicted in 1970). Under these conditions, the vanguard became more receptive to the arguments of the market reformers.

Ideas can be a material force when they seize the minds of the vanguard. And, in the Battle of Ideas, the constrained capitalists had strong weapons. They had economists as their ideological representatives. Those economists were not would-be capitalists or necessarily conscious representatives of capital. However, as Marx commented about the spokespersons of the petit bourgeoisie:

> What makes them representatives of the petit bourgeoisie is the fact that in their minds they do not get beyond the limits which the latter do not get beyond in life, that they are consequently driven, theoretically, to the same problems and solutions to which material interest and social position drive the latter in practice.[6]

In this case the economists definitely tended to be stuck within class limits. In particular, their blind spot was the working class. The alternative they offered to the hierarchical rule of the vanguard did not challenge the domination of workers within the workplace and society. Instead, the economists stressed the constraints upon the managers. They did not talk about dynamic inefficiency as the effect of the separation of thinking and doing upon the capacities of workers. Instead, they began and ended with the inefficiencies that managers confronted on a daily basis as the result of their domination from above.

"Free the manager" was their solution, and that was the direction reforms within "real socialism" took. It shifted from viewing the economy as a whole to looking at the enterprise as the basic unit of the economy. The managers in this respect were success-ful in wresting clear property rights over the enterprises from the vanguard. But acceptance of the enterprises as the "basic unit" of the economy was only one part of the struggle to free the man-agers. The other aspect of the Battle of Ideas for the managers and their ideological representatives was the necessity to attack the social contract—in particular, the job rights of workers, a property right that linked them to particular means of production. In other words, the second side of the Battle of Ideas for the economists was the assault on the working class.

And, with echoes of Thatcher and Reagan when capital moved to reverse inroads made by the working class, the ideological spokesmen of capital within "real socialism" went into full attack mode. "Socialism is not philanthropy automatically guaranteeing everyone employment irrespective of his or her ability to do the job," declared Stanislav Shatalin, who was chosen by Gorbachev to prepare his 500-Day Plan for reform. Similarly joining in the attack on job rights in the Soviet Union, Nikolai Shmeliov complained about the "economic damage caused by a parasitic confidence in guaranteed jobs," and he urged the government to consider the advantages that a "comparatively small reserve army of labor" could bring to a socialist political economy. The problem was that "excessive full employment" produced "a host of social ills"; accordingly, he argued, "the real danger of losing a job . . . is a good cure for laziness, drunkenness and irresponsibility." [7]

Why, ultimately, did the vanguard party yield to a class perspec-tive that challenged vanguard relations and attack the working class that the vanguard had supported with the social contract? Aside from a growing loss of confidence given the crisis and their weakness in the face of the weapon of "science" (the science of neoclassical economics) wielded by capital, the choice was not made by a vanguard party pure in its commitment to the logic of the vanguard but rather by one infected in the course of its inter-action with the logic of capital. That disease spread throughout the party, affecting both existing members and the nature of new recruits. Capital ultimately won the Battle of Ideas in "real socialism" because it successfully invaded the vanguard party.

The Logic of the Working Class

Was there no alternative to vanguard relations other than the restoration of capitalism? In *Contradictions of "Real Socialism,"* I identified a third logic, that of the working class. This logic was repressed both in reality (insofar as only social organizations functioning as transmission belts for the vanguard were allowed to exist) and ideologically (insofar as the distortion of Marxism that I call Vanguard Marxism disarmed the working class). However, in the behavior of and interactions within the working class, there was a particular moral economy—a sense of what was right and just. In the moral economy of the working class of "real socialism," the seeds of a socialist alternative are implicit. In their orientation toward egalitarianism, we can see glimpses of one such characteristic—the focus upon the common ownership of the means of production, which implies the right to share equally as owners.

Similarly, from the individual workplace came a particular common sense, a sense of their own collective power as workers and latent support for workers' control. No organized campaign for worker power was possible in normal circumstances under the conditions imposed by the vanguard. But workers protected each other in the workplace. There was a broad consensus among workers and support for resistance to domination and exploitation from above, and the spontaneous eruption of workers' councils at points of weakness in the system—for example, Hungary in 1956 and Poland in 1980—allows us to infer the existence of an underlying consensus among workers in support of worker management.

We see then two elements latent in the moral economy of the working class in "real socialism," which are social ownership of the means of production and social production organized by workers, two sides of what I described in my book, *The Socialist Alternative*, as socialism as an organic system, two sides of what President Chávez called "the socialist triangle." Together they imply the concept of "the cooperative society based on the common ownership of the means of production." Yet cooperation within a society involves more than cooperation within the sphere of production. It also encompasses cooperation with respect to the determination of the *purpose* of productive activity. Fully developed, such a society focuses directly upon social needs, that is, on production for communal needs and purposes—the third side of the socialist triangle. This side is also latent in the moral economy of the working class within "real socialism."

For that third side, the key concept is solidarity. In the solidarian society, people do not relate as owners, demanding a *quid pro quo* for parting with their property or their labor. Their starting point is not that of self-oriented owners, but rather the concept of a community. The germ of such relations was revealed within "real socialism" when people helped one another without demanding an equivalent in return. In contrast to a relation in which alienated, mutually indifferent individuals exchange alienated things, there was a gift relation within networks among people who have a bond, people who have a past and hope to have a future, and its product is the enhancement of solidarity. The solidarian society is precisely a "gift economy," one in which those who give are rewarded not by the anticipation of what they may receive at some point in return but rather because *not* to give violates one's own sense of virtue and honor.

In the moral economy of the working class in "real socialism," we can glimpse not only the orientation to social ownership of the means of production and social production organized by workers but also communal needs and purposes as the goal of productive activity—the three sides of the socialist triangle. Latent is the potential for a different type of society, a cooperative society in which people relate consciously as members of a community. It is the society of associated producers, a society based upon the recognition that the free development of each depends upon the free development of all.

No one could confuse this impulse with the logic of the vanguard, nor is it the logic of capital. This is the logic of the working class, the logic of associated producers. It is a logic that places full human development at its core and insists that people develop through their activity. It places at its center protagonism in the workplace and the community because it grasps the importance of "revolutionary practice"—"the coincidence of the changing of circumstances and of human activity or self-change."

Contested Reproduction in Yugoslav Self-Management?

None of this focus upon the key link of human development and practice was occurring in "real socialism." Workers were not able to develop their capacities. This fundamental contradiction was inherent in vanguard relations of production. Within these productive relations, the domination over workers prevents the development of their capacities, ensures their alienation from the production process, and holds back the development of productivity, that is to say, the development of the productive forces of workers. That is one side of the vanguard relation. The other side is the drive of the vanguard to push for growth, for the expanded reproduction of means of production, with the explicit purpose of building socialism.

Given the nature of the workers produced under vanguard relations, the vanguard relies upon managers to act on its behalf to ensure the achievement of its goals. Yet the managers, who have a particular relation to the means of production (in fact, possess those means of production), increasingly become conscious of their own particular interests; they act according to a logic of their own, which is not identical to the logic of the vanguard. The managers emerge as a class in itself, and their efforts to pursue their own interests interact with the attempts of the vanguard to enforce its property rights.

Thus the struggle between vanguard and managers displaces the relation between vanguard and workers as the contradiction producing the particular movement of "real socialism." That contested reproduction generated a crisis with the result that the logic of capital subordinated the logic of the vanguard.

Are there any insights from this consideration of "real socialism" with respect to the experience of self-management in the former Yugoslavia? Certainly we know that there were important differences. Both before and after the war, the concept of the vanguard party in Yugoslavia mirrored that of "real socialism"; however, there was a significant change around 1950. While retaining the belief in the need for a political instrument and a centralized, united, and disciplined vanguard party, there was a break with the concept of the society being constructed in the Soviet Union. Party leaders charged that state ownership and state management were insufficient for socialist relations of production and that it was essential to introduce worker management in order to build a new socialist society.

The immediate steps taken were the new law on worker self-management, which made enterprise management responsible to workers' councils, and the law on planned management of the economy, which replaced detailed central planning of production by instructions as to basic proportions of investment. Though these initial acts have been viewed as steps to the production of a new whole, it is useful to consider whether they latently contained within themselves two different logics, that of capital and that of the working class. Insofar as these measures involved the creation of workers' councils with power within enterprises, this certainly was a start toward the realization of the side of the logic of the working class, which stresses production organized by workers. Combined with the earlier end to capitalist ownership of the means of production, this pointed toward a process of building two sides of the socialist triangle.

Yet there was another aspect to these changes. Certainly the elimination from the central plan of detailed instructions from above was the beginning of a shift in property rights from the vanguard, a shift described as one from state ownership (which meant in fact vanguard ownership) to social ownership. The agents of possession in this case were becoming agents of property. There was a shift from state ownership to ownership by groups of workers. However, we always need to distinguish between juridical and real ownership. *Who* were those emerging owners? It is important to think back about "real socialism" and to recall that the demands for ending detailed central planning and allowing individual enterprises to make their own decisions in the market without interference from planners were the demands of the managers and represented the logic of capital.

So what was different in Yugoslavia? Obviously, what makes us think differently about this was the role assigned to workers' councils in each enterprise. Implicit was the idea that the *workers* were now the real owners, with all of the attributes of ownership (that is, the entire bundle of property rights) with the exception of the ability to sell or bequeath the means of production. The question, though, is whether workers were able to *exercise* those rights and whether the process was one of their growing capability to do so.

Let me suggest that there was in fact contested reproduction between the logic of capital and the logic of the working class in each enterprise and that the focus upon self-interest and the maximization of income within each individual enterprise strengthened the logic of capital and weakened the realization of the logic of the working class. How else do we explain why despite Tito's insistence in 1950 that workers would "be able to master the complicated techniques of management of factories and other enterprises" through the very process of management and that "only through practice will workers be able to learn," that twenty-five years later Joze Goricar described the gap between workers and the managers, noting that the worker had "only meagre opportunity for developing, in performing his duties, any substantial measure of freedom of thought, imagination and inventiveness"?[8]

How else can we explain the growing inequality between workers in the same industry, between workers in different industries, between workers in different regions, between urban and rural workers? Can we speak of *social* ownership of the means of production when so much depended upon differential access to *particular* means of production and when so many were separated from *all* means of production because they were either unemployed or had left Yugoslavia to be guest workers? Further, with respect to the third side of the socialist triangle, rather than solidarity and a sense of community, there was separation and indifference among workers of different enterprises. Indeed, Che Guevara worried in 1959 about the competition among workers that he observed, noting that it could "introduce factors that distort what the socialist spirit should presumably be." It would be difficult to argue that the logic of the working class was being realized.

On the contrary, the logic of capital was increasingly hegemonic as demonstrated by the successful struggle to remove still-existing regulations instituted by the vanguard and to reduce taxation of enterprises—the revenues of which were used by the vanguard state to establish new enterprises and to equalize regions. More of the revenue was left in the individual enterprises to decide upon its distribution, and those decisions were proposed by managers and their technical experts and rubber-stamped by the workers' councils. The essence of this trajectory was revealed completely by the constitutional amendments of 1968, in particular the removal of regulations that ensured the participation of manual workers in workers' councils with the juridical power to manage the enterprises. This period, in reality, was one in which advances in the direction of both social ownership of the means of production and production organized by workers were reversed. Rather than workers being real owners, those who turned possession of the means of production into property were increasingly the managers.

Add to this picture the growing invitations to foreign investors to set up firms in mergers with the Yugoslav enterprises and the changing nature of the League of Communists, which was less and less composed of manual workers and more and more dominated by managers and experts. Those who ruled over expanded reproduction were the bearers of the logic of capital, and they were removing all obstacles to the fulfillment of that logic.

And yet the logic of the vanguard and the logic of the working class were not entirely defeated. It is well known that there was a strong reaction against the trajectory of the 1950s and 1960s. As Yugoslavia entered the early 1970s, there were growing protests among manual workers and from the poor republics. They said we don't have power anymore; inequality is growing; unemployment is growing. And in response to these movements, the vanguard changed course. Over and over in the party literature, you see the following argument: we're fighting a battle on two fronts. On one front we're fighting against the state bureaucracy, the bureaucratic class that wants to run everything from the top. But the other battle, the other front, is a battle against capitalism. And we *forgot* about the second front.

In order to attack the power of capital, presented as a "techno-bureaucracy," there were a series of initiatives introduced in the 1970s. These included new legislative changes, the "workers' amendments" to the constitution, regulations intended to compress wage differentials by determination of socially warranted wages, as well as a new law that focused upon planning from below through self-managing agreements between the workers of different enterprises.

Without question, the new regulations and laws introduced constraints upon the managers; they introduced a check upon the logic of capital that reflected to some extent the logic of the vanguard and the logic of the working class. There was contested reproduction in Yugoslavia. Accordingly, it is wrong to look at self-management as a single system with particular characteristics. Rather, it is essential to consider the experience of self-management in Yugoslavia as a particular concrete phenomenon, the product of the interaction of differing productive relations in a process of contested reproduction.

Interaction of Differing Logics in Yugoslav Self-Management

It is important to think about ways in which the differing logics of the vanguard, capital, and the working class interacted to generate dysfunction and to deform each other in practice. To approach this question adequately, a serious study would be needed, but let me suggest some aspects of these interactions in no special order.

Consider, for example, the workers' orientation toward common ownership of the means of production. The form that this took in Yugoslavia was to reject the inequality arising from differential access to particular means of production. Workers in less profitable firms expected their wages to rise much like those in the more profitable firms. The effect was to reduce significantly the liquidity of the weaker firms and to compel them to turn to the banks to secure funding not merely for expanded reproduction but even to meet the personal income requirements of workers. This was entirely contrary to the official perspective on "socialist commodity production" in which personal incomes were to be the result of commodity sales not of bank loans. A similar effect upon the liquidity of firms was that, unlike capitalist firms, a slowdown in sales did not mean that members of the collective were laid off; rather, the concept of a workers' collective meant that at such times firms continued to function by producing for inventory. Adding to the effect of all this was the vanguard's position (as reflected in the arguments made by the representatives of the commune governments on banks) that enterprises should not be allowed to fail because that would generate unemployment, leaving commune governments to deal with that problem. We see from this the basis for both a soft budget constraint familiar in Hungary for the same reason and the internal tendency to generate significant inflation as a result of bank lending.

The logic of the working class (supported by the vanguard) interfered in other ways with the ability of the managers to run the enterprises in a way they considered efficient. Having to spend time in meetings of the workers' councils was clearly viewed as a waste by the managers, but it was one imposed as a constraint by the vanguard. Similarly, the imposition of self-managing agreements as the basis for a plan from below was also a factor that went counter to the ability of individual enterprises to function as they wished in the economy. Not surprisingly, the managers lost little time in breaking the self-management agreements when conditions changed that were contrary to the individual welfare of their own firms.

While the vanguard constrained the logic of capital and supported elements consistent with the logic of the working class (the development of a plan from below, workers' councils, protection against enterprise bankruptcy), it at the same time thwarted the realization of the logic of the working class by its unbending insistence upon the supremacy of self-interest. Arguments suggesting that people should relate to each other in any way other than self-interest were attacked as ultra-leftism, voluntarism, and anarchism, as were criticisms that the managers had become a new class with power over workers.

Rather than focusing upon building an alternative based upon solidarity and cooperation of people within a community, rather than building upon the basis of the moral economy of the working class and looking to reinforce the logic of the working class, the premise of the vanguard was that the way to encourage workers to cooperate is to argue that they will make more money this way. Although they used the term "solidarity," in practice it meant "solidarity is built by workers recognizing that by working together they will make more money and will succeed better." There was both a theoretical and class basis for this position. Theoretically underlying that premise was the same position as that of the vanguard in "real socialism"—the Vanguard Marxism that distorted Marx to argue the necessity of two separate stages with a first stage based upon a socialist principle of "to each according to his contribution." And, in practice, underlying that premise was the logic of capital and the power of the commodity-producing enterprises whose agents of property were the managers.

Vanguard Marxism is a one-sided Marxism.[9] It looks at workers only as workers. In other words, it doesn't look at workers as human beings with other sides, as human beings within society. That is a point that Marx grasped clearly in his criticism of the formula of "to each according to his contribution" in his *Critique of the Gotha Program*. It was a critique of the focus upon material interest, one understood by Che Guevara in his reflection that "the pipe dream that socialism can be achieved with the dull instruments left to us by capitalism; for example, the commodity as an economic cell, individual material interest as the lever, etc., can lead you into a blind alley; and you wind up there after having traveled a long distance with many crossroads and it's hard to figure out just where you took the wrong turn."[10]

Yugoslav self-management did end up in a blind alley. The failure to build upon the logic of the working class and the continued interaction of the differing logics produced an impasse in which the logic of capital was dominant but constrained, deformed, and dysfunctional. In the end that impasse was resolved by external force, namely the IMF conditionality that enabled the supporters of capital to take the logical step in the 1988 law on enterprises to substitute the power of stockholders for the legal constraint of decision making by workers' councils.

My purpose in this brief sketch of the Yugoslav experience has been to encourage you to explore that history by seeing it as the result of a particular process of contested reproduction. But I confess that I hope that I conveyed another message as well. The point is not to interpret history differently. Rather, it is to *make* history.

5. Proposing a Path to Socialism: Two Papers for Hugo Chávez

This article was published in March 2014 in Monthly Review, *one year after the unfortunate death of Hugo Chávez on March 5, 2013. The Editors earlier had quoted a letter from István Mészáros to John Bellamy Foster that described Chávez as "one of the greatest historical figures of our time" and as "a deeply insightful revolutionary intellect" ("Notes from the Editors" in the May 2013 issue of* Monthly Review *65/1). On this occasion, I wrote that whether Chávez will be remembered over time this way depends significantly on whether we build upon the foundations he began. As important as his vision and his deep understanding of the necessary path, so clearly demonstrated by his focus upon communal councils as the basis of a new socialist state—"the most vital revolutionary achievement in these years," as the Editors indicated—was Chávez's ability to communicate both vision and theory in a clear and simple way to the masses. As demonstrated by Chávez's articulation of the concept of "the elementary triangle of socialism" that is what revolutionaries must learn to do.*

In 2006, it was clear that Chávez would be reelected in December to a new term of office as president of Venezuela. For those of us

actively involved in Centro Internacional Miranda (CIM), an insti-
tute initiated following a proposal of Marta Harnecker to Chávez
in late 2004, it was also clear that, following the election, Chávez
would be thinking seriously about directions for the new mandate.
Accordingly, we decided in advance of the election to prepare a series
of papers proposing initiatives that we felt could advance the process
of building socialism in Venezuela.

Although several of us engaged in these discussions, ultimately
only three of the CIM directors, Marta Harnecker, Haiman El
Troudi, and I, completed papers for transmission to Chávez in early
December. In what follows, I include an excerpt from one paper I
prepared plus a second paper subsequently developed in response to
Chávez's reaction to the first.[1]

Building New Productive Relations Now

Everyone understands that it is impossible to achieve the
vision of socialism for the 21st century in one giant leap
forward. It is not simply a matter of changing property
ownership. This is the easiest part of building the new world. Far
more difficult is changing productive relations, social relations in
general, and attitudes and ideas.

To transform existing relations into the new productive relations, we need first of all to understand the nature of those existing
relations. Only then can you identify the mechanisms by which
the new relations can be introduced. At this time, there is a great
variety of experiments and approaches to changing productive
relations that are being pursued. There is no attempt to set out specific proposals here but only to provide the framework in which
such changes should be explored in order to move toward socialist
productive relations.

The first step is to understand the *direction* of change. The
precise *pace* of transformation will depend upon the existing conditions, the conjuncture, and the correlation of forces (national
and international).

Transitional Steps for Transforming Existing Relations

A. EXISTING PRODUCTIVE RELATIONS

It is essential not to confuse property relations with productive relations. For example, a state-owned firm could be (a) worker-managed and functioning in a market with the goal of maximizing income per worker, as in the self-managed enterprises in the former Yugoslavia; (b) a profit-maximizing state capitalist firm; or (c) what we call for our purpose here a "statist" firm—a productive unit directed by the state to achieve specific targets in terms, for example, of output or revenue. Similarly, a cooperative may be focused upon maximizing the income of its members or solving local needs. And, in all these cases, there is always the possibility of managers and managerial elites directing the enterprises in their own personal interests because of the difficulties in monitoring and sanctioning their activity (as occurred in the old PDVSA).[2]

1. CAPITALIST PRODUCTIVE RELATIONS

We understand capitalist productive relations as those in which workers enter into a relationship with capitalists in which they surrender their ability to work and their claim upon what they produce to capitalists. What workers get from this transaction is a wage that provides for their maintenance; what capitalists get is the right to direct their employees in such a way as to profit from their ability to work, the right to own everything that workers produce, and the right to determine what is produced and how it is produced. These relations may take different forms. For example, workers may have more or less control over the production process and may receive a portion of their wage in the form of profit-sharing (which means that they share in the risks of the capitalist). However, characteristic of capitalist productive relations is that everything is subordinated to the generation of profits and the accumulation of capital and that the capitalist works constantly to increase those profits however he can.

Thus the system drives toward the greatest possible exploitation of workers and the greatest possible use of resources for which the capitalist does not have to pay (such as clean air and water); workers and society may succeed in winning some battles from time to time, but the logic of capital is always to attempt to undermine and reverse those victories sooner or later. Because the logic of capital is opposed to the logic of human development and human needs.

2. COOPERATIVE PRODUCTIVE RELATIONS

Cooperative relations exist when workers are associated in enterprises in their mutual interest as producers. Both in the case where workers are the owners of the means of production and in the case where the means of production are owned by the state and entrusted to the collective of workers, the inherent logic of the cooperative as a separate unit is the same: maximize the income per member of the cooperative. Accordingly, characteristic of a cooperative is that it looks upon members of other cooperatives and members of society as a whole as either competitors or as potential sources of income as customers. The logic of the cooperative is the self-interest of the group; in this respect, taxation of the cooperative by the state, by reducing the net income of its members, appears as a burden contrary to the interests of the group.

Thus the logic of the cooperative as such is not a focus upon human development and solidarity within society as a whole. The cooperative retains the self-orientation of the capitalist firm and may function atomistically on a market in the same way as capitalist firms. Nevertheless, the differences between cooperatives and capitalist firms are immense. In the cooperative, workers don't surrender their ability to work, their right to determine how they will produce or their claim over what they produce. Rather, they combine or pool their capacities in their common interest, and, instead of keeping their tacit knowledge to themselves and finding ways to minimize their work, the logic of the cooperative leads them to share their knowledge and their ability because they are the beneficiaries.

Precisely because of this collective interest and this conscious combination of activity, cooperatives build solidarity within the specific group and teach a lesson about the benefits of coopera- tion. At the same time, this orientation toward the interests of the specific group—and toward "group property"—is consistent with the exploitation of other workers (non-cooperative members) as wage-laborers and with actions in the interest of the group that are contrary to the interests of society. Nevertheless, the two-sided nature of relations within cooperatives suggests the potential of building new productive relations upon them.

3. Statist Productive Relations

Characteristic of statist relations is that enterprises are given spe- cific directives by the state and are expected to fulfill these. Insofar as the goal of the state is to meet a specific output or revenue target or to maximize revenue for the state budget, the resources of the statist unit will be directed toward meeting this goal.[3] Further, the counterpart of the directive or command given to the statist enterprise will be the directive or command transmitted *within* that enterprise. Characteristic of the statist enterprise is hierarchy: orders are transmitted downward. Thus, democracy and worker decision making are not characteristic. Rather than the disrup- tions in state goal achievement that may result from the differing goals of workers, the preferred role of an organization of work- ers from the statist perspective is to mobilize human resources to meet the selected goal and thus, to serve as a transmission belt for state directives. In this respect, from the perspective of workers, the statist firm may be no different than the capitalist firm.

Similarly, insofar as meeting the chosen output or revenue targets is paramount, efficient use of resources (including the environment) may tend to be sacrificed in the interests of reach- ing those targets. Despite state goals that are formulated in the interests of society as a whole, the fact that specific directives are given to individual productive enterprises means that efforts to achieve them may stimulate behavior that is in the interests of the particular enterprise rather than those of the whole. Such a pattern is particularly likely when the income or career path of enterprise managers depends upon their success in meeting these assigned targets. In fact, the private interests of those managers may yield many antisocial effects, with the result that the statist firms do not act in the interest of society as a whole. Where state enterprise managers are not committed to the goals of the state and where their behavior is not easily monitored, the performance of these enterprises will appear incoherent because they reflect the presence of a different set of relations. The existence of managers with their own goals and the difficulty of monitoring them from above was characteristic of enterprises in the former USSR.[4]

The logic of the statist enterprise, accordingly, is two-sided. Though it potentially can be directed in the interests of society as a whole and is essentially oriented toward production of use-values rather than profits, in the absence of specific directives that stress the interests of workers and society as a whole and the transparency that is a precondition for monitoring and empowering of workers and communities, the statist enterprise can be captured by particular interests.

B. TRANSFORMING EXISTING PRODUCTIVE RELATIONS

The steps that must be taken to make a transition from existing relations to the new productive relations and the pace at which the changes can be made depends upon the starting point.

1. TRANSFORMING STATIST ENTERPRISES

Without question, the easiest transition can be made in the statist firm, which is already at the threshold of new productive relations. Unlike the explicit private interests in capitalist and cooperative productive relations, the statist firm is in form the property of society as a whole and has as its explicit directive to act in the interests of society as a whole.

The path to transform the logic of statist enterprises is to change the directives that they are given by the state. If the new productive relations to be built emphasize as a goal the full development of human potential and the creation of new socialist human beings, the nature of these institutions and the instructions given by the state must include the conditions necessary for the realization of this goal. With the development of workers' councils and the growing orientation of their activity toward meeting the needs of communities (as expressed by those communities themselves) and with the transparency that allows waste, corruption, and bureaucratic self-interest to be challenged, statist enterprises increasingly can be characterized by socialist productive relations. This is not an easy process, because the habits, traditions, and common sense of both capitalist and statist firms is that decisions should be made at the top and transmitted downward. For this reason, success in this process depends upon the selection of managers who share the vision.[5]

To the extent that the statist enterprise moves in the direction of new socialist relations emphasizing the full development of human capacity, it no longer can be evaluated by the measures of traditional capitalist accounting. State directives such as, for example, transformation of the workday to include education in the workplace, transitional phases in the development of worker participation, and improvement of environmental conditions are directives to invest in human development. Thus, rather than view the specific enterprises that follow such social policies as "uneconomic" or money-losing, these policies are social investments whose cost must be borne by society as a whole.

2. TRANSFORMING COOPERATIVES

The transformation of cooperatives concerns not only those in which the means of production are owned by a group of workers but also the case of state-owned enterprises that are self-managed and enterprises that are a combination of state and group ownership. Despite the difference in property ownership, common to all is that the prevailing logic is to maximize income per worker within the group.

Besides this group self-interest, however, this institution contains the essential ideas of cooperation and democracy, which are at the core of the new relations to be built. The transition here, then, must take the form of encouraging the cooperative to move beyond its narrow self-orientation and to develop organic links to society.

A first step would be to develop links between groups of workers, such as members of different cooperatives. With the establishment of a Council of Cooperatives in each community, it would be possible to explore the way in which these groups of workers could cooperate in activities rather than compete and, in general, to investigate ways in which cooperatives can integrate their activities directly without being separated by market transactions. Further, links could be established between the Councils of Cooperatives in each community and communal councils. With the support of the communal banks, the needs of local communities could in this way be communicated to the organized cooperatives as a way of moving toward production for communal needs and purposes.[6]

The process of transforming the productive relations of cooperatives is one of guiding them step-by-step beyond their own narrow interests into a focus upon the needs of communities. In other words, cooperatives are at *another* threshold of socialism for the 21st century. Both the statist enterprises and the cooperatives have in common that they are not capitalist enterprises; rather, they are part of the social economy that can "walk on two legs" on a path toward socialist productive relations.

However, there is nothing automatic about this process. The logic of capital can dominate both: it can turn statist firms and cooperatives into complements and supports for capitalism. Being on the threshold of socialist productive relations does not mean you will ever cross that threshold.

3. TRANSFORMING CAPITALIST ENTERPRISES
Capitalism is not at that threshold, and it will never be. The essence of capitalism is the exploitation of workers and the orientation

toward profit at the expense of every human being and every human need. We can never use the logic of capital to build new social relations. Rather, it is necessary to go beyond capital and to subordinate its logic to the logic of the new society.

Part of the process of subordinating capitalism to a new social logic is by introducing the transparency necessary to monitor the activity of capitalist enterprises. With a new law on transparency, making the financial records (including records of transactions with other entities) of all business enterprises of a minimum size (for example, over twenty-five workers) available to inspection by workers and tax officials, the information available for a democratic, participatory, and protagonistic society would be increased. Those enterprises unwilling to provide this information would be understood to be acting against the public interest and would instead have to be operated in a transparent way by the state or groups of workers.

A rupture of property rights in this way—that is, nationalization by the state or a takeover by collectives of workers—is one of three ways to subordinate existing capitalist enterprises within a country. Certainly, this does remove these capitalist enterprises and the capitalist interests behind them as threats to a new social-ist society. As noted earlier, changing property rights is not the same as developing new productive relations. At best, this only takes us to the threshold (in the form of statist firms and coopera-tives) of those new relations. In fact, a private capitalist firm may simply be replaced by a state capitalist firm that exploits workers and destroys the environment, all in the interests of maximiza-tion of profits. Thus, though *existing* capitalist enterprises may be subordinated in this way, we have seen that more is needed to introduce new productive relations.

A second way to subordinate existing capitalist firms is by extracting and transferring the surpluses generated in those firms. Through taxes or administered prices, surpluses generated within these firms may be siphoned off to other sectors (such as new firms) and to the support of social programs rather than realized as profits. A similar assault on the profitability of these enterprises could be through competition with state-owned firms or subsidized cooperatives. Certainly, such inroads upon the profits of capitalist firms will reduce their viability, and their subsequent absorption by the state or workers would likely follow in the public interest in order to maintain jobs and production.

Whereas the above cases involve an external assault on existing capitalist firms, a third approach to their subordination involves the invasion of an alien logic, the logic of new productive relations *within* those enterprises. The premise here is not that capitalism can be reformed or that it can change but, rather, that its orientation toward profit-maximization will be constrained by the existence of new requirements. For example, the existence of strict environmental standards compels the capitalist enterprise that wants to remain in operation to accept these as a cost of doing business and to continue, within this new constraint, to attempt to maximize profits. In the same way, government directives requiring enterprises to transform the workday to include educational training, introduce specific forms of worker decision-making (such as workers' councils), and devote a specific portion of resources to meet local community demands will impose costs upon these firms that would be still consistent with the logic of capital and its drive to maximize profits.

Why would capitalist enterprises accept such imposed costs when they can go to other locations in the world where those particular costs are not present? They would do so if this were a condition to having access to scarce local resources, to credit from state banks and to the market that state enterprises and the state offer. In other words, the state can use its leverage to change the ground rules under which capitalist enterprises that are not footloose can do business.

Does this change them from being capitalist firms? Does it mean that they no longer exploit workers? Obviously not. Why, then, would a state that wishes to transform productive relations accept the continued existence of these capitalist firms? It would do so only if the limited economic and technical resources at its disposal make it rational for it to work for a period with capitalist firms constrained in this way.

The process of introducing these conditions—socialist conditionality—means the insertion of new, alien productive relations within the capitalist firm. The combination of state directives that enforce the development of workers' councils (with increasing responsibilities) and a growing orientation toward meeting community needs makes the capitalist enterprise contested terrain. And the struggle within these firms will continue: just as capitalist firms in this case will be constantly attempting to lessen and reduce the burden of "socialist conditionality," the state, in cooperation with workers and communities, will be working to introduce into these enterprises *further* elements characteristic of the invading socialist society.[7] In short, we are describing here a process of class struggle in which the goal of socialism for the 21st Century is the complete replacement of the logic of capital by the logic of a new socialist society.

In the following week, Marta Harnecker received a call from Chávez in relation to our papers. Could Michael look at the paragraph from István Mészáros's Beyond Capital *in which he described capitalism as an organic system of production, distribution, and consumption, a system in which everything is connected? If everything is connected, how is it possible to change anything? So, ask Michael to indicate concrete proposals for change in this context.*

*Frankly, I was blown away by the question, and my immediate reaction when she passed this message to me was—**what** paragraph? Happily, I had Mészáros's book with me in Caracas, so I searched for the paragraph in question. It wasn't easy to isolate a single section because the whole book is about the necessity to go beyond all sides of capital if socialism is to be built. Ultimately, I concluded that the paragraph Chávez had in mind was within section 20.3.5 where*

Mészáros talked about "the inescapable dialectical relationship" between production, distribution, circulation, and consumption, stressing that "the capital relation is made up of many circuits, all intertwined and mutually reinforcing one another." Here, then, was why Mészáros concluded that "it is inconceivable to achieve the socialist objectives without going beyond capital, i.e., without radically restructuring the totality of existing reproductive relations."[8] And here was the problem that concerned Chávez and that now concerned me. What concrete measures were possible in this context? That led to the second of these papers for Chávez in December 2006.

From Mészáros to Concrete Proposals
for Transforming Venezuela

Rereading István Mészáros's *Beyond Capital*, I am impressed by the way he goes to the heart of the new society that must be built. It is true that he draws heavily upon Marx's discussion in the *Grundrisse* (and I have often stressed this point); however, what is so remarkable is how sharply he hones Marx's point. Especially significant is the way he stresses a "twofold tyrannical determination" in capital (to which the market socialist reformers in the USSR were oblivious): (a) "the authoritarianism of the particular workshops" and (b) "the tyranny of the totalizing market."[9]

Precisely because this double tyranny is so clear for him, Mészáros is unequivocal in identifying as characteristic of the new socialist society that (a) control of production be "fully vested in the producing individuals themselves"; and (b) "the social character of labor is asserted directly," not *after the fact.* In other words, productive activity in this socialism is social not because we produce for each other through a market but because we *consciously* produce for others. And, it is social not because we are directed to produce those things but because we ourselves as people within society *choose* to produce for those who need what we can provide.

Here is the core of this new socialism as Mészáros saw it—"the *primacy of needs.*" Our needs as members of society—both as producers and as consumers—are central. This is a society centered on a conscious exchange of activity for communal needs and communal purposes. It is a society of new, rich human beings who develop in the course of producing *with* others and *for* others; these are people for whom the desire to possess and the associated need for money (the real need that capitalism produces, as Marx noted) wither away. We are describing a new world in which we have our individual needs, needs for our own "all-round development," but where we are not driven by material incentives to act. It is a world in which our activity is its own reward and is, indeed, "life's prime want," because we affirm ourselves as conscious social beings through that activity, a world in which we produce use-values for others and produce ourselves as part of the human family.

But obviously such people do not arise spontaneously. They are formed by every aspect of their lives, not only their activity as producers but also in the spheres of distribution and consumption. In this complex dialectic of production-distribution-consumption, Mészáros stresses, no one part can stand alone. It is necessary to radically restructure the *whole* of these relations because capitalism is a "structure of society, in which all relations coexist simultaneously and support one another."[10] So, how can you make any real changes if you have to change all relations, and you can't change them all simultaneously?

Think about how capitalism developed. Capitalism developed through a process of "subordinating all elements of society to itself" and by creating for itself the organs it lacked. The new socialist society similarly must develop through a process of subordinating all the elements of capitalism and the logic of capital and by inserting its own logic centered in human beings in its place. It proceeds by assembling the elements of a new dialectic of production-distribution-consumption.

Elements of the New Socialism

What are those elements? At the core of this new combination are three characteristics: (1) social ownership of the means of production, which is a basis for (2) social production organized by workers in order to (3) satisfy communal needs and communal purposes. Let us consider each in its turn and their combination.

Social ownership of the means of production is critical because it is the only way to ensure that our communal, social productivity is directed to the free development of all rather than used to satisfy the private goals of capitalists, groups of individuals, or state bureaucrats. Social ownership, however, is not the same as state ownership. State property is consistent with state capitalist enterprises, hierarchical statist firms, or firms in which particular groups of workers (rather than society as a whole) capture the major benefits of this state property. Social ownership implies a profound democracy, one in which people function as subjects, both as producers and as members of society.

Production organized by workers builds new relations among producers, those of cooperation and solidarity. It furthermore allows workers to end "the crippling of body and mind" and the loss of "every atom of freedom, both in bodily and in intellectual activity" that comes from the separation of head and hand characteristic of capitalist production. As long as workers are prevented from developing their capacities by combining thinking and doing in the workplace, they remain alienated and fragmented human beings whose enjoyment consists in possessing and consuming things. Further, as long as this production is carried out for their private gain rather than that of society, they look upon others as means to their own ends and thus remain alienated, fragmented, and crippled. Social production, therefore, is a condition for the full development of the producers.

Satisfaction of communal needs and purposes has as its necessary condition a means of identifying and communicating those needs and purposes. It requires the development of the democratic institutions at every level that can express the needs of society. Production reflects communal needs only with information and decisions that flow from the bottom up. However, in the absence of the transformation of society, the needs transmitted upward are the needs of people formed within capitalism, people who are "in every respect, economically, morally and intellectually, still stamped with the birthmarks of the old society." Within the new socialist society, the "primacy of needs" is based not upon the individual right to consume things without limit but upon "the worker's own need for development"—the needs of people in a society in which the free development of each is the condition for the free development of all. In a society like this, where our productive activity for others is rewarding in itself and where there is all-round development of individuals, we can place upon its banner: to each according to his need for development.

As consideration of these three specific elements suggests, realization of each element depends upon the existence of the other two, which is precisely Mészáros's point about the inseparability of this distribution-production-consumption complex. Without production for social needs, no real social property; without social property, no worker decision making oriented toward society's needs; without worker decision making, no transformation of people and their needs. The presence of the defects inherited from the old society in any one element poisons the others. We return to the essential question: How is a transition possible when everything depends upon everything else?

Building Revolutionary Subjects

In order to identify the measures necessary to build this new socialist society, it is absolutely critical to understand Marx's concept of "revolutionary practice," which is the simultaneous changing of circumstances and human activity or self-change. To change a structure in which all relations coexist simultaneously and support one another you have to do more than try to change a few elements in that structure; you must stress at all times the hub of these relations, namely human beings as subjects and products of their own activity.

Every activity in which people engage forms them. Thus there are two products of every activity: the changing of circumstance or things (for example, in the production process) and the human product. This second side of production is easily forgotten when talking about structural changes. However, it was not forgotten in the emphasis of the Bolivarian Constitution upon practice and protagonism, in particular, the stress upon participation as "the necessary way of achieving the involvement to ensure their complete development, both individual and collective."[11]

What's the significance of recognizing this process of producing people explicitly? First, it helps us to understand why changes must occur in all spheres; every moment that people act within old relations is a process of reproducing old ideas and attitudes. Working under hierarchical relations, functioning without the ability to make decisions in the workplace and society, focusing upon self-interest rather than upon solidarity within society, produces people on a daily basis. It is the reproduction of the conservatism of everyday life.

Recognizing this second side also directs us to focus upon the introduction of concrete measures that explicitly take into account the effect of those measures upon human development. For every step two questions must be asked: (1) How does this change circumstances?; and (2) How does this help to produce revolutionary subjects and increase their capacities? There are often several ways to make changes, but the particular battles that will more certainly build this new socialism will be those that not only win new ground but also produce an army capable of fighting new, successful battles.

Choosing Concrete Steps

When we focus upon human beings and their development, it is easy to see how the elements within the new dialectic of production-distribution-consumption are connected. The process is one of synergy. The effects of changes in the sphere of production will be felt in the spheres of distribution and consumption; this whole is greater than the sum of its individual parts. Let us consider each of the elements in turn.

PRODUCING FOR COMMUNAL NEEDS AND COMMUNAL PURPOSES

The Bolivarian Revolution has taken a giant leap into the 21st century with the creation of the Communal Councils, an essential cell of socialism for the 21st Century. The Communal Councils provide a means by which people can identify communal needs democratically and learn that they can do something about these by themselves as a community. In this respect, these new community organizations are a school of socialism, one in which there is simultaneously a changing of circumstance and the development of people, "both individual and collective."

They are also a base upon which to build. As the councils begin to function successfully, they can take further steps in identifying the needs of the community: what are those needs (both individual and collective) and what are the local resources that can satisfy those needs? For example, the councils can conduct a census of the local cooperatives and other enterprises that could produce for local needs. Further, they can bring together workers and the community to discuss ways to produce for communal needs and purposes.

The Communal Councils in this respect are a paradigm for this process. Not only are they a vehicle for changing both circumstances and the protagonists themselves, but they also move step-by-step to a deepening of the process. Inevitably, all councils will not develop at the same pace, so uniformity cannot be imposed; however, this unevenness provides an opportunity for more advanced communities to share their experiences (a process that helps to build solidarity among communities). Further, the transmission of their needs upward for participatory budgeting at higher levels is an essential part of the process of developing planning from below for communal needs and purposes.

Of course, not all decisions to satisfy social needs belong at the level of the neighborhood and community. The decisions to reject neoliberalism, to pursue endogenous development, to seek food sovereignty, to create new education and health programs, to create a new transportation infrastructure, to build new socialist relations are decisions that must be made at the national level. So, in such cases, where is the place for revolutionary practice, the simultaneous changing of circumstances and self-change?

There is no automatic place for the protagonism of the people in such state decisions. Perhaps someday a new state based upon the communal councils will emerge, and perhaps at some point computers will permit instant referenda on a host of national issues. On such matters at this point, however, the participation from below that allows people to develop their capacities will only occur as the result of a political commitment, one that makes real the constitution's understanding that the sovereign people must become not only the object but also the subject of power.

National-level decisions can all be made at the top, which is characteristic of both dictatorships and representative democracies, *or* there can be a dedicated search for mechanisms that incorporate people below so they not only can affect the nature of the decisions but also recognize the decisions as *theirs*. The "Parliament of the streets" is an obvious example of a mechanism that can incorporate people into the discussions of laws, improve the quality of information available for good decisions, and create an identification with these decisions. However, finding ways to institutionalize this process so that people view it as their *right* to participate (and punish National Assembly deputies who do not honor this right) is important both in empowering people and attacking bureaucracy and elitism.

National decisions on such matters as the sectors of the economy that should be expanded and the social investments that need to be made are most critical at a time when the rapid and dramatic transformation of the structure of the economy from an oil economy is desired. These decisions have the profoundest effect upon which needs of society can be satisfied in the present and future. The significance of such decisions is precisely why it is important that they be pursued transparently, that the information people need to understand the logic behind these proposals be circulated in a simple and clear way, and that the proposed plans and directions be discussed in advance in assemblies of workers and communities.

Just as in the case of discussions in communal councils and the development of links between the community needs and local producers, the dissemination and discussion of information about nationwide needs and purposes will be important in mobilizing support and initiatives from below in communities and workplaces to meet the needs of society. Sometimes, too, it will prevent serious errors when national initiatives do not take into account local and regional impacts, especially their environmental effects. Thus, not only do these democratic processes disseminate information downward, they also are an essential means of transmitting information upward.

For goals identified at both the community and national levels, the greater the spread of information and discussions through which people take ownership of the decisions, the more likely that productive activity will occur to ensure the successful achievement of those goals (rather than out of self-interest). In this way, producing for communal needs and purposes emerges as common sense.

SOCIAL PRODUCTION ORGANIZED BY WORKERS

The preconditions for successful worker organization of production are dissemination of the information necessary to carry out the activity and the ability to use this information efficiently. Transparency ("open books") and worker education, through a transformation of the traditional workday to include education should be introduced in state, private capitalist, and cooperative enterprises.

Whereas some aspects of enterprise activity such as production statistics and information about purchasing decisions can be monitored by workers relatively easily, examination of financial data and evaluation of management proposals require the development of more skills. Therefore, for an interim period, workers should have access to worker auditors and advisors who can serve on their behalf. These specialists could be part of the group of educators assigned to the enterprise or could be provided to the enterprise by the Ministry of Work or by a trade union or trade union federation.

The steps in which workers assume direction of the organization of production should be set out clearly in advance in each enterprise; these steps and the pace pursued will vary in accordance with the history, culture, and experience in each case. While individual cases will vary, one of the first areas where workers can demonstrate the benefits of worker decision making is through the reorganization of production. With their knowledge of existing waste and inefficiency, workers should be able to improve productivity and reduce costs of production.

To encourage the efficient production of use-values and to deepen the development of social production, the gains from these worker initiatives should not accrue to the enterprise (especially in the case of private capitalist firms!). Rather, in principle, these benefits should be divided among enterprise workers and the local community following discussions in worker assemblies and the direct coordination of worker representatives with local communal councils. The links between workers and community built upon this basis are then an important part of the creation of these new relations.

In general, the process by which worker decision-making advances in the enterprise should start from the bottom up. Beginning from worker veto over supervisors (on the logic that supervisors unacceptable to workers are inconsistent with any worker management), the degree of worker decision making would grow on a step-by-step basis. Starting from a phase in which workers identify the profile of acceptable managers and begin discussions of production and investment proposals of managers, the development of knowledge and worker capacities through this process would proceed toward the goal in which workers, including the managers who represent them and society as a whole, organize social production for communal needs and purposes.[12]

Under ideal circumstances, the steps in this process will be determined through negotiation and agreement between workers and management of enterprises and will be filed with the Ministry of Work as a social contract. Where timely agreement is not possible, enterprise workers can bring the matter to the Ministry of Work for its action, and for referral to the National Assembly in the case of privately owned enterprises.

It should be pointed out that two characteristics often identified with co-management—worker election of top directors and worker ownership shares—play no role in the above discussion. Both measures contain within them the potential for old ideas and familiar patterns to penetrate into the new relations of worker management and to make them simply new forms of the old relations.

As in the case of representative democracy in the political sphere, worker election of enterprise directors has often served to create a separation between those directors and the people they presumably represent. The club of directors develops its own logic, which is one distinct from the interest of workers. In particular, within the contested terrain of capitalist firms, co-management in this form means co-optation, a means of incorporating workers into the project of capitalists. In contrast, the process described here in which workers organize production is one of protagonistic democracy in which workers' power proceeds from the bottom up and does so for the purpose of serving communal needs.

Similarly, the idea that workers' interests in enterprises (state-owned or private capitalist) should be secured by giving workers shares of ownership, whether those shares are individually held or owned by a cooperative, is a case where co-management can be deformed into self-oriented private ownership. Instead of workers functioning as socially conscious producers, expressing themselves as cooperating producers and members of society, they are transformed into owners whose principal interest is their own income, which means the economic success of their particular company. This is not the way to build social production, that is, the exchange of activity based upon communal needs and purposes.

SOCIAL OWNERSHIP OF THE MEANS OF PRODUCTION

Social ownership of the means of production is often presented as a matter of ideology. However, in a society oriented toward "ensuring overall human development" and "developing the creative potential of every human being," social ownership of the means of production is common sense.

The point of social ownership is to ensure that the accumulated products of the social brain and the social hand are subordinated to the full development of human beings rather than used for private purposes. If the private ownership of the means of production does not support the creation of food sovereignty, endogenous development, and investment that generates good jobs, then the interest of society is advanced by introducing social ownership in its place.

Similarly, if private owners are not prepared to be transparent, to introduce education into the workplace, to accept growing worker decision making, and to direct their activity increasingly to satisfying communal needs and communal purposes, then they thereby declare that they rank the privileges and prerogatives of private ownership over ensuring overall human development. Where they refuse to support public policies oriented toward creating a society based upon the logic of the human being, they demonstrate that there is no alternative for such a society than social ownership of the means of production.

Thus, it is not the socialist project that excludes them. They exclude themselves by demonstrating that they are incompatible with the full development of human potential.

One month later, on his regular Sunday "teach-in" ("Alo President" #264, 28 January 2007), Chávez drew upon the concepts developed in this second paper and introduced (to my excitement as I watched!) what he called the elementary triangle of socialism: social property, social production, and satisfaction of social needs. He did this by setting out three points on his desk and explaining each side.[13] This was one of many examples of his unique ability to take complex theoretical concepts (most evident in his regular references to Meszaros's Beyond Capital*) and to communicate these to the masses of viewers without a theoretical background.[14] With simple commonsense language, Chávez succeeded in grasping the minds of the masses, and that was an essential aspect in the combination that was building a path to socialism in his (truncated) lifetime. If we can learn to do that, then Chávez no se va.*

6. Socialism: The Goal, the Paths, and the Compass

At the February 2010 Havana Book Fair, I presented my short book, El Socialismo no Cae del Cielo: Un Neuvo Comienzo, which had been published in 2009 by Ciencias Sociales (Cuba) and earlier in 2007 by Monte Avila (Venezuela). The book contained sections from Build It Now; Socialism for the 21st Century *(in particular, "Socialism doesn't fall from the sky," well-known in Venezuela because of Chávez's many references to it on television and available in several free editions), and this was supplemented for Monte Avila with a new beginning, "New Wings for Socialism" from* Monthly Review *(April 2007). The talk provided an opportunity to introduce Cubans explicitly to the concept of "the elementary triangle of socialism," the goal developed in "New Wings" but not named in the new book. It also was an occasion to talk about difficulties and obstacles along the path to the goal—obstacles such as those faced by Cuba then and now. Without mentioning Cuba at all, I spoke about what I had observed in Vietnam a few months earlier, and I am certain that the Cubans present understood my cautionary tale. Discovering a new path without getting lost is always challenging, and I hope that the publication by Ciencias Sociales in 2015 of* The Socialist Alternative: Real Human Development, *in which the argument of the socialist triangle is fully developed, will be useful.*

There's an old saying that if you don't know where you want to go, any road will take you there. As I've said on many occasions, this saying is mistaken. If you don't know where you want to go, *no* road will take you there. In other words, you need an understanding of the goal. You need a vision for the future.

Marx had a very clear vision. It was a vision of a society that would permit the full development of human beings, a society that allowed all people to develop their potential. And that would occur not because of gifts from above but as a result of the activity of human beings. This was his concept of revolutionary practice—the simultaneous changing of circumstances and human activity or self-change. Human development and practice—this "key link" in Marx reminds us that there are always two products as the result of our activity, the change in circumstances and the change in people themselves. It reminds us that what Marx called rich human beings, socialist human beings, produce themselves only through their own activity.

The Goal

The Bolivarian Constitution of Venezuela incorporates Marx's key link. It stresses that the goal of society must be the full development of every human being and that participation and protagonism is "the necessary way of achieving the involvement to ensure their complete development, both individual and collective." In 2007, President Chávez of Venezuela reinforced this vision by introducing what he called "the elementary triangle of socialism": Social ownership of the means of production, social production organized by workers, and production for social needs and purposes make up this triangle.

Firstly, social ownership of the means of production is the way to ensure that our communal social productivity is directed to the free development of all rather than used to satisfy the private goals of capitalists, groups of producers, or state bureaucrats. Secondly, social production organized by workers permits them to develop their capacities by combining thinking and doing in the workplace and thus to produce not only things but also themselves as self-conscious collective producers. Thirdly, satisfaction of social needs and purposes is the necessary goal of productive activity in the new society because it substitutes for the focus upon self-interest and selfishness an orientation to the needs of others and relations based upon solidarity.

The Paths

This concept of socialism is the vision of the society we want to build. This is where we want to go. And if we don't know that, no road will take us there. However, knowing where you want to go is not enough. It's not true that if you do know where you want to go, any road will take you there. Isn't there a relationship between the goal and the road you take to get there? Are these independent of each other? For example, can you get to the goal by going in the *opposite* direction? Do you build social ownership by relying upon capitalist ownership of the means of production and the capitalist monopoly of our social heritage and of the products of our labor? Do you build a society of associated producers and social production by preventing decision making by workers and retaining the gap between thinking and doing? Do you build a society based upon solidarity, where production is for social needs, by stressing selfishness? In other words, do you go forward by going backwards?

Maybe. Maybe sometimes it is necessary. Socialism does not fall from the sky. It is necessarily rooted in particular societies. We all start from different places—in our development, in our histories. Therefore, there cannot be one single path. All paths will be different. Some will be longer than others. Some will be relatively

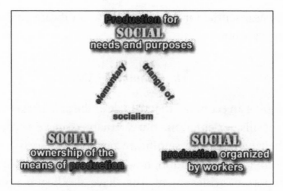

Elementary triangle of socialism[1]

straight, while others will require switchbacks because of the obstacles along the road. As we have learned, the biggest mistake is thinking that there is one road and one model.

The Compass

But there is a problem. When you are *not* going directly toward the goal, how do you avoid getting lost? How do you avoid the problem of the growth of capital and capitalist interests, the alienation of workers in the process of production and thus an emphasis upon possessing things and consumerism, and the growth of self-interest at the expense of solidarity? Some would say that there is no problem as long as we have a compass, as long as we have a directional finder. And that the party is that compass; the party can point in the direction of the goal when obstacles have temporarily forced you to go in the opposite direction.

I agree with that in principle. But I also believe that we need to learn from historical experience that the party is not itself immune, that it does not stand outside society and thus does not always point to the true north. This was certainly the case, for example, in Hungary, Yugoslavia, and China. And not only there. I have just returned from an intense month in Vietnam. There is no question in my mind that under the conditions facing Vietnam in the

1980s, it was essential for them to make a significant change in the path they were on.

The Example of Vietnam

By developing an economy that they describe as a market economy with a socialist orientation, the Vietnamese have succeeded in lifting their people from significant poverty. Whereas previously people were facing starvation, now Vietnam exports food. This is a very important achievement. They have also begun a process of industrialization.

However, there are serious problems. Young people are overwhelmingly oriented toward capitalism. They say openly that Vietnam needs more foreign investment, and they credit foreign investment with ending poverty. They want capitalism, and they look upon Marxism as having no relevance to their lives. I stress this point because the students we met were not selected randomly. They came largely from the young communists.

The dominant views are, in fact, no different from those in other countries in Southeast Asia. Thailand, Malaysia, and other nearby countries relying upon foreign investment and export-oriented industrialization are the basis of constant comparison in Vietnam. In other words, capitalism is winning in Vietnam. There is growing inequality; there is the emergence of millionaires (not as many as in China so far); and there is a significant process of privatization, called "equitisation," of state-owned industry.

And then there is the party, "the socialist orientation." It is my sense that a growing portion of the party is looking to Sweden and social democracy as the appropriate model. This was openly advocated at the conference I attended at the Ho Chi Minh National Political Academy, the party school. In other words, an emerging goal is not the socialist vision but, rather, capitalism plus social policies that reduce inequality—a capitalist welfare state.

There is an infection in Vietnam, and the party is not immune to it. I suspect that the next Party Congress will involve a struggle over this direction. Some party leaders are very worried about these tendencies. Certainly, the direction of change in the party in recent congresses has been to strengthen capitalist tendencies; for example, they have removed the prohibition on membership in the party by capitalists.

Something has been missing in Vietnam. Missing so far has been a sufficient emphasis upon the participation and protagonism that is "the necessary way" to ensure the complete development of human beings, "both individually and collectively." While there has been some focus upon grassroots democracy (for example, in Ho Chi Minh City), there has been very little decision making by workers in workplaces (outside of annual congresses in state-owned industry), and there has been little emphasis upon conscious production for social needs. The results have been predictable. In the absence of social production organized by workers and production for social needs, the third side of the socialist triangle, social ownership, is withering away. Increasingly, the human product is people who embrace the logic of capital.

I think that Vietnam reinforces the lesson that every step to the market must be accompanied by two steps in the direction of building a socialist society: building worker decision making in workplaces and building institutions based upon solidarity. If we recognize that people produce themselves through their activity, then their activity should unleash their potential rather than be left to an orientation to the market and self-interest. What I stressed in Vietnam was that the party needs to create the conditions in which people can develop their capacities as protagonists within their workplaces and their communities, institutions such as the communal councils and workers' councils being developed in Venezuela.

I suggest that through such a process of producing rich human beings with confidence and dignity, both the people and the party will be inoculated against the infection that can prevent us from reaching the socialist goal. That won't be achieved, however, by a one-sided focus upon developing productive forces.

We should never forget the essential insight of Che Guevara of the necessity to build productive forces and socialist human beings simultaneously.

Struggling to Build

Socialism Now

7. What Makes the Working Class a Revolutionary Subject?

In 2008, I received a request from an Iranian militant outside Iran to respond to a series of ten questions on the theme of "Is the Proletariat an Agent of Socialism?" in a left journal, Bidar. *Among the questions asked were whether the proletariat had been incorporated and absorbed into the system, if its victory is inevitable, whether it should be identified with the industrial proletariat, and why it is a revolutionary subject. My answer in 2008, included below, was framed as an answer to these questions. Later in the year, I learned that this answer would appear both in the journal and as the foreword to my book* Beyond Capital, *which had now been translated into Farsi. Although there were concerns as to whether publication in Iran itself would be possible, it was published outside and in 2009 we were happy to learn that it had been approved by the Ministry of Publications. (I was sent a copy of its cover and was told it would be available in a month in Iran.) Unfortunately, publication was subsequently delayed and then once again approved, and I am not certain about its current fate in Iran. Aside from the history of this note, it is included here because it is a clear statement of my broad conception of the working class and because of its stress upon struggle. This piece appeared subsequently in* Monthly Review *in December 2012 and more recently in Turkey.*

What makes the working class a revolutionary subject? Not Hegelian mysticism—that it is the universal class or the vulgar copy of the Absolute Spirit. Nor is the working class a revolutionary subject because of its physical location—that it is strategically placed to stop the wheels of industry.

From the sublime to the crude, there can be little surprise that these explanations convince few. Of course, there are some who had better explanations as to why the working class was revolutionary but who now say that the working class's time has come and gone. Once upon a time, capital concentrated workers, allowed them to come together to organize and struggle; today, though, capital has decentralized workers and turned them against one another in a way that prevents them from struggling together. Once upon a time, the working class had nothing to lose but its chains; but now it has been absorbed within capitalism, is a prisoner of consumerism, and its articles of consumption own and consume it.

Those who conclude that the working class is not a revolutionary subject because capitalism has changed the working class reveal that they do not understand the ABC's of Marxism. *The working class makes itself a revolutionary subject through its struggles—it transforms itself.* That was always the position of Marx—his concept of "revolutionary practice," which is the simultaneous changing of circumstances and self-change. The working class changes itself through its struggles. It makes itself fit to create the new world.

Why do workers struggle? Underlying all the struggles of workers is what Marx called the "worker's own need for development." We know that Marx understood that wage struggles in themselves were inadequate. But not to engage in them, he recognized, would leave workers "apathetic, thoughtless, more or less well-fed instruments of production." In the absence of struggle, Marx argued that the workers would be "a heartbroken, a weak minded, a worn-out, unresisting mass." Struggles are a process of production: they produce a different kind of worker, a worker who produces herself as someone whose capacity has grown, whose confidence develops, whose ability to organize and unite expands. Moreover, we should not think that this is limited to wage struggles. Every skirmish in which people assert themselves, every battle in which they push for social justice, every struggle to realize their own potential and their need for self-development builds the capacities of the actors.

And these struggles bring us up against capital. Why? Because capital is the barrier that stands between us and our own development. It is so because capital has captured the fruits of all civilization; it is the owner of all the products of the social brain and the social hand; and it turns our products and the products of workers before us against us. All of this is for one sole purpose, which is its own gain, profit. If we are to satisfy our needs, if we are to be able to develop our potential, we must struggle against capital and, in doing so, we working people create ourselves as revolutionary subjects.

But who are we? What is this working class that is the revolutionary subject? You will not find the answer in *Das Kapital*. Marx's *Capital* was not about the working class, except insofar as the working class was an object. What *Capital* explains is the nature of capital, its goals and its dynamics. But it only tells us about the working class insofar as capital acts against it. And, since it does not present the working class as subject, it also does not focus on the way in which capital struggles against this subject. So we have to look elsewhere in Marx for his comments about how the capitalist class maintains its power by dividing and separating workers (in Marx's example, Irish and English workers). Further, although Marx explicitly commented that "the contemporary power of capital rests" upon the creation of new needs for workers, there is no place where he explored this question.

Thus this critical question of the nature of the contemporary working class is one for which the answers will not be found in a book. We must develop the answers ourselves. Who is "not-capital" today? Who is separated from the means of production and must approach capital as a supplicant in order to survive? Surely, it is not only those who sell their labor power to capital but also those *unable* to sell their labor power to capital. Not only the exploited but also the excluded. And surely, it includes those who, in the context of a massive reserve army of the unemployed, work within the sphere of circulation of capital but are compelled to bear the risks themselves, that is, those who struggle to survive in the informal sector. They may not correspond to the stereotype of the working class as male factory worker, but that stereotype was always wrong.

Certainly, we need to begin with the recognition of the heterogeneous nature of the working class. As Marx knew, differences within the working class make it possible for capital to continue to rule. But, as Marx also knew, in the process of struggle we build unity. We can build that unity by recognizing as our common goal the need for our own development and by recognizing that "the free development of each is the condition for the free development of all." Capital has been winning the battle of ideas by convincing us that there is no alternative, and those who dismiss the working class as revolutionary subject reinforce that message. We can fight the battle of ideas, however, by stressing our right for self-development. As Marx and Engels knew, for workers "this appeal to their right is only a means of making them take shape as 'they', as a revolutionary, united mass."[1] We have a world to win—the world we build every day.

8. Three Perspectives on Democracy

This essay originated with a panel on Democracy under Capitalism and Socialism at the International Seminar, Democracy, Socialism and Visions for the Twenty-first Century in Hyderabad, India, in March 2014. Placed on this panel, along with participants from India and Nepal, I was stimulated to develop my thinking on the inadequacies of concepts of democracy in capitalism and in "real socialism," including Cuba, and to stress the importance of redefining democracy. This is its first publication.

Everyone agrees that democracy is a good thing. But democracy means something different to different people. How those views differ depends on particular premises. I want to identify three different general premises and then to consider democracy in light of these perspectives:

1. The individual's freedom to choose is the value to be maximized.
2. The coordination of individuals should be maximized in order to advance the interests of all efficiently by avoiding disharmony and dysfunction.
3. The development of human capacities is the value to be maximized.

I call these three perspectives consumer choice, the orchestra conductor, and human development, respectively.

Consumer Choice

Let us consider the first of these, the consumer choice perspective. The argument in this case is that we are free if we have complete freedom to choose. If we as individuals can choose whatever we want, if we can freely choose what we want to consume, whatever job we want, whatever candidate or political party we want, we are free and we are equal in that freedom. In each case the starting point is the atomistic, isolated individual who is free to choose.

From this perspective, unfreedom and dictatorship exist if we are restricted in our ability to choose commodities, jobs, and candidates in an election. That is the ideological perspective of democracy in capitalism: individuals appear free if they can choose. However, it is important to distinguish between appearance and the essential, underlying structure.

Consider the choice of a job. In the capitalist workplace, as the result of the sale of labor power, capital determines the purpose of production, has authority over the worker in the workplace and owns the products of labor. There is no freedom in the capitalist workplace. Rather, there is the dictatorship of capital. This perspective would say, however, that if you are free to choose another job, you cannot be exploited. After all, you can always go elsewhere. The freedom to move from job to job, however, is the freedom to seek a different capitalist exploiter, a different dictator. In other words, there is freedom to choose but what is there to choose from? What is the choice set?

Consider choice in the market. Marx's comment on market exchange was that despite their all-round dependence upon one another, the social connection of people in the market is the connection of "mutually indifferent persons." Rather than understanding and acting upon our links, our connection via the market appears as "external to the individuals and independent of them."[1]

Accordingly, isolated and indifferent individuals take the data from that social connection (the market) and make their own best decisions based upon that data. We are free to seek our self-interest. We choose. We are the masters of our fate. We are free.

Marx's point, though, is that we are in fact dominated by our social connection, dominated by the market. These "seemingly independent individuals," he argued, are in fact ruled by the market. They are "ruled by abstractions" that are "nothing more than the theoretical expressions of these material relations which are their Lord and master." Insofar as we are producers, we are driven by the market. We are driven by the need for money (the real need produced in capitalism), and if the market tells us we will get the money we need by engaging in a particular act, we do so. Rather than free, those seemingly independent individuals, Marx commented, are subject to "complete dependence on the so-called world market."[2]

Insofar as we are "mutually indifferent" consumers, we are also dominated by that social connection. Rather than direct links with those who produce, we choose from what is available in the market, what has been produced. But what is produced is not determined by a conscious social decision; rather, in the market, money decides. And, rather than reflecting equality, the market is dominated by those who have the most money. Atomistic individuals are free to choose, but the choice set, what there is to choose from, is dominated by those who have capital.

Finally, consider the seemingly independent individuals in the process of voting. Here, too, the choice set is a function of those who have money. Those who control the media, those who control the banks, the companies, etc., choose the candidates who can win. Again, it is the question of the choice set and the dictatorship of capital. There is apparent freedom—the individual possibility of choosing someone else, someone with little chance of being elected.

The apparent freedom of these seemingly independent individuals is certainly real for those individuals but in fact there is domination by the power of capital. Further, the appearance of individual freedom is central to the reproduction of these mutually indifferent persons. That is, the appearance of democracy as the individual ability to choose plays a central ideological role in capitalism. What kinds of people are produced in democracy understood as the individual's right to choose? Atomistic, isolated individuals indifferent to each other and divided. People who can be ruled.

The Orchestra Conductor

Consider the second perspective, the orchestra conductor. This perspective entirely rejects a focus on isolated, atomistic individuals. It stresses instead the unity of individuals and the importance and necessity to coordinate those individuals. Marx in this respect stressed the need for a directing authority to ensure a "harmonious cooperation of the activities of individuals." The orchestra conductor was his metaphor for the need to coordinate many people: "A single violin player is his own conductor; an orchestra requires a separate one."[3]

The job of considering the whole, Marx noted, is the "special work" of particular individuals. What, then, is the self-perception of the conductor? For the conductor, according to Elias Canetti, music is the only thing that counts. No one is more convinced than the conductor that "his business is to serve music and to interpret it faithfully." As I proposed in *Contradictions of "Real Socialism": The Conductor and the Conducted*, the perspective of the conductor is: "I am necessary. Without me, there would be chaos."[4]

Consider in practice what democracy is from this perspective. In this case it is the right to participate collectively in discussions and to offer suggestions that can improve a predetermined course of action. In other words, democracy here is collective participation, sometimes considerable participation. But not participation in the development of the goal. Rather, it is the opportunity to comment and to improve the plan of the conductor.

For example, the principal function of trade unions in the Soviet Union as set out in Article 96 of the Fundamental Labor Legislation was to serve as a transmission belt to mobilize workers in support of state goals. Article 97 of that legislation, on the other hand, noted the right of workers to take part in discussions and to "submit proposals on improving the work of enterprises, institutions and organizations." In other words, workers had the right to make suggestions. The article continued, "The officials of enterprises, institutions, organizations must promptly consider proposals made by factory workers and office employees, and inform them regarding the steps taken on these matters." Not much power there for workers. Rather, the company will be happy to receive suggestions from workers, and the company will decide which ones, if any, it will follow.[5]

A more recent example of the concept of democracy as consultative participation was the extensive discussion in Cuba over the "*lineamientos*," the guidelines for the party that were circulated by the party. These were the guidelines that have set Cuba on its current path to "update" the model. Everyone was mobilized for discussions—in workplaces, neighborhoods, everywhere. The party coordinated these discussions in each separate location, and, on the basis of reports, made adjustments. For example, the great concern expressed in many meetings about the phasing out of the *libreta* (the set of subsidized necessities) and the release of large numbers of people from state employment led to a slowing down (although, it must be noted, not the reversal) of these decisions.

Subsequently in Cuba there were discussions of a new labor code. Here again there was extensive discussion of the document initiated by the party. As in the case of the discussions of the guidelines, this participation plays an important role in transmitting concerns from below, while at the same time educating those below as to the proposal. However, these discussions are constrained. For example, in the case of the labor code, there was no place for a general discussion of worker management. Further, there was no means for communicating from one workplace to another; rather, collective atomization characterized the process.

All of this is logical from the perspective of the conductor: he is the one who knows the score. He alone knows the whole and, therefore, activity outside this framework is to be discouraged. Further, the logic of the conductor is such that there can be only one conductor; it is, after all, essential that there be unity at the top because in its absence this would confuse the players.

There is absolutely no doubt that extensive discussions, for example, in Cuba, distinguish that society from many others. However, participation in this case is not the same as the opportunity to develop capacities through protagonistic democracy. What kinds of people are produced in this relation? Not what Marx called rich human beings. Not people who have transformed themselves through their activity and are confident in their own powers. As the Soviet Union, China, and other countries characteristic of the "real socialism" of the twentieth century demonstrated, such relations do not build the protagonistic subjects who have the strength to prevent the restoration of capitalism. The people produced within this relation are people without power.

Human Development

This brings me to the third perspective, human development. Rather than privileging unconstrained individual choice or efficient centralized decisions improved by consultation, this perspective explicitly sets as its goal the full development of the potential of all members of society, that is, "the rich individuality which is as all-sided in its production as in its consumption." It is, simply, Marx's vision of that "society of free individuality, based on the universal development of individuals and on the subordination of their communal, social productivity as their social wealth."[6]

This conception of a society that encourages the development of rich human beings has reappeared explicitly in the vision of socialism for the twenty-first century. The Bolivarian Constitution of Venezuela, for example, insists in Article 299 that the goal of a human society must be that of "ensuring overall human development." "Everyone," it declares, "has the right to the free development of his or her own personality"; it focuses on "developing the creative potential of every human being and a full exercise of his or her personality in a democratic society." Human development is the overriding theme.[7]

But human development doesn't just happen. On the contrary, it comes only with practice—revolutionary practice. This was the point of Marx's third thesis on Feuerbach. Marx strongly rejected the view of some people (such as Robert Owen) that changing circumstances for people will produce changes in their nature. On the contrary, he argued that this doctrine "forgets that it is men who change circumstances and that the educator must himself be educated. Hence this doctrine is bound to divide society into two parts, one of which is superior to society." Human development, in short, does not come as a gift to those below; rather, "the coincidence of the changing of circumstances and of human activity or self-change can be conceived and rationally understood only as *revolutionary practice*."

Marx was entirely consistent on this point throughout his life. The combination of the change of circumstances and self-change is the red thread that runs through his work. Workers, for example, struggle in order to change circumstances and, in doing so, they change themselves; they thereby make themselves fit to build a new world. And it is not only worker struggles that lead to these two changes. *Every* human activity has two products. This is clear in the sphere of production, where every activity has two products: the material product and a joint product, the human being involved in production.

For example, under capitalist relations of production there is a growth of material output but also a particular human product—the fragmented, crippled human being, incapacitated by the separation of head and hand. Marx insisted that production under capitalist relations of production destroys human beings and nature. It produces workers whose alienation from their own products leads to the desire to fill the emptiness with things.

Yet, as noted earlier, Marx envisioned an alternative in which means of production are used to serve "the worker's own need for development," and he stressed the need to invert the capitalist inversion. Working under new relations of production, that of associated producers, allows for the development of a different human product. As Marx commented, "When the worker cooperates in a planned way with others, he strips off his individuality and develops the capabilities of his species." Through revolutionary practice, rich human beings are produced, the rich individuality that is as all-sided in its production as in its consumption.

Focus on the key link of human development and practice distinguishes the concept of socialism for the 21st century from the theory and experience of 20th century attempts at building socialism. Explicitly evoking that link of human development and practice, the Bolivarian Constitution declares in Article 62 that participation by people in "forming, carrying out and controlling the management of public affairs is the necessary way of achieving the involvement to ensure their complete development, both individual and collective." The *necessary* way. Only through practice does human development occur. The same emphasis upon a democratic, participatory and protagonistic society necessary for the development of our capacities is present in the economic sphere, which is why Article 70 stresses "self-management, co-management, cooperatives in all forms" and why Article 102's goal of "developing the creative potential of every human being" emphasizes "active, conscious and joint participation."

Central to the concept of socialism for the 21st century is protagonistic democracy—protagonistic democracy in the workplace, the community, and throughout society. Thus this concept of socialism implies a particular definition of democracy as a process of production, a process of producing "the all-round development of the individual."

Redefining Democracy

Think about the literal meaning of democracy. In Greek, the term comes from *demos* (people) and *kratos* (power or rule). *Dēmokratía* literally means the power or the rule of the people. Yet people cannot rule if they themselves lack power; they cannot rule if they lack the capacity to rule.

For the people to rule, we must develop their capacities to do so. Democracy from this perspective is defined as the process of developing capacities. And "the necessary way of achieving the involvement to ensure their complete development, both individual and collective" is through protagonism and practice.

The importance of creating institutions and forms by which people can develop their capacities was understood by Hugo Chávez, as evidenced by his stress upon the communal councils as the cells of a new socialist state, his statement that without workers' control you don't have socialism, and his insistence in one of his last talks that without the communes, there is *nada*. But we can also see the focus upon democracy as practice in the talk given by Alvaro Garcia Linera, the vice president of Bolivia, to the Party of the European Left in December 2013. In proposing "What is to be done?" today, Garcia Linera insisted that the left "must recover the concept of democracy," and he continued that "we must free ourselves from a purely institutionalized conception of democracy." We are, indeed, "prisoners of a liberal, fossilised conception of democracy."[8]

What, then, is the *non*-fossilized conception of democracy? Garcia Linera was clear:

> Democracy is practice, a collective action—it consists of increasingly taking part in the management of the common areas of society. There is democracy if we take part in the common good. If our heritage is water, then democracy is taking part in the management of water. If our heritage is a language, then democracy is defending that common good.

If our heritage is forests, land, knowledge, then democracy is managing, administering them in common. We must have an increasing participation in the management of forests, water, air, natural resources. Democracy exists, living not fossilised democracy, if the population and the left are taking part in the management in common of common resources, institutions, rights and riches.

Practice, collective action, struggle of the people to rule the commons—these are the ways to build the rule of the people; this is the protagonistic democracy by which both circumstances and people are transformed. In contrast to the concepts of democracy as individual choice or collective consultation, which are means of reproducing fossilized relations, democracy understood as the key link of human development and practice is the way to build a new, socialist society.

As noted in chapter 2, the organs and institutions that permit people to produce themselves as rich human beings are critical for the reproduction of the society of associated producers. The struggle to build those new organs and institutions is the struggle for democracy in the 21st century. And that struggle for protagonistic democracy must occur in every sphere of life. As Garcia Linera noted, we need to understand that it is important but not enough for democracy to knock at the factory gates: "It must also knock at the doors of banks, firms, institutions, resources—everything that belongs to people." Very simply, if socialism is to be the future, we have to build it now. Everywhere.

9. The Concept of "Fairness": Possibilities, Limitations, Possibilities

This chapter originated as the keynote address to the Fourth Annual Conference in Critical Social Research: Faultlines of Revolution!, in Ottawa, 4 May 2012, and was revised for publication in Studies in Political Economy: A Socialist Review *(2013). Although I had explored the moral economy of the working class in "real socialism" in* Contradictions of "Real Socialism," *here I focus upon moral economy as a basis for struggle, its inadequacies and the importance of socialists discovering and making explicit what is implicit in the moral economy of the working class in order to redefine "fairness."*

A specter is haunting the working class—the specter of communism. For the working class, that frightful hobgoblin is a society of little freedom, a society of workers without power (in the workplace or community), and a society where decisions are made at the top by a vanguard party that views itself as the sole repository of truth. This was not what communism meant for Marx and Engels, nor, indeed, for Lenin. For the visionaries of the nineteenth century, communism was a society that would foster human development, a society, in Marx's words, in which "objective wealth is there to satisfy the worker's own need for development."[1]

But now, in the twenty-first century, it is not the nineteenth century dream that the working class thinks about. Rather, it is the experience of the twentieth century. That memory, both real and exaggerated, has seized the minds of masses; it acts therefore as a material force not easily dissolved by the mantra, "Communism! Communism!" chanted by philosophers and other magicians of the word. And therein lies today's tragedy. Despite the intensification of capital's class war against the working class, despite capital's insistence that workers must bear the burden of capital's own failures, the working class sees no alternative than to try to say "NO." No to cutbacks, no to austerity, no to new user charges, no to the destruction of our lives and our environment. But *not* yes to a socialist alternative. Faced with the living nightmare of twenty-first-century capitalism, workers have seen no apparent alternative other than to mitigate the damage, individually or collectively. That is the tragic result of the destruction of the dream of socialism that occurred in the twentieth century.

We need a new vision, a new dream. As Hugo Chávez declared in Porto Alegre in 2005, "*We have to reinvent socialism.*"[2] But where will that vision come from and how will it displace the specter of twentieth-century communism? It will not spring full-grown from the forehead of Zeus. Rather, the starting point for the development of a vision of a socialist alternative can only come from the struggles of resistance of working people themselves against capital's assault.

There is a reason that people struggle. They do so when their sense of fairness is violated. Sometimes they protest, sometimes they erupt like a volcano, sometimes they riot—and sometimes they organize. Sometimes, of course, they don't struggle. They grumble over unfairness and injustice but conclude that there is no alternative and accordingly focus upon individual escapes and exits. There are both possibilities and limitations in the concept of fairness.

Possibilities

Referring to social norms and beliefs as to right and wrong, E. P. Thompson introduced the concept of "the moral economy of the poor." In his classic article, "The Moral Economy of the English Crowd in the Eighteenth Century," Thompson argued that the food riots of this period reflected a broad and passionate consensus on what was right, leading to a sharp reaction to egregious violations of that conception of justice.[3] Commenting on Thompson's account, a recent Chinese analyst of worker protests in China, Li Jun, observed that those "rioters were legitimized by the belief that they were defending traditional rights or customs that were supported by the wider consensus of the community."[4]

Similarly, James Scott, in his work on "the moral economy of the peasant," focused upon the notion of economic justice among peasants and pointed to revolts and rebellions that erupted when notions of fairness were violated. For Scott, these conceptions of justice had their roots in the need for maintaining subsistence rather than opposition to exploitation (that is, the extraction of the fruits of their labor) as such. "The test for the peasant," Scott proposed, "is more likely to be 'What is left?' than 'How much is taken?'"[5]

From this perspective, exploitation in itself does not generate riots, revolts, and rebellions. "Moral economists," Jeffrey Kopstein commented, in his study of worker resistance in East Germany, "posit the existence of a tacit social contract in almost every long-standing social formation in which subaltern groups tolerate their own exploitation." Those groups tolerate exploitation as long as they are left enough for themselves and are able to secure their expected subsistence. When the prevailing norm is violated, however, Kopstein proposed that it generates "resistance ranging from shirking, grumbling, foot dragging, false compliance, dissimulation, and other 'weapons of the weak,' to open strikes and other forms of collective action." But only to *negate* that violation. According to moral economists, Kopstein reported, "exploited groups simply want to restore their previous standards before the downturn. Rarely do they try to overturn the existing order altogether."[6]

The underlying concept here is one of an *equilibrium*—a concept that Thompson employed explicitly in talking about "a particular set of social relations, a particular equilibrium between paternalist authority and the crowd."[7] When that equilibrium is disturbed, there is a feedback mechanism: masses (peasants, crowd, workers) react to restore the conditions corresponding to the social norms supported by the consensus of the community. Thus, all other things equal, there is a tendency toward stability.

We can see this phenomenon in the "real socialism" of the latter part of the twentieth century, a term introduced in the Soviet Union to distinguish its actual experience from merely theoretical ideas about socialism. In what has been described as the social contract characteristic of "real socialism," workers had definite expectations as to their entitlement. They expected rising income over time, subsidized necessities, relative egalitarianism and especially job rights. The latter embraced not only the guarantee of a job, which was supported by a full employment policy, but also protection from any changes in their existing jobs that they did not want. In return, workers accepted the rule of the vanguard party in the workplace and society and comprehensive restrictions upon any power and, indeed, initiatives, from below.

"There was a system of mutual obligations," Boris Kagarlitsky explained with respect to the Soviet Union:

> We use the term "obligatory social contract" or asymmetrical social contract, meaning that the population was forced into this social contract. The social contract was definitely not free. On the other hand, if you lived in the country you understood that, though the population was forced into this contract, it was accepted, not just because there was no other way, but because people liked certain aspects of the contract.[8]

The right of everyone to subsistence and a growing standard of life, the importance of stable prices and full employment, the orientation toward egalitarianism (and thus small income differentials)—all these were part of the norms that formed the moral economy of the working class in "real socialism." While that social contract did not exclude exploitation, it did yield something workers wanted. Kopstein argued, for example, that "along with job security, East German workers had the power to demand a rough-and-ready sort of wage egalitarianism and consumer prices that remained low relative to wages."[9]

The same argument for a moral economy of the working class and the support that the social contract provided is explicit in Li Jun's examination of strikes in China: "Simply put, in the Chinese socialist setting, workers view themselves as having a relationship with the state, a relationship which operates according to the norm of reciprocity: the state is expected to have committed itself to ensuring that the workers have a decent living by providing job security and a prodigious welfare package, while workers, in return, advocate the party ruling by giving their political support and loyalty to the state." To support what Li Jun calls "the workers' moral economy," it was expected that the state authority would fulfill "its responsibility to protect and benefit its working class in the form of the 'iron rice bowl.'"[10]

What occurred in "real socialism" when this popular consensus of justice and fairness was violated? According to the Hungarian economist Janos Kornai, a process of feedback tended to restore an equilibrium. When the economy generates "results which deviate from existing norms (the result of 'habit, convention, tacit or legally supported social acceptance, or conformity'), the system generates signals that are fed back into the system." Kornai argued that central decision-makers in Hungary had as a target a normal rate of growth of real consumption per head of 3–4 percent with the result that "if the growth of consumption remains below its normal rate, the scale of investment will be reduced so as to leave more of the national income for consumption."[11]

It was clear to Kornai why those at the top acted in this way. They were limited by what "the population is content to accept, and where dissatisfaction begins." There was a potential cost to violating the norms. "Holding back increases in living standards, or their absolute reduction, and infringing the lower limit . . . sooner or later entails serious political and social consequences, tension and even shocks, which after a shorter or longer lag force a correction." Behind the attempt of the vanguard to avoid deviations from the norm was the anticipation of the responses of workers (for example, to increased prices). People, Kornai stated, wanted price stability, "and after a time they even expect the government to guarantee it. Any important price increase gives rise to unrest."[12]

Kornai argued that those at the top were limited. The barrier "depends on the actual socio-political situation, what level and growth rate of consumption the population is content to accept, and where dissatisfaction begins. And, if there is dissatisfaction, at what point it starts to endanger the stability of the system. It is a historical fact that unrest may be so great that it induces leaders to change economic policy."[13]

Thus we can see in "real socialism" that the moral economy of the working class was reinforced during this period by the honoring of the existing social contract. Those at the top understood that people would respond to perceived violations of the social contract, as they did in riots in 1962 in the Soviet Union in response to price increases, and they took those potential responses into account in their actions. When ideas grasp the minds of masses, Marx noted, ideas are a material force. And, when people struggle to reverse violations of their concepts of right and wrong, those concepts are clearly a material force rather than disembodied ideas.

However, in such struggles more occurs than just the return to an initial equilibrium. Even though people may not be struggling against exploitation as such, something more than what they themselves intend is produced in that process. This was Marx's concept of revolutionary practice. Very simply, people change in the course of struggle. Despite the limited goals involved, Marx commented in 1853 that wage struggles prevented workers "from becoming apathetic, thoughtless, more or less well-fed instruments of production"; without them, workers would be "a heartbroken, a weak-minded, a worn-out, unresisting mass." He returned to the same point in 1865, noting that workers who did not engage in wage struggles "would be degraded to one level mass of broken wretches past salvation."[14]

Can we doubt this point? After all, those who are not engaged in struggle are producing themselves as people of a particular type. So, even though the moral economy of the working class as such is not an immediate challenge to exploitation, it can be the basis for a process by which workers themselves change in the course of struggle. This, then, is the possibility inherent in the concepts of right and wrong and of fairness characteristic of the moral economy of the working class. It is the possibility of building upon those existing beliefs to the point of challenging exploitation and the system itself directly.

Limitations

And yet, the example of "real socialism" points to the real limits of that moral economy. It demonstrates that concepts of fairness and a consensus of what is right and what is wrong are not sufficient to prevent their violation. In "real socialism," the social contract that embodied and reinforced the moral economy of the working class was not merely unfulfilled in some respect. On the contrary, it was unilaterally *revoked* by the vanguard.[15] But rather than this leading to resistance by the working class to restore the social contract, there was no appreciable resistance to the ending of the social contract whether it was in the Soviet Union, Eastern Europe, China or, currently, in Cuba.

What is more, this problem is not simply a particular characteristic of "real socialism." Consider what happened to the "moral economy of the poor" discussed by E. P. Thompson. The historic "particular set of social relations, a particular equilibrium between paternalist authority and the crowd" that he described also came to an end. As in the case of "real socialism," Thompson observed that "the 'nature of things' which had once made imperative, in times of dearth, at least some symbolic solidarity between the rulers and the poor, now dictated solidarity between the rulers and 'the Employment of Capital.'"[16]

If we add to these cases the experience in the developed capitalist world in the period after the Second World War when the so-called Golden Age and "capital-labor accord" were dissolved from the top without serious resistance from the working class, there appears to be a definite pattern. In every tacit social contract based merely upon inherited concepts of fairness, the "subaltern groups" cannot prevent the social contract from being abandoned entirely by those who rule.

To understand why, consider Marx's discussion of the spontaneous concepts of fairness characteristic of workers in nineteenth-century capitalism. Marx understood that the attitudes and notions of moral economy exist at the surface of society; rather than revealing the actual relations, they reflect how things appear (and may necessarily appear) to the real actors. What is apparent in everyday life spontaneously produces the ideas that grasp the minds of masses and underlie their actions.

What did workers in mid-nineteenth-century Europe struggle about? In his *Value, Price and Profit*, Marx observed that 99 percent of wage struggles followed changes that had led wages to fall. "In one word," he noted, they were "reactions of labour against the previous action of capital." These wage struggles were an attempt to restore the "*traditional standard of life*" that was under attack.[17]

The spontaneous impulse of workers under these conditions was to struggle for "fairness" against the violations of existing norms—indeed, to fight a guerilla war against effects initiated by capital. The explicit goal of workers, Marx noted, was to struggle for "a fair day's wage for a fair day's work." In doing so, they were not attempting to change the system or struggling against exploitation, except insofar as exploitation was understood as unfairness. Marx described the demands of workers as "conservative" and argued that, instead of those demands for fairness, "they ought to inscribe on their banner the *revolutionary* watchword, 'Abolition of the wages system!'"[18]

Yet Marx understood quite well *why* the workers' slogan focused upon fair wages and a fair workday: it flows from the necessary appearance of a transaction in which workers yield the property right to use their capacity to work, their labor power, for a given period. "On the surface of bourgeois society," Marx pointed out in *Capital*, "the worker's wage appears as the price of labour, as a certain quantity of money that is paid for a certain quantity of labour."[19] The conscious struggle of workers is over the *fairness* of "the certain quantity of money" and the *fairness* of the "certain quantity of labour." What is perceived as just and fair is that they receive an equivalent for their labor, that they are not "cheated." This follows from the way the wage necessarily appears. From the form of the wage as the payment for a given workday, Marx commented, comes "all the notions of justice held by both the worker and the capitalist."[20]

"Nothing is easier," he declared, "to understand than the necessity, the *raison d'être*, of this form of appearance" that underlies the moral economy of the working class in capitalism. This appearance is not an accident; nor is the moral economy of workers based upon appearances an accident. On the surface, the worker sells his or her labor to the capitalist. However, this form of appearance "makes the actual relation invisible, and indeed presents to the eye the precise opposite of that relation." Specifically, there appears to be no exploitation, no division of the workday into necessary and surplus labor; rather, all labor appears as paid labor. Precisely because exploitation is hidden on the surface, it is necessary to delve below the surface: "The forms of appearance are reproduced directly and spontaneously, as current and usual modes of thought; the essential relation must first be discovered by science."[21]

At the level of appearances, we cannot understand capitalism. "The interconnection of the reproduction process," Marx commented, "is not understood."[22] Accordingly, he rejected a focus on individual commodity transactions and examined the underlying structure of capitalism. What is the nature of the system and how is it reproduced? This is the central question in *Capital*. Considering the working class as a whole, Marx assumed that, in return for yielding to the capitalist the use of their capacities, workers receive their "traditional standard of life," that which is necessary to reproduce themselves as wage-laborers in a given time and place. This concept of a given level of necessity (the basis for the value of labor-power) allowed him to demonstrate how the workday is divided into necessary labor and surplus labor and how exploitation of workers is the necessary condition for the reproduction of capitalists.

For this critical deduction, however, Marx did not have to explain the basis of this existing standard of necessity. He simply *assumed* it as given—an assumption he intended to remove in his projected book on wage-labor.[23] With this approach, Marx was able to reveal the nature of capital and its inherent tendencies, something that a focus upon appearances can never reveal. Thus the case was made for the necessity to end capitalist relations of production rather than to struggle for "fair wages."

How else could we understand what capital is *without* the critique of those forms of appearance that underlie the moral economy of the working class in capitalism? The apparent relation of exchange between capitalist and worker strengthens the rule of capital: it "mystifies" the actual relation and "ensures the perpetuation of the specific relationship of dependency, endowing it with the deceptive *illusion* of a transaction."[24] To enable workers to go beyond that conservative motto to the "*revolutionary* watchword," Marx offered the weapon of a critique based upon an alternative political economy, the political economy of the working class.[25]

However, the political economy of the working class introduced by Marx in *Capital* was incomplete. What determines the standards underlying concepts of fairness, that is, the equilibrium that is the basis of consensus? This is not a question that Marx explicitly considered theoretically. Marx began with the assumption that the traditional standard of life, the standard of necessity, was *given*. While that assumption was sufficient to demonstrate that capital is the result of the exploitation of workers, with this assumption we cannot explore theoretically what determines the standard of necessity. This means that we are unable to consider the factors which cause the standard of necessity to *change*. What allows it to be driven downward? And what prevents this?

Beyond **Capital** demonstrates that with the *removal* of this assumption of a fixed standard of life, it is no longer possible to argue that the automatic effect of productivity increases is the growth of exploitation (relative surplus value).[26] To understand the determination of the standard of necessity and the rate of exploitation (and any movements in these), the state of class struggle is essential to consider. For this purpose, I introduced as a variable the concept of "the degree of separation among workers," a concept that draws upon Marx's observations in *Capital* that "the dispersal of the rural workers breaks their power of resistance, while concentration increases that of the urban workers" and "the workers' power of resistance declines with their dispersal."[27]

By explicitly articulating this variable, we acknowledge that the potential for collective struggle (both its emergence and its prospect for success) will be significantly influenced by the degree of separation of workers. If workers are isolated and atomized, if they are separated from other workers and indeed view them as enemies, then there is little prospect for collective action. As Marx commented with respect to the antagonism between English and Irish workers, this is "the *secret of the impotence of the English working class*, despite its organization."

It should be obvious that workers are separated not only by purely economic factors. Racism, sexism, geographical location, and legal and ideological barriers to collective action all contribute to separation among workers. They thereby contribute to the maintenance of existing structures. Marx noted with respect to the impotence of the English working class that the separation of English and Irish workers is "the secret by which the capitalist class maintains its power. And that class is fully aware of it." [28]

While clearly relevant to capitalism, this aspect of class struggle transcends capitalism itself. In *Beyond* **Capital**, I stressed that in any society "those who mediate among producers have an interest in maintaining and increasing the degree of separation, division and atomization among producers in order to continue to secure the fruits of cooperation in production." [29] And we can see what happens, all other things equal, when there are significant increases in the degree of separation among workers.

When overaccumulation of capital and the ensuing increase in the intensity of capitalist competition (a process that began before the much-evoked more recent process of globalization of capital) brings with it an assault upon the apparent capital-labor accord, and when the economic crisis in "real socialism" leads to attacks upon the egalitarian impulses and job rights of workers—upon the social contract of "real socialism"—we see clearly that the equilibrium characteristic of an existing moral economy is only an *apparent* one, one that rests upon the reproduction of a given degree of separation of producers.

As long as the degree of separation (or the balance of class forces) is constant, this implies the reproduction of an equilibrium in which any deviations produce feedback tendencies to restore the norms. And insofar as such deviations are temporary, it strengthens the belief in the permanency of those particular norms. But the existing moral economy can never explain its basis, that is, *why* those particular beliefs as to what is fair are present—and thus why those norms can change. To grasp the conditions underlying concepts of fairness at a given moment, it is necessary to move from the moral economy of the working class to the political economy of the working class.

For revolutionaries who would help to put an end to existing structures of exploitation and deformation, it is essential to recognize the importance of the moral economy of the working class but to go beyond it. We need to understand how the system is reproduced and how divisions among producers play an essential role in that reproduction. With that understanding, there is possibility.

Possibilities

Understanding the nature of the system as the source of the anger and unhappiness of people, however, is not a sufficient condition for going beyond the system. It is also essential to focus upon the alternative implicit in the political economy of the working class—what Marx called in *Capital* "the worker's own need for development."[30] For people whose sense of fairness has been violated, the vision of an alternative is necessary. It must be one that can appear to workers as a new common sense, as *their* common sense. Just as in every labor process "a result emerges which had already been conceived by the worker at the beginning, hence already existed ideally," so also for the revolutionary labor process we must build that goal in our minds before we can construct it in reality; only this conscious purpose can ensure the purposeful will required.[31]

Rather than the abstract proletarians that are characteristic of bad theory, though, the starting point should be real people with particular ideas and concepts that are reflected in an existing moral economy. By considering current social norms and beliefs as to what is right and what is wrong, we can avoid the tendency to begin with a preconceived theory and to see nothing else. If we are to put an end to existing structures of exploitation and deformation, it is essential to recognize the importance of the moral economy of the working class and to go beyond it.

As we have seen, the existing concepts of fairness as reflected in the moral economy of the working class are limited. Not only is it impossible at this level to understand the basis of those current concepts but the spontaneous tendency of moral economy is to look *backward*. Characteristic is an attempt to restore a previous equilibrium, either an immediate one or an idealized one from the past. This is a vision of the past rather than one for the future.

To build a vision of the future that can resonate with today's actors, we need to search for the necessary raw materials in the present. To articulate what is implicit in current concepts and struggles is essential for the development of a conscious vision of a new society. Guided by the political economy of the working class, we may be able to identify elements in the moral economy that potentially point beyond toward a new society, a society of associated producers.

In *The Contradictions of "Real Socialism,"* for example, I identified three elements in the moral economy of the working class in "real socialism" that contain implicitly within them characteristics of a society of associated producers.[32] In the orientation of workers toward egalitarianism, we can see glimpses of one such characteristic, namely, the focus upon the common ownership of the means of production, which implies the right to share equally as owners. As the repeated exhortations of the vanguard against egalitarianism demonstrate, this sense of entitlement had real lasting power in the minds of workers.

Further, solidarity of workers within their individual workplaces as manifested in their mutual support in protecting each other against managers and through their spontaneous cooperation in making production possible generated a sense of their collective power and latent support for workers' control. Just as the spontaneous food riots of the eighteenth century revealed the underlying moral economy of the crowd, so also does the spontaneous emergence of workers' councils, as in Hungary in 1956 and Poland in 1980, allow us to infer the existence of an underlying consensus among workers. This orientation toward worker management was acknowledged by the vanguard when it sought to shore up support for its role—as in Yugoslavia in 1950, Czechoslovakia in 1968, and initial gestures in perestroika.

Finally, within that moral economy was a tendency for people to help each other without demanding an equivalent in return. An "economy of favours" is how Ledeneva described the Soviet Union. Rather than relations in which alienated, mutually indifferent individuals exchange alienated things, characteristic of "real socialism" is the presence of gift relations within networks of friends and family. That gift relation, she notes, is "created and preserved by a mutual sense of 'fairness' and trust."[33] It presumes people who have a bond, people who have a past and hope to have a future, and its product is the enhancement of solidarity within these bounds. In this third element of the moral economy of the working class in real socialism, there is latent a society based upon solidarity and community, one where we support others to the best of our ability.

Three glimpses of an alternative society present within "real socialism." But *only* glimpses, isolated appearances of a hidden alternative structure. As long as they remain isolated and unarticulated as integral parts of a whole, they appear simply as anomalies and inefficiencies in a structure dominated by a different logic. From the perspective of the logic of the vanguard and the logic of capital (the two contesting logics that made "real socialism" dysfunctional), these elements within the moral economy of the working class were irrational vestiges of peasant society, anti-proletarian, and were opposed to the development of productive forces. In the absence of a theory that articulated the logic of the working class, that implicit alternative was (and continues to be) easily defeated.[34]

But that logic can be articulated. In the moral economy of the working class in "real socialism," we can glimpse three sides of what I identified in *The Socialist Alternative* as the organic system of socialism (which Hugo Chávez of Venezuela called in 2007 the "elementary socialist triangle"): social ownership of the means of production, social production organized by workers, and communal needs and purposes as the goal of productive activity.[35] By articulating the characteristics of this particular combination of production, distribution, and consumption, it is possible to present a coherent vision that transcends the moral economy of the working class in "real socialism."

These elements are not only implicit in "real socialism." Each side of this socialist triangle relates directly to elements of current struggles within capitalism—social ownership of the means of production to the fight against privatization, social production organized by workers to the sense of emptiness and powerlessness of life within the workplace and community under capitalist domination, and production for social needs in relation to the struggle against capitalist-imposed austerity. By themselves, these themes represent partial rejections of existing structures; however, to the extent that they remain partial, they cannot offer a vision that goes beyond the existing moral economy of the working class in capitalism. By demonstrating their interdependence within an organic socialist system, however, it is possible to offer an alternative common sense, one that contains a *new* sense of fairness, the potential for a *new* moral economy, one that goes beyond the limits of the existing moral economy.

The potential is there because of a new vision of socialism that has emerged in the twenty-first century as an alternative to the barbarism of capitalism. It is a vision that can be a weapon in struggle because it explicitly rejects not only capitalism but also the specter of twentieth-century communism.[36] At its core is the alternative that Marx evoked in *Capital*: in contrast to a society in which the worker exists to satisfy the need of capital for its growth, Marx pointed to "the inverse situation, in which objective wealth is there to satisfy the worker's own need for development." Human development is at the center of this vision of the alternative to capitalism.

From his early discussion of a "rich human being" to his later comments about the "development of the rich individuality which is as all-sided in its production as in its consumption," the "development of all human powers as such the end in itself," and "the all-around development of the individual," Marx focused upon our need for the full development of our capacities. This is the essence of his conception of socialism—a society that removes all obstacles to the full development of human beings.[37]

Marx always understood that human development requires practice. It does not come as a gift from above. Starting from his articulation of the concept of revolutionary practice, the red thread that runs throughout his work, Marx consistently stressed that through their activity people simultaneously change as they change circumstances. [38] We develop ourselves through our own practice and are the products of all our activities: the products of our struggles (or the lack of same), the products of all the relations in which we produce and interact. In every human activity, there is a *joint product,* both the change in the object of labor and the change in the laborer herself.[39]

Marx's unity of human development and practice constitutes the *key link* that we need to grasp if we are to talk about socialism. What kind of productive relations can provide the conditions for the full development of human capacities? Only those in which there is conscious cooperation among associated producers; only those in which the goal of production is that of the workers themselves. Worker management that ends the division between thinking and doing is essential, but clearly this requires more than worker-management in individual workplaces. They must be the goals of workers in society, too, as members of their communities.

Implicit in the emphasis upon this key link of human development and practice is our need to be able to develop through democratic, participatory, and protagonistic activity in every aspect of our lives. Through revolutionary practice in our communities, our workplaces, and in all our social institutions, we produce ourselves as "rich human beings"—rich in capacities and needs— in contrast to the impoverished and crippled human beings that capitalism produces. This concept is one of democracy in *practice*, democracy *as* practice, *democracy as protagonism.* Democracy in this sense—protagonistic democracy in the workplaces, neighborhoods, communities, and communes—is the democracy of people who are transforming themselves into revolutionary subjects.

Social production organized by workers is essential for developing the capacities of producers and building new relations of cooperation and solidarity. If workers do not make decisions in their workplaces and communities and develop their capacities, we can be certain that *someone else will*. Protagonistic democracy in all our workplaces is an essential condition for the full development of the producers.

However, as I have suggested, there are other elements in this socialist combination. The society we want to build is one that recognizes that "the free development of each is the condition for the free development of all." How can we ensure that our communal, social productivity is directed to the free development of *all* rather than used to satisfy the private goals of capitalists, groups of individuals, or state bureaucrats? *Social ownership of the means of production* is that second side. Remember, though, that it is essential to understand that social ownership is not the same as state ownership. Social ownership implies a profound democracy, one in which people function as subjects, both as producers and as members of society, in determining the use of the results of their social labor.

Are common ownership of the means of production and cooperation in the process of production sufficient for "ensuring overall human development"? What kind of people are produced when we relate to others through an exchange relation and try to get the best deal possible for ourselves? This brings us to the third side of the triangle: *satisfaction of communal needs and communal purposes*. Here the focus is upon the importance of basing our productive activity upon the recognition of our common humanity and our needs as members of the human family. The premise is the development of a solidarian society, in which we go beyond self-interest and where, through our activity, we both build solidarity among people and at the same time produce ourselves differently.

Unifying this vision of socialism for the twenty-first century is the concept of human development, the full development of human potential, a concept that can appear as common sense when people think about what they want for their children. We need to find ways to articulate this vision. To this end, I proposed in *The Socialist Alternative* a simple set of propositions, a "Charter for Human Development" that can be recognized as self-evident requirements for human development:

1. Everyone has the right to share in the social heritage of human beings—an equal right to the use and benefits of the products of the social brain and the social hand—in order to be able to develop his or her full potential.
2. Everyone has the right to be able to develop his and her full potential and capacities through democracy, participation, and protagonism in the workplace and society—a process in which these subjects of activity have the precondition of the health and education that permit them to make full use of this opportunity.
3. Everyone has the right to live in a society in which human beings and nature can be nurtured—a society in which we can develop our full potential in communities based upon cooperation and solidarity.[40]

The goal of such a charter is to try to *redefine* the concept of fairness. It is *unfair* that some people monopolize the social heritage of all human beings; it is *unfair* that some people are able to develop their capacities through their activities while others are crippled and deformed and it is *unfair* that we are forced into structures in which we view others as competitors and enemies.

Possibilities-Limitations-Possibilities: the repositing of possibilities based upon understanding and transcending limitations. If we can begin to redefine the concept of fairness and to build a new moral economy based upon the political economy of the working class, then instead of NO's that look backward to a good old past, we can struggle for a YES based upon a vision of socialism for the twenty-first century. Again, we need to try to articulate what is implicit in current concepts and struggles and to develop a conscious vision of a new society.

Communicating that vision is not easy. The Battle of Ideas is never easy, especially in times of crisis, when the spontaneous tendency is to look backward to the old moral economy and to search for scapegoats to explain what has gone wrong. There is no lack of alternative visions rooted in existing cultures and religions that foster the focus upon scapegoats. But communicating the vision of socialism for the twenty-first century and struggling to make it real is essential. The choice before us is familiar: socialism or barbarism.

10. The State and the Future of Socialism

This chapter revises and develops a talk originally presented as the Fourth Annual Poulantzas Memorial Lecture in December 2010 and published as Building Socialism for the 21st Century: The Logic of the State *(Athens: Nicos Poulantzas Institute, 2011). I took the opportunity on the occasion of the talk to stress the importance of a new state based upon communal councils and workers' councils (as opposed to some combination of this and parliamentary democracy as a goal). In this subsequent version (published in the* Socialist Register 2013*), I developed further organizational mechanisms for this new state, expanding the discussion in my book* The Socialist Alternative.

Crises and Class War

We are in the midst of a class war. That's not unusual. There is always class war in capitalism, although sometimes it is hidden and sometimes there is the interlude of an apparent Carthaginian Peace. But the class war has intensified because of the crisis in capitalism, one rooted in the overaccumulation of capital. And, in this crisis, capital has intensified the class war against the working class. Austerity, cutbacks, and the need to sacrifice are the demands of capital as it calls upon workers to bear the burden of capital's own failures. This is a war conducted by capitalist states against workers to compel them to give up their achievements from past struggles. In some places, we see that the working class is saying "no." In some cases, we see that workers are fighting to defend their past successes within capitalism and that they are fighting against the racism and xenophobia that are the default position when workers are under attack but are not in struggle against capital. Such struggles, as Marx knew, are "indispensable." They are the only means of preventing workers "from becoming apathetic, thoughtless, more or less well-fed instruments of production."[1] But, who will win this class war?

In his recent book, *The Communist Hypothesis*, Alain Badiou describes the past defeats of May 1968, the Chinese Cultural Revolution, and the Paris Commune, as well as those of factory occupations and other such struggles as defeats "covered with glory."[2] Because they remain in our memory as inspirations, they must be contrasted, he insists, to the "defeat without glory" that social democracy brings.[3] This is certainly true. However, we need to acknowledge that the current struggles against capital's attempt to make the working class rescue it from yet another of its crises may yet be added to the list of glorious defeats.

Certainly, it is necessary to try to stop the cutbacks and to communicate to capital how high its costs will be for attempting to shift the burden of its own failures to workers. And we must celebrate those struggles taking place wherever the working class has not been anesthetized as a result of previous defeats without glory, leaving only what Marx once described as "a heartbroken, a weak-minded, a worn-out, unresisting mass."[4] However, it is not enough to say no. There are those who think that an accumulation of loudly screamed no's can be sufficient. These poets of negation demonstrate thereby that they don't understand why and how capital reproduces itself.[5] Why is it that after so many defeats, so many still cannot see what Marx grasped in the nineteenth century, that capital has the tendency to produce a working class that views the existence of capital as *necessary*? "The advance of capitalist production," he stressed, "develops a working class which by education, tradition and habit looks upon the requirements of this mode of production as self-evident natural laws."[6]

Marx understood that capitalism tends to produce the workers it needs, workers who look upon capitalism as common sense. Given the mystification of capital (arising from the sale of labor-power), which makes productivity, profits, and progress appear as the result of the capitalist's contribution, it followed that "the organization of the capitalist process of production, once it is fully developed, *breaks down all resistance*." Marx added that capital's generation of a reserve army of the unemployed "sets the seal on the domination of the capitalist over the worker" and that the capitalist can rely upon the worker's "dependence on capital, which springs from the conditions of production themselves, and is *guaranteed in perpetuity* by them."[7] Obviously, for Marx, capital's walls will never be brought down by loud screams.

Even with a certain resistance marked by struggles over wages, working conditions, and the defense of past gains, as long as workers look upon the requirements of capital as "self-evident natural laws," these struggles occur within the bounds of the capitalist relation. In the end, workers' subordination to the logic of capital means that faced with capitalism's crises they sooner or later act to ensure the conditions for the expanded reproduction of capital. Nowhere is this clearer than in the defeats without glory of social democracy.

Defeat when capitalism is in crisis means that capital can emerge from the crisis by *restructuring* itself, as it did internationally with the Bretton Woods package after the crises of the 1930s and the 1970s. As is often noted, there is a big difference between a crisis *in* capitalism and a crisis *of* capitalism. The latter requires conscious actors prepared to put an end to capitalism, to challenge and defeat the logic of capital. But this requires a vision that can appear to workers as an alternative common sense, as *their* common sense.

Like the architect who first "builds the cell in his mind," we must construct our goal in our minds before we can construct it in reality; only this conscious focus can ensure the "purposeful will" required to complete the defeat of the logic of capital.[8] To struggle against a situation in which workers "by education, tradition and habit" look upon capital's needs "as self-evident natural laws," we must struggle for an *alternative* common sense. But what is the vision of a new society whose requirements workers may look upon as "self-evident natural laws"? Clearly, it won't be found in the results of twentieth century attempts to build socialism, which, to use Marx's phrase, ended "in a miserable fit of the blues."[9]

The "Key Link": Human Development and Practice

"We have to reinvent socialism." With this statement, Hugo Chávez, president of Venezuela, electrified activists in his closing speech at the January 2005 World Social Forum in Porto Alegre, Brazil. "It can't be the kind of socialism that we saw in the Soviet Union," he stressed, "but it will emerge as we develop new systems that are built on cooperation, not competition." If we are ever going to end the poverty of the majority of the world, Chávez argued, capitalism must be transcended. "But we cannot resort to state capitalism, which would be the same perversion of the Soviet Union. We must reclaim socialism as a thesis, a project, and a path, but this must be a new type of socialism, a humanist one, which puts humans and not machines or the state ahead of everything."[10]

There, at its core, is the vision of socialism for the twenty-first century. Rather than expansion of the means of production or direction by the state, human beings must be at the center of the new socialist society. This marks a return to Marx's vision, to the contrast he drew in *Capital* between a society subordinate to the logic of capital—where "the worker exists to satisfy the need of the existing values for valorization"—and the logic of a new society, that "inverse situation, in which objective wealth is there to satisfy the worker's own need for development."[11] This concept of the worker's need for development is the culmination of Marx's consistent stress upon the centrality of the development of human capacity, the "development of the rich individuality," as the real wealth and explicit goal of the new society. Here was the "inverse situation" that would allow for "the all-round development of the individual," the "complete working out of the human content," the "development of all human powers as such the end in itself," a society of associated producers in which "the free development of each is the condition for the free development of all."[12]

But this is only one side of Marx's perspective. A focus upon the full development of human potential was characteristic of much socialist thought in the nineteenth century.[13] What Marx added to this was his understanding of *how* the development of human capacities occurs. In his *Theses on Feuerbach*, he was clear that it is not by giving people gifts, not by changing their circumstances for them. Rather, we change only through real practice, by changing circumstances ourselves. Marx's concept of "revolutionary practice," that concept of "the coincidence of the changing of circumstances and of human activity or self-change," can be found throughout his work.[14] Marx was most consistent on this point when talking about the struggles of workers against capital and how this revolutionary practice transforms "circumstances and men," expanding their capabilities and making them fit to create a new world.[15]

This process of changing ourselves, though, is not limited to the sphere of political and economic struggle. In the very act of producing, Marx indicated, "the producers change, too, in that they bring out new qualities in themselves, develop themselves in production, transform themselves, develop new powers and new ideas, new modes of intercourse, new needs and new language."[16] And, certainly, the relations within which workers produce affect the nature of the workers produced. This was Marx's point about how capitalist productive relations "distort the worker into a fragment of a man" and degrade him and "alienate from him the intellectual potentialities of the labour process."[17] Every human activity, Marx understood, has as its result a *joint product*—both the change in the object of labor and the change in the laborer himself.[18] Unfortunately, that second product is often forgotten.

Marx's combination of human development and practice constitutes the *key link*. Taken seriously, it has definite implications for relations within the workplace. Rather than capitalism's joint product—the fragmented, crippled human being whose enjoyment consists in possessing and consuming things—it implies a person who is able to develop all her potential through her activity. Taken seriously, that key link has definite implications for the nature of the state. Rather than allowing us every few years to elect those who misrule us as our representatives to a state that stands over and above us, it implies what Marx called the "self-government of the producers," the "reabsorption of the state power by society as its own living forces."[19] Taken seriously, that key link has definite implications for the nature of the party. Rather than a body that sees itself as superior to social movements and whose members are meant to learn the merits of discipline in following the decisions made by infallible central committees, it implies a party that learns from popular initiative and unleashes the creative energy of masses through their own practice. Taken seriously, that key link has obvious implications for building socialism.

Socialism for the 21st Century

Consider the characteristic of socialist production implicit in this key link.[20] What are the circumstances that have as their joint product "the totally developed individual, for whom the different social functions are different modes of activity he takes up in turn"?[21] Given the "dialectical inversion" peculiar to capitalist production that cripples the body and mind of the worker and alienates her from "the intellectual potentialities of the labour process," it is clear that to develop the capacities of people the producers must put an end to what Marx called, in his *Critique of the Gotha Program*, "the enslaving subordination of the individual to the division of labour, and therewith also the antithesis between mental and physical labour."[22]

For the development of rich human beings, the worker must be able to call "his own muscles into play under the control of his own brain." Expanding the capabilities of people requires both mental and manual activity. Not only does the combination of education with productive labor make it possible to increase the efficiency of production; this is also, as Marx pointed out in *Capital*, "the only method of producing fully developed human beings."[23] Here, then, is the way to ensure that "the productive forces have also increased with the all-around development of the individual, and all the springs of co-operative wealth flow more abundantly."[24]

The activity through which people develop their capacities, however, is not limited to the sphere of production as narrowly defined within capitalism. Every activity with the goal of providing inputs into the development of human beings needs to be understood as an aspect of production. And the goals that guide production must be democratically established so that people can transform both their circumstances and themselves and thereby produce themselves as subjects in the new society.[25] The implication is obvious. *Every* aspect of production must be a site for the collective decision-making and variety of activity that develops human capacities and builds solidarity among the particular associated producers.

When workers act in workplaces and communities in conscious cooperation with others, they produce themselves as people conscious of their interdependence and of their own collective power. The joint product of their activity is the development of the capacities of the producers, which is precisely Marx's point when he says that "when the worker cooperates in a planned way with others, he strips off the fetters of his individuality, and develops the capabilities of his species."[26] Creating the conditions in workplaces and communities by which people can develop their capacities is an essential aspect of the concept of socialism for the twenty-first century. But it is only one element. How can the worker's own need for development be realized if capital owns our social heritage, the products of the social brain and the social hand? And how can we develop our own potential if we look upon other producers as enemies or as our markets, if individual material self-interest is our motivation?

Capitalism is an organic system, one that has the tendency to reproduce the conditions of its existence (including a working class which looks upon its requirements as "self-evident natural laws"). That is its strength. To counter that and to satisfy "the worker's own need for development," the socialist alternative also must be an organic system, a particular combination of production, distribution and consumption, a system of reproduction. What Chávez named in January 2007 as "the elementary triangle of socialism" (social property, social production, and satisfaction of social needs) is a step forward toward a conception of such a system.[27]

Consider the logic of this socialist combination, this conception of socialism for the twenty-first century:

1. *Social ownership of the means of production* is critical within this structure because it is the only way to ensure that our communal, social productivity is directed to the free development of all rather than used to satisfy the private goals of capitalists, groups of producers, or state bureaucrats. This concerns more than our current activity. Social ownership of our social heritage, the results of past social labor, is an assertion that all living human beings have the right to the full development of their potential—to real wealth, the development of human capacity. It is the recognition that "the free development of each is the condition for the free development of all."

2. *Social production organized by workers* builds new relations of cooperation and solidarity among producers. It allows workers to end "the crippling of body and mind" and the loss of "every atom of freedom, both in bodily and in intellectual activity" that comes from the separation of head and hand. Organization

of production in all spheres by workers is a condition for the full development of the producers, for the development of their capabilities, a condition for the production of rich human beings.

3. *Satisfaction of communal needs and purposes* as the goal of productive activity means that, instead of interacting as separate and indifferent individuals, we function as members of a community. Rather than looking upon our own capacity as our property and as a means of securing as much as possible in an exchange, we start from the recognition of our common humanity and thus of the importance of conditions in which everyone is able to develop their full potential. When our productive activity is oriented to the needs of others, it both builds solidarity among people and produces socialist human beings.

These three sides of the "socialist triangle" mutually interact to form a structure in which "all the elements coexist simultaneously and support one another," as Marx put it. "This is the case with every organic whole."[28] Yet the very interdependence of the three sides suggests that realization of each element depends upon the existence of the other two. Without production for social needs, no real social property; without social property, no worker decision making oriented toward society's needs; without worker decision making, no transformation of people and their needs.

The State's Place within Socialism as an Organic System

Is there a place for the state in socialism as an organic system? In the absence of a mechanism by which this particular combination of production, distribution, and consumption can be realized, it remains only a vision. Implicit in the concept of socialism as an organic system is a set of institutions and practices through which all members of society can share the fruits of social labor and are able to satisfy their "own need for development." To produce and reproduce "rich human beings" in a society based upon solidarity requires a conscious attempt to ensure that the necessary conditions for full human development infuse all levels of society.

Consider one possible scenario for a process of participatory diagnosis and planning.[29] At the level of an individual neighborhood, it is possible for neighbors to discuss directly the kind of community they want to live in and what they see as necessary for the development of their capacities and that of those around them.[30] While this process identifies needs, the discussion also allows this community to explore its own ability to satisfy those needs itself. In other words, it identifies the capabilities of the community. At the level of the community, there is a direct attempt to coordinate the system of needs and the system of labors.

In addition to being able to identify its needs and the extent to which those can be satisfied locally through the labor of community members, this process, which occurs under the guidance of elected neighborhood councils, has a second product. By sharing and attempting to reconcile views of the most urgent needs of members of this community, there is a learning process, one in which protagonism builds and reinforces solidarity. That is, the process of participatory diagnosis produces particular people, a particular joint product as well as the diagnosis itself.

In practice, the probability of a precise match between capabilities and needs within this community is negligible. The community is likely to have needs it cannot satisfy locally and capacities it does not need. In this situation, autarky supports neither the ability of people to secure the use-values they identify as important for their development nor the satisfaction in meaningful activity that can come from meeting the needs of others outside their immediate neighborhood. To satisfy "the worker's own need for development," the community needs to go beyond this barrier in order to coordinate with other communities in a larger body.

The commune represents a further step, bringing together the information transmitted by local neighborhood councils about the needs and capabilities of their communities as well as drawing upon the knowledge of workers within units of production in this geographical area.[31] Do workers have the capacity to satisfy the needs identified by the communities? By exploring this question in their workers' councils, workers engage in conscious consideration of production options within their workplaces and focus upon the logic of producing for communal needs. However, to answer this question adequately requires more than responses from individual production units. By combining their knowledge and capabilities, workers in particular workplaces can achieve results that are greater than the sum of their individual parts taken separately. But, here again, more than a process of producing for communal needs and purposes occurs. Cooperation within and between units of production generates solidarity among the combined workers and reinforces their understanding of the goals of production.

Throughout this process, community members and workers can interact through communal meetings and a communal parliament. The result of the process is that the commune councils have at their disposal data on (a) needs that can be satisfied from within the commune; and (b) the needs that cannot be satisfied locally. Further, there is information on (c) the potential output of workplaces that can be provisionally utilized within the commune; and (d) the potential output of workplaces that is unutilized. Thus there is both an indication of the level of needs that provisionally can be satisfied locally as well as identification of the excess demand and excess supply within each commune.

To stop here would reproduce the problem of remaining at the level of the individual neighborhood. To create the conditions for the free development of all, it is necessary to go beyond geographical barriers. The process is therefore extended to larger areas: the data from communes is transmitted upward to cities (communal cities), to the states or provinces and ultimately to the national level—to bodies composed of delegates from the communes, cities, and the states, respectively. At the national level, it is now possible to identify (a) provisionally satisfied needs, (b) unsatisfied needs, (c) provisionally assigned output, and (d) provisionally unassigned output.

It is fair to assume that there will not be a balance between needs and capacities at the first iteration. Therefore, the process of reconciling the system of needs and the system of labors is an essential requirement of the set of institutions and practices characteristic of socialism as an organic system. If there are excess needs, there are two logical resorts: (1) find a way to increase output (a question for workers' councils to explore); and (2) recognize the necessity to reduce satisfaction of some needs. [32] A critical discussion must then occur to answer the question—What needs are to be unsatisfied?

Exploration of this question requires an examination of the relative requirements of different areas and the different types of needs to be given priority. It is only at this level that identification of national and regional inequality occurs, as well as a discussion of priorities and choices for the society as a whole. This dialogue needs to take place not only at the national level but at every level down to the neighborhood. It is absolutely essential, because, through such a process of participatory planning, people learn about the needs and capacities of others elsewhere in the society. There is no other way to build solidarity than to put faces upon other members of society. As is the case with all social activity, throughout this process there are two products: development of the plan and the development of the people who participate in its construction.

The result of this scenario is a process of production for communal needs and communal purposes in which protagonism within the workplace and community ensures that this is social production organized by the producers. Further, social ownership completes the socialist triangle in that the means of production here are not the property of capital, any individual, any group of producers, or any particular community; rather, they are our common social heritage, there "to satisfy the worker's own need for development." In each workplace, workers are conscious that their productive activity is for society. In short, begin with communality, and the product of our activity is "a communal, general product from the outset."[33]

Could the concept of socialism as an organic system be made real *in the absence* of institutions and practices such as these? The answer must be no. This combination and articulation of councils and delegates at different levels of society is necessary to ensure the reproduction of a society in which the "free development of each is the condition for the free development of all." We are describing a *state*—a particular type of state, a state from below, a state of the commune type. This state does not wither away. Rather, it is an integral part of socialism as an organic system.

Some people may not wish to call this set of institutions a state because these are society's "own living forces," not "an organ standing above society" but "one completely subordinate to it."[34] How would designation of this as a state be compatible with the view that, by definition, as Holloway puts it, "The state is the assassin of hope"?[35] Like those who conceive of labor as inherently a burden and can think of nothing better than to reduce it to zero, those who reject these institutions as a state demonstrate that they are trapped in the categories of old societies.

Old habits die slowly. And taxonomy should not trump content. So, if some people prefer to call these articulated councils a non-state or the "Unstate," this should not present a problem as long as they agree that socialism as an organic system requires these institutions and practices in order to be real.

Subordinating the Old Society

However, an organic system does not drop from the sky: In socialism as an organic system, "every economic relation presupposes every other in its [socialist] economic form, and everything posited is thus also a presupposition; this is the case with every organic system."[36] Yet a new system *never* produces its own premises at the outset. Rather, when a new system emerges, it necessarily inherits premises from the old. Its premises and presuppositions are "historic" premises that are produced outside the system; that system does not develop initially upon its own foundations.

Every new system as it emerges is inevitably defective: it is "in every respect, economically, morally and intellectually, still stamped with the birthmarks of the old society."[37] The development of an organic system is a process of *becoming*. "Its development to its totality," Marx indicated, "consists precisely in subordinating all elements of society to itself, or in creating out of it the organs which it still lacks. This is historically how it becomes a totality."[38]

In the 1920s, the Soviet economist Evgeny Preobrazhensky made this very point about how a new system develops. "Not a single economic formation," he argued, "can develop in a pure form, on the basis merely of the immanent laws which are inherent to the particular formation. This would be in contradiction to the very idea of development. The development of any economic form means its ousting of other economic forms, the subordination of these forms to the new form, and their gradual elimination."[39] *So, what is to be subordinated?* If socialism is to develop into an organic system, social ownership of the means of production must supplant private ownership; worker management must replace despotism in the workplace; and productive activity based upon solidarity and community must subordinate individual self-interest. What is more, the old state must be transcended, replaced by the new organs that foster the simultaneous changing of circumstances and self-change.

These things cannot happen overnight. However, that doesn't mean that they take place in distinct *stages*. The idea of putting off some questions until a later stage is prepared is alien to the concept of an organic system. The continued presence of elements of capitalism does not simply mean that socialism is as yet incomplete because a few parts are missing. After all, what kinds of people are produced within the old relations? In fact, every moment that people act within old relations is a process of reproducing old ideas and attitudes. Working within a hierarchy, functioning without the ability to make decisions in the workplace and society, and focusing upon self-interest rather than upon solidarity are activities that produce people on a daily basis; this is the reproduction of the conservatism of everyday life—indeed, the reproduction of elements of capitalism.

The concept of socialism for the twenty-first century as an organic system theoretically posits what the experience of the twentieth century has demonstrated, which is the need to build all sides of the socialist triangle: *one war, three fronts*. In the absence of a struggle to subordinate all the elements of the old society, the new society is inevitably *infected* by the old society. The matter is even worse if we choose homeopathic medicine to cure the infection. In short, rather than *build* upon defects (such as the orientation toward material self-interest that Marx warned about in his *Critique of the Gotha Program*), the point is to *subordinate* them.[40]

Contested Reproduction

However, in the same way that capitalism required the development of a specifically capitalist mode of production to be an organic system, socialism does not subordinate all elements of society to itself until it develops a specifically socialist mode of production. Consider capitalism before it developed to the point where it produced its own premises in their capitalist form, when it was still becoming. That process of becoming necessarily involved the subordination, the contracted reproduction, of the *existing* relations—relations Marx described as ones in which the producer "as owner of his own conditions of labour, employs that labour to enrich himself instead of the capitalist." It took the separation of producers from those means of production and the compulsion to sell their labor-power to mark the beginning of capitalist relations. Wherever possible, however, workers attempted to *extract* themselves and to become independent producers rather than to sell their "birth-right for a mess of pottage." This possibility was always present when wages increased with the accumulation of capital in the absence of the specifically capitalist mode of production. "Two diametrically opposed economic systems" coexisted both in the

Old World and in the colonies, where the problem of non-reproduction of wage-laborers was most marked.[41]

Thus the struggle over the subordination of the elements of production did not end with the original (or primitive) development of capitalist relations of production. Reproduction of those new relations was not secure until the development of the specifically capitalist mode of production. "As soon as capitalist production stands on its own feet," Marx wrote, "it not only maintains this separation [between workers and the means of production] but reproduces it on a constantly extending scale."[42] Until capital developed upon its own foundations, however, differing relations and differing logics existed simultaneously.

So what happens when differing relations coexist? Rather than peaceful coexistence, there is *contested reproduction,* with each system attempting to expand at the expense of the other. Considering the Soviet Union in the 1920s, Preobrazhensky argued that the state economy was in "an uninterrupted economic war with the tendencies of capitalist development, with the tendencies of capitalist restoration."[43] This, he proposed, was a "struggle between two mutually hostile systems," a war between two regulating principles—one the result of the spontaneous effects of commodity-capitalist relations (the law of value), and the other based upon the conscious decisions of the regulatory organs of the state, which he called "the law of primitive socialist accumulation." Preobrazhensky argued that each of these regulating principles was "fighting for the type of regulation which is organically characteristic of the particular system of production-relations, taken in its pure form." However, the result of their interaction was that the Soviet economy was regulated by *neither* in its pure form. There was not a simple combination or addition of the productive relations and their associated regulating principles; rather, they *interpenetrated*—coexisting, limiting, and (significantly) deforming each other.[44]

Preobrazhensky's insight was that in the process of becoming a new system, two systems and two logics do not simply exist side-by-side. They *interact*. They interpenetrate. And they *deform* each other. Rather than the combination permitting the best of both worlds, the effect can be the *worst* of both worlds. Precisely because there is contested reproduction between different sets of productive relations, the interaction of the systems can generate crises, inefficiencies, and irrationality that would not be found in either system in its purity. Accordingly, Preobrazhensky argued that rather than search for balance between the two, it was essential that what he called primitive socialist accumulation *subordinate and replace* the law of value.

Contested reproduction implies the possibility that the new relations cannot be sustained. Consider how capitalist relations of production were reproduced in the absence of the specifically capitalist mode of production. The interaction between what Marx had called "two diametrically opposed economic systems" was definitely producing problems that would not occur outside that combination. This was exactly what was occurring when the labor-intensive accumulation of capital produced a tendency for the non-reproduction of wage-labor as the result of rising wages. How did capital ensure the reproduction of capitalist relations of production under these conditions? Marx detailed the measures undertaken with the emergence of capitalism—"the bloody discipline," the "police methods," "the state compulsion to confine the struggle between capital and labour within limits convenient for capital." In direct contrast to the conditions for the reproduction of capitalist relations once the specifically capitalist mode of production has been developed, he argued that "the rising bourgeoisie needs the power of the state, and uses it to 'regulate' wages."[45]

Until capital produced its own premises with the development of the specifically capitalist mode of production, it needed what I have called a "capitalist mode of regulation," one that could ensure the compatibility of the behavior of workers with the requirements of capital.[46] In the absence of what Marx called "the sheer force of economic relations," that specific mode of regulation relied upon the coercive power of the state to prevent wages from rising and to compel workers, through "grotesquely terroristic laws," "into accepting the discipline necessary for the system of wage-labour."[47]

The Necessity of a Socialist Mode of Regulation

Can the associated producers, in their turn, use such a state to support socialist productive relations before the development of socialism as an organic system? Consider the situation described in the *Communist Manifesto* in which the "battle of democracy" has been won—through a revolutionary rupture or a longer process— with the result that a government representing workers exists. At every step in the process of the becoming of socialism, the elements of capitalism and socialism, "two diametrically opposed economic systems," will interact and produce systemic incoherence and crisis. For example, when capitalist elements dominate, attempts to subordinate or make "despotic inroads" upon them will tend to generate a capital strike and an economic crisis. If a government is prepared to break with the logic of capital, it will understand (as the *Manifesto* indicates) that it is "compelled to go always further" and to make "further inroads upon the old social order" and thus to "wrest, by degrees, all capital from the bourgeoisie, to centralise all instruments of production in the hands of the State."[48] In contrast, the sorry history of social democracy has been that, sooner or later, it yields to the logic of capital and reinforces its rule.

A socialist mode of regulation must achieve consciously what a specifically socialist mode of production will tend to do spontaneously—ensure the reproduction of socialist relations of production. The building and reproduction of those relations (represented by the sides of the socialist triangle) "consists precisely in subordinating all elements of society to itself, or in creating out of it the organs which it still lacks." Thus the socialist mode of regulation must subordinate consciously every element that supports the old society, both the institutions and the common sense that supports those old relations. Further, it must create new socialist elements that can become the premises and foundation for the new society.

The socialist mode of regulation, accordingly, must embrace the Battle of Ideas, the ideological struggle oriented toward human development. It must stress how the logic of capital is contrary to the development of our potential, and it must use every example of capital's response to measures supportive of human development as yet another demonstration of the perversion of capitalism. Further, the acceptance of the logic of capital as "self-evident natural laws" must be challenged by development of a coherent alternative that stresses the importance of democratic, participatory, and protagonistic practice in workplaces and communities and emphasizes a new social rationality based upon cooperation and solidarity.

But an ideological struggle cannot succeed by itself. Without the creation of institutions like workers' councils and neighborhood councils, which provide the necessary space for human development through practice, the Battle of Ideas lacks a real basis for the development ("both individual and collective") of new socialist subjects. Indeed, this mode of regulation requires a state that supports this struggle ideologically, economically, and militarily, thus serving as the midwife for the birth of the new society.

The State within the Socialist Mode of Regulation

What, though, do we mean by *the state*? Do we mean the *old* state or the emerging new state based upon workers' councils and neighborhood councils as its cells? How could the old infected state whose very institutions involve a "systematic and hierarchic division of labour," a state that has the character of a public force organized for social enslavement, of an engine of class despotism, possibly be part of the socialist mode of regulation?[49]

Marx and Engels grasped that the working class "cannot simply lay hold of the ready-made state machinery, and use it for its own purpose."[50] *At last*, Marx proclaimed, following what he saw as the spontaneous discovery by workers in the Paris Commune of an alternative form of state—a new democratic and decentralized state where the legitimate functions of the state were to be "wrested from an authority usurping pre-eminence over society itself, and restored to the responsible agents of society." At last, the necessary form of the workers' state has been discovered: the Commune, which combined legislative and executive functions, was "the political form at last discovered under which to work out the economical emancipation of Labour." Here was the state that would "serve as a lever for uprooting the economical foundations upon which rests the existence of classes, and therefore of class-rule."[51]

The commune form represented the destruction of centralized state power insofar as that state stands above society. Marx called it "the reabsorption of the state power by society as its own living forces instead of as forces controlling and subduing it, by the popular masses themselves, forming their own force instead of the organised force of their suppression—the political form of their social emancipation." With the conversion of the state "from an organ superimposed upon society into one completely subordinate to it," self-governing producers thus wield the state for their own purposes, continuously changing both circumstances and themselves.[52]

This new type of state, based upon direct protagonistic democracy in workplace and community, is indeed essential for the development of socialism as an organic system. Not only does it permit the unleashing of tacit knowledge and popular energy to link the capacities of people to communal needs and purposes but it has as its joint product new social subjects with new capacities, pride, and dignity. With the transparency that is necessary for any control from below, councils in workplaces and communities can police waste, sabotage, and other attempts to reverse the process effectively; and, this too, reinforces the sense that the process belongs to the people and is not alien to and above them.

Yet this new state does not drop from the sky. For one, given the effects of the "education, tradition and habit" of those formed within the old society, we should not be surprised at the power of the old ideas to undermine efforts to build the new state from below. Although people transform themselves through their practice in workers' and communal councils, they do so in small units and the spontaneous focus of these cells of the new state inevitably will be one of localism and self-interest (both individual and collective). The development of solidarity and a concept of community that goes beyond the local to other communities and workplaces (and beyond the self-interest that is manifested as consumerism) will tend to emerge only through practice.

These cells need to be connected if they are to emerge as the new state. They need to develop horizontal and vertical links with other workplaces and communities, as well as with bodies that consolidate these. But the creation of such links through the delegation of spokespersons on their behalf is not the same as the development of solidarity that transcends local self-interest. It takes *time* before the concept of the whole develops organically in these units and is internalized. Although the course of development of socialism as an organic system requires the creation of links based upon solidarity from below and the acceptance of collective democracy that transcends the particular, this process cannot be instantaneous. The new state is not capable initially of making essential decisions that require concentration and coordination of forces.

In contrast, the old state is more likely to be able to see the overall picture at the outset. With the presence of revolutionary actors in the government of the old state, it is possible to confront not only individual capitals but the power of capital as a whole. This is essential because the process of subordinating capital requires the working class to take the power of the existing state away from capital (and thereby to remove its access to the military forces of the state). This is the strength of the old state; it is well situated to identify critical bottlenecks and places for initiatives that require a concentration of forces, including actions to defend the process militarily against internal and external enemies determined to reverse every inroad. Can we imagine building a new society *without* taking the existing power away from those who possess it in the old society? In contrast to modern fantasists, Marx understood that "the transfer of the organised forces of society, viz., the state power, from capitalists and landlords to the producers themselves" is necessary. He understood that you cannot change the world without taking power.[53]

However, as might be expected from this "engine of despotism," with its "systematic and hierarchic division of labour" and "ready-made state machinery," the old state has the tendency to act from above to change circumstances for people rather than to foster revolutionary practice. It remains above society and divides society into two parts, one part of which is superior to society and which would bestow socialism as a gift to an underlying population. How could the old hierarchical state, even if made more democratic, foster the key link of human development and practice? Inherent in the logic of representative democracy is the separation of governing from the governed. Rather than the necessary involvement of people that "ensures their complete development, both individual and collective," the spontaneous tendency of such a state is to reproduce "the delusion as if administration and political governing were mysteries, transcendent functions only to be trusted to the hands of a trained caste." The faces may change in the legislative branch, but the face of the old state to those below is that of the functionary, "an authority usurping pre-eminence over society itself." That is precisely why the Commune's combination of legislative and executive bodies is so central to the development of a state that is society's "own living forces instead of . . . forces controlling and subduing it."[54]

During the interregnum when the old state cannot yet die and the new state is not yet able to stand upon its own feet, a great many morbid symptoms appear. Both states are necessary at the outset for the subordination of the old society and the nurturing of the new. However, the inherent tension between the top-down orientation from within the old state and the bottom-up emphasis of the worker and community councils is obvious. In their interaction over a period of indeterminate length, each state will tend to deform the other.

Thus the desire on the part of revolutionaries in the old state to enact national policies according to a predetermined time-table, for example, tends toward the creation of uniform rules that ignore differences in the history and practices of the cells of the emerging state from below. In both those cases where organic development is lagging and where it is more advanced, the effect of demands placed by the old state upon the new shoots will tend to deform their development, as the impatience of functionaries of the old state will either turn the cells of the new into instruments of the old state or impose a uniformity that tends to reverse unique advances and thereby to discourage initiative and enthusiasm.

Nor, viewed from the other angle, can the old state easily achieve goals of coherent planning, balance, and equality when workers' and communal councils assert their right to self-determination. As long as these local units insist upon their unique character and the right to pursue their own collective self-interest without inter-ference, the tendency will be to foster relations of exchange (the *quid pro quo*), inequality, and a lack of solidarity. Here, again, the combination of the two states produces incoherence rather than the best of both worlds.

In the context of growing tension and crises produced by the interaction of two diametrically opposed systems, there will be those in the old state who see the solution as the enforcement of power from above. Similarly, there will be those in the new cells who will see the solution as the removal of any authority above the individual unit in order to permit the unfettered pursuit of their particular collective interest. Both those tendencies must be struggled against because each leads to a different deformation of the socialist triangle of social production organized by workers, using socially owned means of production for the purpose of sat-isfying social needs.

The socialist mode of regulation requires a combination of revolutionary actors within both the old state and the new.

Within the old state, it is essential that the policies pursued focus upon both the changing of circumstances and the changing of human beings. This calls for the rejection of capitalist measures of accounting and efficiency and their replacement by a concept of socialist accounting explicitly recognizing the joint product that emerges from the key link of human development and practice.[55] Within the cells of the new socialist state, on the other hand, the struggle must be against the defects associated with the self-orientation inherited from the old society. In both workplaces and communities, it is essential to find ways to build solidarity with other communities and society as a whole and to develop the understanding that the free development of each has as its condition the free development of all.

The socialist mode of regulation involves a combination of the nurturing of the new state and the withering away of the old. In this process, there is a natural alliance within both the old and the new, not with the goal of achieving a balance between the two states, but unified in the commitment toward building a new socialism oriented explicitly toward human development and defined by the socialist triangle.

The State and the Struggle for Socialism

The combination of old and new states is not only essential for ensuring the reproduction of socialist relations, however. A struggle against one-sidedness must be at the core of a strategy to end capitalism and to build socialism. Some people focus only upon the new state—or, if you will, the "Unstate"—and reject the idea of using the old state. "The very notion that society can be changed through the winning of state power," John Holloway argues, is the source of all our sense of betrayal. We need to understand, he announces, that "to struggle through the state is to become involved in the active process of defeating yourself." Why? Because "once the logic of power is adopted, the struggle against power is already lost." And why even try? After all, the existing state cannot "be made to function in the interests of the working class" because as a capitalist state "its own continued existence is tied to the reproduction of capitalist social relations as a whole." The state is "just one node in a web of social relations" and, indeed, is "not the locus of power that it appears to be."[56]

From this perspective, the need to use the state, the *armed* "node," to rip apart that web of social relations is just so old-fashioned, so nineteenth and twentieth century. Forget the military, police, judicial, and legislative apparatus now at the disposal of capital. The alternative to capital's power is already there: "Ubiquitous power implies ubiquitous resistance. Ubiquitous yes implies ubiquitous no."[57] With the Hegelian magic by which things can be miraculously transformed into their opposites (as long as we don't watch too closely), we come to understand that electoral abstention is victory, lack of leadership is leadership, and the "Many" (the multiplicity of negative struggles against capitalism) is by definition "One." Negating the existing state through the mind means that it continues in the hands of capital in reality.

The other form of one-sidedness focuses exclusively upon the capture of the old state. Whether choosing the electoral road or invoking glorious victories of the past to support a direct assault upon state power, from this perspective the process of building the institutions and practices characteristic of the new state must be subordinated to the principal task. Social movements essential for the organic development of a new socialist consciousness based upon practice are viewed instrumentally, as fodder for election committees or as the source of cadres for the party. Subordinate, subordinate—that is, Holy Moses and the prophets! Thus, whether due to the imperatives of electoral rhythm or to the perceived need to rehearse military discipline, the tendency of parties fixated upon the old state is to draw the lifeblood from the incipient elements of the new state and to suppress within their own ranks those who would argue otherwise.

According to Marta Harnecker, this lack of respect for the autonomous development of popular movements was characteristic of elements of the political left in Latin America and brought with it a "verticalism, which cancels out people's initiative" and a "traditional narrow conception of politics" that "tends to reduce politics to the struggle that has to do with political-legal institutions and to exaggerate the role of the state."[58] And the tendency for "hierarchization" is the kernel of truth, too, in Holloway's argument that the party, "whether vanguardist or parliamentary," subordinates "the myriad forms of class struggle to the overriding aim of gaining control of the state."[59]

However, rather than inherent in a party as such, this "hegemonist" characteristic is precisely the result of a one-sidedness focused upon the old state. A different left is possible. As Harnecker argues, to build the left essential for socialism in the twenty-first century, we have to change the traditional vision of politics and overcome the narrow definition of power. The new political instrument must grasp the importance of practice for developing consciousness and capacities, and it needs to learn to listen to popular movements and to respect and nourish them. But it also has a special role. It should not "try to gather to its bosom all the legitimate representatives of struggles for emancipation but should strive to coordinate their practices into a single political project," that is, to create the spaces where they can learn from each other.[60]

There is an organic link between state and party, and a party that recognizes the necessity for the articulation of an old and a new state in the process of building socialism differs substantially from one that focuses solely upon the capture of the old state.[61] It is necessarily "a political organisation which, as it advances a national programme which enables broad sectors of society to rally round the same battle standard, also helps these sectors to transform themselves into the active subjects building the new society for which the battle is being waged."[62] The party that is needed is one that learns to walk on two legs.

Two sides, two struggles: a party determined to defeat capital and to build the new state from below must always be conscious of the danger of one-sidedness. If crises within capitalism propel a political organization into government, it must not only use that opportunity to defeat the logic of capital and to reduce capital's power over the old state but also to use the power it has to foster the accelerated development of the sprouts of the new state. If conditions do not permit a party to grasp the reins of power in the old state, then it must work to *create* those conditions by encouraging the autonomous development of social movements through which people can develop their powers and capacities and by building unity among them based upon *recognition* of difference.

Just as a socialist mode of regulation requires the articulation of the old and the new state in the process of building socialism as an organic system, so must we walk on two legs in order to defeat capital and to build collective power. At no time is it more possible to demonstrate clearly the gap between the logic of capital and the logic of human development than in the intensified class war when capital is in crisis and the nature of capital comes to the surface. It provides the opportunity to shatter the idea that accepting the demands of capital is common sense. But to show there is an alternative, we need the vision of a society in which the free development of each is understood as the condition for the free development of all. And we need to reinforce that vision with more than rhetoric. Unless we are creating through our struggles the spaces that prefigure the new society, we face more glorious defeats.

When capital is in crisis, there are always two options—to give in or to move in. If masses are armed with a clear conception of the socialist alternative, they can turn a crisis *in* capitalism into the crisis *of* capitalism. It is possible that, as the result of our ideological disarmament, the current struggles against the capitalist offensive ultimately may lead to a glorious defeat. It is possible, but we must take that chance.

11. End the System

This chapter, written especially for this volume, reflects my growing understanding of the natural disaster that capitalism is producing and that we must waste no time in accelerating the socialist imperative.

In 1989, Herman Daly and John Cobb Jr. wrote that "at a deep level of our being we find it hard to suppress the cry of anguish, the scream of horror—the wild words required to express wild realities. We human beings are being led to a *dead* end—all too literally. We are living by an ideology of death and accordingly we are destroying our own humanity and killing the planet.... Before this generation are set two ways, the way of life and the way of death. May humanity choose life!"[1]

A quarter of a century later, it is apparent that the generation in question did not choose the way of life. Consider the current situation. Among the natural phenomena identified by Fred Magdoff and John Bellamy Foster in 2010 are the following: global warming, glacier melting, rising ocean levels, devastating droughts, water shortages, extinction of species, acidification of oceans, pollution of air and water, pesticides in water and food, ozone depletion, decline in biodiversity, soil erosion, deforestation, and exhaustion of finite non-renewable resources.[2] More recently, considering only the climate change patterns, the Intergovernmental Panel on Climate Change (IPCC) in November 2014 acknowledged that "recent anthropogenic emissions of greenhouse gases are the highest in history," that "atmospheric concentrations of carbon dioxide, methane and nitrous oxide . . . are unprecedented in at least the last 800,000 years," and that these and other human-generated effects are "extremely likely to have been the dominant cause of the observed global warming since the mid-twentieth century."

And the IPCC's prognosis? Even with an immediate end to all anthropogenic emissions of greenhouse gases, the projection for centuries is that of further warming, for increased "likelihood of severe, pervasive and irreversible impacts for people and ecosystems," that "heat waves will occur more often and last longer," and for rising "risks of abrupt or irreversible" climate change.[3] Add to that all the non-climate-specific changes noted above, and it is apparent that we are indeed "being led to a *dead* end," that we are on a path to death.

Capital as Finite

To understand in general the underlying situation, we begin with a simple premise: the idea of a constrained economy. Specifically, we begin with a view of economic processes as a subsystem within a finite earth system, that is essentially a closed system. This conception seems like common sense: we know that economic activity has grown and grows, and we know that the biosphere, the natural world, though not unchanging, is fixed. Yet, as Daly and Cobb point out, this very conception, which allows us to pose questions about the relationship between the subsystem and the total system, represents a paradigm shift when it comes to thinking about economic activity.

Economists, they note, have managed to avoid the question of "how big the subsystem should be relative to the total system" in two ways: "first by viewing the economic subsystem as infinitesimally small relative to the total system" and "second, by viewing the economy as coextensive with the total system." In the latter case, the question of appropriate scale of the economy cannot arise—by definition—and in the former case, the question is irrelevant.[4] In both cases, the conjuring trick is by assumption—now you see it, now you don't.

Once we *do* see it, that is, once we do recognize the economy as a subsystem of a larger but finite total earth system, then several propositions follow. First, there are limits to the ability of an earth system to support the continued growth of the economy, and these will be reached sooner or later. "Continuous growth in the scale of the aggregate economy could only make sense in the context of an unlimited environment." Second, the closer the approach to those limits, the more that problems associated with that growth appear: "The economy (subsystem) becomes larger relative to the ecosystem and stresses the parent system to an ever greater degree."[5] In this respect, the greater the signs of "generalized stress," the higher the probability that the economy is approaching its limits.

But there is more to consider. Once we explicitly reject the paradigm that economic activity occurs within infinite space, then the question of distribution comes to the fore. If there is a limit to the extent of the commons, upon what basis is access to the commons to be determined? As discussed in this book's opening chapter on the capitalist nightmare and the socialist dream, inequality is the elephant in the room. Given finite space, we cannot ignore the implications of vast differences in access to the means of production, both those supplied by nature and those that are the result of previous activity of the social hand and the social brain.

However, though it is useful to talk about a relation in general between an economic subsystem and the ecological system, economic activity always takes place within and through a *particular* society, which is to say, within particular social relations. The character and dynamics of a particular economy are determined by its specific relations of production. We need to be concrete: it is not inherent that an economic system will be oriented to continuous growth with respect to its demands upon the ecological system. Where collective decisions are made in full knowledge of the limits of the commons, there is no necessary approach to the limits of the ecological system. But, clearly that is not the case within capitalist relations of production.

As discussed in chapter 1, capital's overwhelming drive is growth, growth as if there were no limits. Inherent in capital's logic, Marx stressed, is "ceaseless striving" to go beyond its quantitative barrier: "The goal-determining activity of capital can only be that of growing wealthier, that is, of magnification, of increasing itself."[6] And, though capital may come up against obstacles to that magnification (including attempts to mitigate its harmful effects), it constantly searches for ways to drive beyond all such barriers. How, then, is it ever possible to talk about regulating capital? Whether it is measures that, for example, try to limit carbon emissions or specific prohibitions of abuses with respect to environmental or financial or matters relating to wages and working conditions, capital finds a way around them because that is the nature of capital. It finds other ways to achieve its goal. For capital, "every limit appears as a barrier to be overcome."[7]

Yet, there is definitely one limit that capital cannot overcome. Because of the limits given by the biosphere, capital is finite. Sooner or later, it will come to an end. But how and when? The central question is whether human beings will come to a "dead end" at the same time as capital. As conscious as Marx was of capital's tendency to destroy "the whole gamut of permanent conditions of life required by the chain of human generations," he did not anticipate the possibility that capital would succeed.[8]

Capital's Potential Gravediggers

Given the growing evidence of the destruction of our natural environment and of a race to the limits of the biosphere, the nature of capital has become increasingly apparent. Capital's treatment of human beings and nature as mere means for its growth (indeed, as *expendable* means) has come to the surface. The ecological crisis, however, is neither the first nor the only demonstration of the need to put an end to capital. And yet, it still moves; it still continues to destroy.

Marx stressed, for example, that capital constantly generates crises because of its tendency for overaccumulation of capital.[9] From time to time, capital demonstrates openly that it contains its own barrier, "a barrier which comes to the surface and, in particular, in *overproduction*—the basic phenomenon in crises."[10] The result is a cutback of commodity production and the casting off of workers as so much excess baggage. At such times, it is obvious that the level of capitalist production is determined by the rate of profit "instead of the proportion between production and social needs, the needs of socially developed human beings." Is this not a clear demonstration that production under capitalist relations "comes to a standstill not at the point where needs are satisfied, but rather where the production and realization of profit impose this"?[11] The necessity to end the capitalist system and to replace it with that inverse situation oriented to the worker's own need for development is undeniable.

Why, then, is capitalism still around and, indeed, dominant? One explanation stresses that capital is strong. Contrary to those who explicitly or implicitly view capital as fragile and weak, this explanation begins from the recognition that capital is able to create the conditions for its own reproduction.[12] As explained in chapter 1, capital produces its necessary premises as results; it tends to produce, in particular, the working class it needs. Precisely because workers have surrendered their creative power to capital in a free exchange, that power (and all that flows from it) necessarily appears as the power of capital. Although workers may struggle over wages and working conditions and even may at moments elect governments to represent their interests, sooner or later they act to ensure the conditions for the expanded reproduction of capital. This is capital's strength; it produces workers who view capital's

requirements as "self-evident natural laws" and see no alternative
to its rule. The result is that the capitalist can rely upon the worker's "dependence on capital, which springs from the conditions of
production themselves, and is guaranteed in perpetuity by them."[13]
This is why capital is able to go beyond all immediate barriers and
to develop qualitatively in the process.

A second explanation of capital's continued existence is the
mirror image of the first—that the working class is weak. But,
rather than this being the result of capital's strength, the stress here
is that the weakness and lack of capacity of the working class is the
source of capital's strength. When we reject the one-sided Marxism
that treats capital as the only subject, then our attention necessarily is drawn to the side of workers.[14] What determines their
strength? How can workers transform themselves and develop
their capacities? The answer for Marx was obvious: only through
their practice, only through that simultaneous changing of circumstances and human activity or self-change that Marx understood
as "*revolutionary practice*" can workers develop the strength to go
beyond capital.

"Every developed personality," the French Marxist psychologist
Lucien Sève proposed, "appears to us straight away as *an enormous
accumulation of the most varied acts through time*."[15] The capacity of people, as we understand from Marx's key link of human
development and practice, is a function of the nature and extent
of practice. But there is another side to this relation. What do we
mean by capacity? Simply, it is the ability to engage in many acts.
Sève defines capacities as "the ensemble of actual potentialities,
innate or acquired, to carry out any act whatever and whatever
its level."[16] The higher the extent of capacity, then, the greater the
potential flow of acts drawing upon that capacity. Capacity is a
stock, one that is expanded (or reduced) as a result of particular
acts, and which is itself the basis for a flow of acts.[17]

Marx understood well this dialectical relationship between
acts and capacities. He understood that the collective struggles of
workers were the source of their strength. Recall his comments on

wage struggles. In 1853, he stressed that such struggles prevent workers "from becoming apathetic, thoughtless, more or less well-fed instruments of production"; without them, workers would be "a heartbroken, a weak-minded, a worn-out, unresisting mass." And he returned to the same point in 1865, noting that workers who did not engage in wage struggles "would be degraded to one level mass of broken wretches past salvation."[18]

As we have seen throughout this book, when people engage in collective struggle, there are two products: change in the particular circumstances and change in the human subjects. By itself, the first may lead only to reforms, which capital can treat as mere barriers; the second develops the strength of the working class and produces the potential gravediggers of capital. Thus, in describing the struggle over the Ten Hours Bill, Engels pointed out in 1850 that through this process the working classes found a way "to organise themselves and to know their strength. The working man, who has passed through such an agitation, is no longer the same as he was before; and the whole working class, after passing through it, is a hundred times stronger, more enlightened, and better organised than it was at the outset." In the same year, Marx also stressed the link between the acts and capacities of workers, telling workers that a continuing process of struggle is necessary "not only to bring about a change in society but also to change yourselves, and prepare yourselves for the exercise of political power."[19]

The accumulated acts that develop workers, however, are not only struggles over wages, hours, and working conditions. Workers are many-sided and produce themselves through all their activities. As indicated in chapter 1, by acting in solidarity with the needs of others, people "construct themselves as certain kinds of people." The simultaneous changing of circumstances and self-change means that we construct ourselves in particular ways through particular activities. But our various struggles (such as struggles over housing, education, inequality, environmental destruction, racism, and patriarchy) do not only produce in us particular characteristics. They also build a potential capacity for

collective action and, in this way, can contribute to the development of a strong working class. This is the hope. Indeed, this is the
condition for putting an end to capital before it puts an end to us.
Yet there is nothing inevitable about the development of capital's
gravediggers.

Someone Is Standing in My Sunlight

When people struggle, it is often because they are losing what they
have previously considered to be an entitlement. Reduced wages,
living standards, employment options, housing possibilities, access
to clean water, air—all can trigger a sense that something is going
wrong. But feelings of unfairness and injustice do not automatically
produce struggle or, at least, sustained struggle. Because sometimes
people adjust. They grumble but ultimately accept, for example,
that their years of education do not entitle them to the secure job
they expected or that they will achieve living standards (especially
housing accommodation) comparable to those of their parents.

Marx certainly understood this phenomenon of adaptive expectations. The reduction of wages, he noted, can produce a tendency
to "degrade" the worker "to the level of the Irish, the level of wage-
labour where the most animal minimum of needs and subsistence
appears to him as the sole object and purpose of his exchange with
capital."[20] The historical or social element in the value of labor-
power (often the product of past historical struggles) is in this case
"extinguished." In short, people may lower their expectations and
adapt them to new conditions. No animal, Marx proposed, is as
able as man "to restrict his needs to the same unbelievable degree
and to reduce the conditions of his life to the absolute minimum."[21]

Yet often people do struggle against the reduction of existing
norms and resist becoming "a heart-broken, a weak-minded, a
worn-out, unresisting mass." Marx pointed out, for example, that
nineteenth-century workers responded to the driving down of
wages by organizing and demanding "a fair day's wage for a fair
day's work." As noted in chapter 9, a characteristic of the moral

economy of the working class (of which this is an example) is that it takes as its reference point the past (real or imagined) and focuses upon ending violations and restoring the norms of the past. In this case, as in many others, we conclude that someone is standing in our sunlight, and we say, "No!"

But who is that enemy standing in our sunlight? Those who identify that enemy do not drop from the clouds; they are not an Abstract Proletariat that discovers its assigned role and proceeds to cast off capital's chains. Rather, they are people with a history, people formed and who have formed themselves in a specific context. Thus we should never be surprised if the spontaneous response to the violation of our expected entitlements takes the form of racism, sexism, xenophobia, and other such rejections of the principle that the free development of each has as its condition the free development of all. Who is the enemy? Blacks, the Irish, Jews, Muslims, immigrants, Chinese workers, women outside the home, modern corporations, the godless. We should always keep in mind Marx's comment about the view of the Irish by English workers: such divisions are "the secret by which the capitalist class maintains its power. And that class is fully aware of it." [22]

There is no lack of potential scapegoats, and the identification of these may bring comfort to those who are aggrieved. The more heartless the world appears, the more the need for a heart. In the absence of a socialist heart for a heartless world, the default position for some is the attempt to turn back the clock—to seek solace, for example, in religious conservatism that enforces the oppression of women. As with workers who have sought to turn the state into their own agency, so too do those who wish to return the world to a real or imagined past seek state power in order to remove the enemies standing in their sunlight.

Although it has been an article of faith (one that Marx himself expressed in short articles and correspondence) that economic crisis brings with it new opportunities for revolution, we need to recognize that crises bring to a head existing contradictions and that their outcome depends upon the relative strength of the respective parties. To the extent that workers accept the logic of capital as common sense, capital is in a position to ensure that the burden of the crisis falls upon the working class. If this ideological domination is not sufficient, however, capital will not hesitate to resort to "the bloody discipline," the "police methods," and "state compulsion to confine the struggle between capital and labour within limits convenient for capital"—methods characteristic of its mode of regulation at the time of its origin. In short, it is not only "the rising bourgeoisie [that] needs the power of the state" and uses it as necessary.[23]

Be careful of what you wish for. Rather than opening the door to revolution, in the absence of a strong working class, crises may bring in their wake fascism and barbarism. The specter of barbarism is haunting the earth, and the economic and ecological crises of capitalism give it more and more substance. All other things equal, the more limits are approached, the more the struggle over resources, the more the prevalence of crises, the closer the realization of the ultimate capitalist nightmare.

What Is to Be Done?

End the capitalist system! For some time, this has been grasped theoretically and practically as the essential condition for ending the destruction of human beings and nature and for creating a society that produces rich human beings and enriched nature that permits "the existence and reproduction of the chain of human generations." The ecological crisis has imparted new urgency to the need to end capital by all means possible. Literally, this is a matter of life and death.

The classic formula for ending the rule of capital has been to begin by taking the state away from capital, by, that is, ending capital's ability to use the police, the judiciary, the army, legislative bodies, and its other oppressive mechanisms to enforce its rule. This was the position advanced by Marx and Engels in the *Communist Manifesto*: "The first step in the revolution by the working class is to raise the proletariat to the position of ruling class, to win the battle of democracy." Workers would then use their "political supremacy to wrest, by degrees, all capital from the bourgeoisie."[24] However, the twentieth century demonstrated that political supremacy of the working class is not achieved simply by winning elections or seizing the state. The *real* battle of democracy, as argued in chapter 8, involves the creation of institutions that provide the space where workers can develop their capacities through their protagonism. The working class cannot win the battle of *Dēmokratía* (the power or the rule of the people) if it is weak.

Twentieth-century states characterized by social democracy and "real socialism" prevented the development of those capacities. Those states maintained the weakness of the working class and ensured that others would rule, whether it was in the name of the working class or in the proclaimed interest of all the people. Precisely because workers did not develop the capacity to rule in the workplace and society, sooner or later capital openly assumed the driver's seat. As I explained with reference to worker management in *The Socialist Alternative*:

> When workers don't manage, *someone else* does. The implication is clear when we recall the key link of human development and practice. If workers don't develop their capabilities through their practice, *someone else* does. This was the experience of efforts to build socialism in the twentieth century, and that experience also demonstrates that however much you may think you have banished capitalism from the house, when production is not based upon worker management, upon the relation of production of associated producers, sooner or later capitalism comes in—first, slipping in through the back door, and then marching openly through the front door.[25]

The practices and outcomes characteristic of twentieth-century parties and states oriented to building a new society have taken their toll. It is not at all surprising that people active in current

movements are inclined to reject the state and the social democratic and vanguard parties that have learned nothing. In contrast
to a verticalism that they identify as power over people, many
now insist upon a horizontalism, a social relationship that literally
implies "a flat plane." As Marina Sitrin describes it, horizontalism
requires the use of direct democracy and consensus; it is non-hier-
archical and anti-authoritarian, a practice carried out in meetings
and assemblies that prefigures the future society through which
people can grow in both capacities and dignity.[26]

Such horizontal social relationships certainly are not unique
to new autonomous movements. Among the places where it
may be found are the communal councils fostered in Venezuela,
in workers' councils, the assemblies of recovered workplaces,
cooperatives, and in traditional communities. Its essential characteristic is community—a coming together of individuals who
exist in and through the community, who share a past and hope
to share a future, who recognize that they face common problems,
and who, in acting together to solve those problems, produce
themselves as members of the particular community. They are
the collective possessors of a particular commons and share an
interest in its maintenance. These relations should be nurtured,
precisely because they can produce people characterized by trust,
confidence, dignity, and solidarity.

Contributing significantly to the success of these communities
are the limited size and the focus upon the shared interests of the
particular group. In chapter 10 I point out, however, that these very
elements can be limitations when it comes to problems and decisions that transcend the particular communities, for example, at
regional, national, and international levels. The spontaneous focus
of these small units is localism and self-interest (both individual
and collective) and the development of solidarity and a concept of
community that goes beyond the local to other communities and
workplaces is not automatic.

Although the horizontal relations of these communities are
offered these days as a model for protest movements, the different

context presents significant additional problems. Lacking the history that allows for mutual trust and understanding to develop, the search for consensus is a new and difficult learning process that can prevent the instant community from being able to act decisively in a timely manner. Further, this community lacks clear boundaries as to its membership; accordingly, rather than common property, the resulting open-access property with no limits to entry and exit and without the commitment to a mutual future diminishes the sense of community.[27] Nevertheless, given the extent to which everyday life in capitalism produces powerless, crippled, alienated people, participation in such horizontal relations is empowering and exhilarating precisely because it suggests that another world is possible.

But how to move from different communities in terms of issues, grievances, and localities to a movement that can put an end to capital? For the advocates of horizontalism, social networks, electronic social media, and the occasional *"encuentro"*—periodic gatherings of meetings such as the World Social Forum and local counterparts—are the horizontal links that permit the sharing of experiences and provide mutual inspiration. For its supporters, the *encuentro* (in particular those initiated by the Zapatistas) represents "a new political strategy," one that "affirms the equality of all the heterogeneous struggles of the world: not only class struggle, or feminism, environmentalism, or antiracism, etc., but all of them equally." Its call is for "mutual global solidarity."[28]

Although these struggles do indeed develop the capacities of their protagonists, there is nothing inherent in them that goes beyond their particular focus to develop an understanding of capital and the need to put an end to it. Rather, the spontaneous result is the development of a particular consciousness—a trade union consciousness, an environmentalist consciousness, a feminist consciousness, an antiwar consciousness, an anti-poverty consciousness, and so forth. While these limited perspectives strengthen those particular struggles, they are susceptible, in the absence of a socialist consciousness that grasps their connection to the inner structure of capital, to being satisfied by the achievement of specific reforms, mere barriers to capital along its destructive path.

For horizontalists, however, the lack of a socialist conscious-ness is not an insurmountable barrier to the process of putting an end to capital. This is because each incident in which people say "No" to existing patterns reveals another crack in capitalism, and the accumulation of cracks points to an end to capital. For John Holloway "the indigenous of Chiapas, university teachers, coal miners, nearly everybody" who struggle openly to make the world anew crack capitalism. And, to those in open negation in one way or another, he adds the hidden world of insubordination—one that encompasses absenteeism from work and the "wise peasant" who, when the great lord passes, "bows deeply and silently farts."[29] In this ubiquitous "substratum of negativity," there is the potential for sudden eruption, and we cannot predict what will release the potential of the "stifled volcano."[30]

What is to be done? Holloway answers: "We have to keep build-ing cracks and finding ways of recognizing them, strengthening them, expanding them, connecting them, seeking the confluence or, preferably, the communing of the cracks."[31] Although this sounds a bit like a call for a party, for Holloway that "we" is "nearly everybody"; all of us constitute the "ubiquitous resistance" implied by ubiquitous power. "We who are without face and without voice: we are the crisis of capitalism," he intones. Precisely because of "the instability, volatility, fragility and unpredictability of capital-ism today," these cracks will sooner or later shatter capital.[32] That is all that needs to be done.

What is *not* to be done according to Holloway is to fall into the trap of thinking that you can use the state to change the world. "The very notion that society can be changed through the win-ning of state power," he argues, is the source of all our sense of betrayal. Indeed, we need to understand that "to struggle through the state is to become involved in the active process of defeating yourself." Rather than being "the vehicle of hope," the state is the "assassin of hope."[33] As with Holloway's unequivocal rejection of the "state illusion," so also does he reject the party. Since the pre-occupation of the party, whether revolutionary or parliamentary, is to gain control of the state, the party is the instrument by which our struggles are impoverished, placing control of the state at the top of the hierarchy and "sensuality, playing, laughing, loving" at the bottom.[34] There is another path. Given the fragility of capital, the "hope of humanity" is that all of our No's to capital's demands will cause it to crumble.[35]

As I argued in my essay on Holloway's book, this faint hope of changing the world without taking power reflects a "period of defeat."[36] The hopelessness of this path is revealed by his admission on the concluding page of his book. There, he asks "How, then, do we change the world without taking power?" He answers, "At the end of the book, as at the beginning, we do not know."[37] Sadder than Holloway's particular impasse, however, is that so many horizontalists share his view of state and party. Now, when capital's destruction of human beings and nature is so obviously threatening our survival, the "hope of humanity" depends upon an unequivocal rejection of the refusal to try to change the world by taking power.

Political Instruments

To end the capitalist nightmare and to build the socialist dream requires the state. But what kind of a state? In chapter 10, I argued that the state that can promote the necessary development of human capacities required for a strong working class is one based upon the communal councils and workers' councils and the mechanisms that link them. Only the new state, the state from below, is an integral part of that socialist dream. Yet that new state doesn't arise spontaneously; rather, it develops as a process that advances only as the result of the revolutionary practice in which circumstances and people are transformed.

Until such time that the new state from below is able to stand upon its own foundations, the old state is required if power is to be taken from capital and if decisive actions to support the interests of the working class, including the removal of barriers to the new state, are to occur. Who else can end immediately capital's ability to use the police, the judiciary, the army, the legislative bodies? In the new society as it emerges, both the new and old state necessarily coexist and interact. "Dual-state socialism" in this transitional period should not be confused, though, with the concept of "dual power," which suggests the existence of two classes. On the contrary, in dual-state socialism, only one class is represented and it is walking on two legs.

The new and the old states are means for achieving the goal of full development of human potential. They are political instruments with which to construct socialism as an organic system, that combination represented by the elementary triangle of socialism (social ownership of the means of production, social production organized by workers, and the satisfaction of social needs). But they are not the only political instruments necessary.

Unless one believes that a spontaneous eruption of the many stifled volcanoes will end the capitalist nightmare and introduce the socialist dream, it is essential to understand that we need a socialist party, one that can "mediate among parts of the collective workers, provide the welcoming space where popular movements can learn from each other and develop the unity necessary to defeat capital." But what kind of a party? Clearly, a party of a different type, one that does not see itself as "superior to social movements and as the place where the masses of members are meant to learn the merits of discipline in following the decisions made by infallible central committees."[38] Rather, what is needed is a political instrument that recognizes the importance of building the strength of the working class. It is a party that can learn from people in motion and that can crystallize and bring back that knowledge to expand their capacity.

As Holloway discerned, there is an intrinsic link between the party and the nature of the state needed to change the world. To take the old state away from capital's grasp and to build the new state, a socialist party (whether it is a single body with multiple tendencies or a front of socialist bodies) must be able to communicate the vision of socialism as an organic system and to encourage the working class to act consciously to realize it. As in the case of the state, a socialist party must learn to walk on two legs.

Consider, for example, social ownership of the means of production. Precisely because capital produces people who view its requirements as "self-evident natural laws," recognition of the necessity to end capitalist ownership of the products of past social labor and nature does not come easily. Even though people spontaneously struggle against violations of what they view as fair, the particular consciousness that flows from particular struggles is surrounded and smothered by the logic of capital. Development of a socialist consciousness, while essential, does not come automatically. A socialist party has to take on the responsibility of patiently explaining why the solution to particular struggles requires the ending of capital's rule.

As long as capital owns the means of production, capital's drive to accumulate rather than "the worker's own need for development" dominates the workplace and society. As indicated earlier, the need to put an end to capitalist property is obvious if people are to develop their capacities. Social ownership, however, involves more than ending capitalist ownership. It implies, as indicated in the Charter for Human Development proposed in *The Socialist Alternative,* that "everyone has the right to share in the social heritage of human beings—an equal right to the use and benefits of the products of the social brain and the social hand—in order to be able to develop his or her full potential."[39]

Equal right! Equality is inherent in the concept of social ownership, which expresses the Marxian principle that "the free development of each is the condition for the free development of all." At the core of this principle is the recognition that "the development of the human capacities on the one side [can no longer be] based on the restriction of development on the other side."[40] This concept implies not only the struggle against capital but also struggles against patriarchy, poverty, and privileged access to our social heritage. And not only within particular countries. Aren't the peasants of the South and the industrial workers of the North, for example, equal in their position as members of human society, equal in their right to human development, and equal insofar as neither has produced our social heritage, which is the result of past social labor?[41] Solidarity campaigns that, for example, support the struggles of the poor of the world, international debt cancellation, and full legal status for immigrant workers necessarily flow from the concept of social property.

What happens if particular campaigns are not linked, if they are pursued one-sidedly? Taken separately, they do not point to the need to end capitalist ownership and may be contrary to development of a socialist consciousness. For example, workers' struggles over wages and working conditions start from the concerns of particular groups of workers. They are, as Marx and Engels stressed, essential for developing the strength and dignity of the working class. However, these struggles by themselves can easily lead to the perception that workers in other countries are the enemy. Such divisions among workers, we understand, are the "secret" by which capital can continue to rule. By emphasizing the degree of international inequality that is the result of past unequal access to the products of social labor, a socialist party can contribute to the linking of workers not on the limited basis of common campaigns over wages and similar conditions of labor, but on the basis of their equal right to satisfy "the worker's own need for development." Connecting issues is one way that a socialist party can help workers go beyond a trade union consciousness to a socialist consciousness that sees the need to end capital.

Similarly, it is essential to go beyond the environmentalist consciousness that flows one-sidedly from specific concerns and struggles over the environment. Environmentalists are very knowledgeable about the relationship between the burning of fossil fuels and climate warming, as well as the many other forms of degradation of local, regional, and global ecosystems, that threaten survival of the human race. They tend to be less so about the poverty and inequality in parts of the world that are the result of exclusion from the common social heritage of humanity. Accordingly, environmentalists are often quick to condemn what they call "extractivism" when poor countries attempt to achieve a more equal share of that heritage by drawing upon the natural resources within their borders.

Certainly, as Marx pointed out, "an entire society, a nation, or all simultaneously existing societies taken together, are not the owners of the earth." Rather, the necessary condition for rational treatment of nature is that it be treated as a commons to bequeath in "an improved state to succeeding generations." For example, since the burning of fossil fuels so clearly destroys that commons, campaigns against fossil fuel and extraction are essential for "the existence and reproduction of the chain of human generations."[42] As indicated in chapter 1, however, global inequality tends to be the elephant in the environmentalists' room. Once we recognize that there are limits imposed by the natural world, the question of distribution must be raised explicitly: "The free development of each has as its condition the free development of all."

What is to be done about the poverty and inequality of poor countries? How are they to obtain their share of the products of past social labor such as adequate health and education without drawing upon the natural resources within their borders? Those who look at countries that are challenging a heritage of poverty and deprivation and declaim "extractivism" need to provide answers to this dilemma. In the absence of real alternatives for the poor, we can be certain they will continue to seek their just share in ways that can produce a tragedy of the commons, which can take many forms, including deforestation and land clearance that leads to desertification.

Left to itself, environmental consciousness in the privileged parts of the world sets itself up against the poor of the world. A socialist party combats this one-sidedness by promoting a consciousness that ensures that discussions of environmental issues incorporate a focus on social justice; and it insists that environmental justice movements go beyond reforms to understand the need to end the capitalist nightmare.

Struggles related to the side of the social ownership of production characteristically involve campaigns to make the existing state stop serving capital and to act implicitly as an agency of the working class. The important contribution the socialist party can make here is to convince those already in motion to demand explicitly that the state must be captured from capital so it can serve the needs of the working class. This emphasis, however, refers to the existing state, which is only one leg upon which the working class must walk. The party's role in relation to the *new* state is critical when we consider the other sides of the elementary triangle of socialism.

Social production organized by workers, a second side of the socialist triangle, immediately poses the importance of the self-development of the working class. As elaborated in the Charter for Human Development:

> Everyone has the right to be able to develop her full potential and capacities through democracy, participation and protagonism in the workplace and society—a process in which these subjects of activity have the precondition of the health and education which permits them to make full use of this opportunity.[43]

The role of the party in this case is to promote by all means possible new democratic institutions, new spaces in which people can develop their powers through their protagonism. In this way, the party promotes the construction of the new state from below. Thus it attempts to convince people to organize communal councils and workers' councils to create their own collective bodies with which to advance their interests against the top-down power of state institutions and despotism in the workplace. In so doing, the working class develops its capacities and the strength to challenge capital and the old state.

"*Dēmokratía*" (the power or the rule of the people) is the principle with which the socialist party should be identified consistently. This is especially important given the extent to which the vanguard parties of the twentieth and early twenty-first centuries are identified with its opposite. Every measure that can transfer power to the people, every measure that can facilitate this revolutionary process should be fought for openly. Rules such as transparency ("open the books!") and the right of veto over local managers and officials are essential demands for those below to be able to control the decisions that affect their lives, both before and after the capture of state power.

The socialist party in such cases listens and leads. By being sensitive to the concerns of people in workplaces and society, it can formulate proposals and slogans that crystallize and focus those concerns. And, in the process of leading struggles centered about democracy, the party can itself be transformed in its internal life to the extent that it listens rather than commands. Through continuous interaction with the democratic struggles of people, the party makes itself fit to play a critical role in the building of a new society that is moving toward realization of the socialist dream.

Without a socialist party able to learn and lead, however, the likely outcomes are, on the one hand, that those who wish to lead will presume that their general view of what needs to be done is sufficient grounds for directing local struggles and, on the other hand, that left to themselves localism and collective self-interest (as explained in chapter 10) will be the spontaneous tendency in emerging democratic forms. Neither outcome (nor, especially, their combination) supports the building of a solidaristic society in which people are able to develop their full human potential.

For this reason, a socialist party has a special responsibility to make explicit what is already implicit in the moral economy of the working class: a concern for the needs of others, the lack of indifference to others. In the absence of such an initiative, islands of cooperation like communal councils and workers' councils logically focus upon advancing their own immediate interests as they emerge. Consistent with the logic of cooperatives (discussed in chapter 5), they look upon those outside the particular island as the Other. Relating, then, to others as separate owners of the means of production, natural advantages, and the products of their labor, they expect a *quid pro quo* in relations with those outsiders. Thus the workplace and the geographical community in such cases are treated in substance as group property, which, as in the case of Yugoslav market-self-management (discussed in chapter 4), is a recipe for inequality and the absence of solidarity within society. Left to themselves, those separate islands of cooperation will never spontaneously produce a society based upon solidarity and community.

If the ideas of equality, democracy, and solidarity were alien to human beings, we could never hope to realize the socialist dream. However, an important element in the moral economy of the working class is the sense that inequality, lack of *dēmokratía* and the indifference and separation of people are *wrong*. Based upon such underlying concepts of right and wrong, a socialist party can make explicit the logic of the working class. It can demonstrate that implicit in the moral economy of the working class are not only social ownership of the means of production and protagonism in the workplace and society but also the concept of a communal society, one characterized by recognition of the needs of others.

In *Contradictions of "Real Socialism": The Conductor and the Conducted*, I examined the moral economy of the working class in "real socialism" and found, as recounted in chapters 4 and 9, that one aspect of the relations of people was a tendency for people to help each other without demanding an equivalent in return.[44] In contrast to an exchange relation between alienated and mutually indifferent individuals, there was a gift relation within networks among people who have a bond, people who have a past and hope to have a future, and its product is the enhancement of solidarity and trust. Latent in such relations is a society based upon solidarity and community, one marked by our recognition of our mutual dependence.

A socialist party can play a key role in expanding and deepening such communal relations—the "communality" that Marx envisioned where characteristic of our productive relations is not an exchange of exchange values (which are a manifestation of private property) but of "activities, determined by communal needs and communal purposes."[45] By stressing the importance of expanding those networks, those islands of solidarity, to encompass the needs of other producers and communities, a socialist party demonstrates its commitment to building the society of associated producers that expends its "many different forms of labour-power in full self-awareness as one single social labour force," that solidaristic society planned from the bottom up (described in chapter 10).[46]

Further, a socialist party can deepen the understanding of communality by articulating the need for decommodification and expansion of the commons. Demands for free education, free health care, free transit, free social services, and free distribution of necessities, for example, stress the need to serve the needs of people and to create conditions for the "free development of all." They point to a new socialist society where, "from the outset," expansion of the commons "grows considerably in comparison with present-day society, and it grows in proportion as the new society develops."[47]

In stressing the importance of this third side of the socialist triangle—the concept of a society that recognizes the importance of producing for social needs and purposes—a socialist party advances the vision of a socialist alternative, a society that Marx described in 1844 as characterized by "the unity of man with man, which is based on the real differences between men."[48] It points to the principle proposed in the Charter for Human Development: "Everyone has the right to live in a society in which human beings and nature can be nurtured—a society in which we can develop our full potential in communities based upon cooperation and solidarity."[49]

The concept of the elementary triangle of socialism brings coherence to the struggle to end capital and build the socialist dream. By struggling on all three fronts (social ownership, social production, and social needs), the working class attempts to make despotic inroads on the rule of capital. In the course of those struggles, their connection can come to the surface. Demands upon the old state, for example, may stimulate the emergence of workers' councils and communal councils as organs of the working class. Similarly, struggles focused upon building the elements of the new state illustrate the necessity to capture the old state. By stressing the connections between struggles and demonstrating that the revolutionary truth is the whole, a socialist party acts as a political instrument by which working people can produce themselves as revolutionary subjects. For socialists, victories are measured not by particular changes in circumstances, which can always be reversed, but by the growth in the strength of the working class.

A socialist party is a revolutionary party. Its goal is not to improve capitalism by removing its bad parts. While it walks on two legs, it moves in only one direction: its guiding purpose is to bring about, by all means necessary, a society oriented to "the worker's own need for development," a society of "free individuality based on the universal development of individuals and on the subordination of their communal, social productivity as their social wealth."[50]

Imagine: The Socialist Dream

To go beyond a situation in which workers "by education, tradition and habit" look upon capital's needs "as self-evident natural laws," it is essential that we make explicit a vision which is implicit in the worker's own need for development—the vision of socialism as an organic system. To end capitalism, the socialist dream must appear to workers as an alternative common sense, *their* common sense.

Constructing that goal in the mind is a premise for the "purposeful will" that is necessary to construct it in reality.

As with every labor process, the revolutionary labor process depends upon the producer's determination to achieve that goal consciously:

> And this is a purpose he is conscious of, it determines the mode of his activity with the rigidity of a law, and he must subordinate his will to it. This subordination is no mere momentary act. Apart from the exertion of the working organs, a purposeful will is required for the entire duration of the work. [51]

The need to combine that vision and the purposeful will to achieve it has never been truer than now because capitalism's destruction of human beings and nature and the prospect of barbarism increasingly haunt us. As Daly and Cobb pointed out, we are being "led to a *dead* end." To awaken from the capitalist nightmare and to begin to construct the socialist dream in reality, we need a socialist party that can combine the socialist vision and particular struggles so we can fight (as noted in the Foreword) with "tomorrow's songs on our lips."

Recently, Kavita Krishnan, secretary of the All India Progressive Women's Association, a leader of the Communist Party of India (Marxist-Leninist) and editor of the magazine *Liberation*, articulated this link between our vision and our struggles in a fine essay, "Re-imagining India."[52] Although its specific reference point is India, it speaks to all of us. With her permission, I share this with you:

> We revolutionaries, who seek to transform society, spend a lot of time re-imagining the world we live in. That does not mean we live in a fool's paradise. It means that we dream dreams that can be achieved.
>
> We don't wish on a star. Our wishes, we know, won't be granted by any gods. The beauty of our dreams lies in the fact that they're made up of human imagination and human will, and can be shaped and brought to life by human will.

When our imaginations are cramped, our realities too are likely to be the same. When an idea comes to life in our imagination, it is the first step towards bringing it to life in our real world.

The other thing about our dreams is that we aren't solitary dreamers. We don't dream our dreams isolated from others. Our dreams are not a private indulgence or a private solace. These dreams are born in the collective minds of fellow fighters. We dream together, as we fight struggles together. And when others are able to see and share our dreams, the dreams acquire a life beyond our own personal lives.

Imagining dreams takes courage. The system survives, not only by jailing or killing revolutionaries—but by killing our dreams. "*Sabse khatarnak hota hai sapnon ka mar jana*" (Most dangerous of all is the death of our dreams), said Paash.

Today, I will attempt to share some of those many dreams with you, the reader.

In my imagination, I see an India where a woman can roam free—free of the labels of "wife," "mother," "daughter," "beautiful," "ugly," "goddess," "slut" . . . Where every child she bears is legitimate, and none seek to know or prove who the father is. Where every woman is valued irrespective of her ability or choice to bear a child.

An India where caring, nurturing and bringing up children is not assigned as "women's work." Instead, all around us we are able to see men and women who change diapers, bathe, feed and clothe children, and feel that mingled feeling of love and pain that being a parent involves.

An India where the birth of a baby is celebrated without worrying about the sex of the child. An India where girls who play sports are not humiliated and accused of being "male," and boys who dance or cook are not taunted for being "effeminate." An India where brothers no longer feel entitled to hold sisters in "bandhan" in the name of "raksha"—and sisters no longer feel obliged to give brothers a right to control their lives.

An India where the love of brothers and sisters is expressed as solidarity with each other's dreams, as respect and support for each other's decisions.

An India where it is unknown for the women to have to worry about "what people will think"—about her clothes, the colour of her skin, who she chooses to love, and what she chooses to do with her life.

An India where love—between people of any community or any sex—will not be a crime.

An India where the ugly hierarchy of castes is a forgotten thing of the past. Where the history of the struggles of the oppressed is recognised and celebrated, and the history of oppression is remembered—so as never to repeat it.

An India where men do not fear women, citizens do not fear "foreigners." An India that does not fear the fullest freedom of the Dalits, the adivasis, the peoples of Kashmir or Manipur or Nagaland. An India that is a free union of free peoples. Where "unity" does not have to mean a regime of fear, or subservience achieved at gun point. An India that does not fear its neighbours—and that does not induce fear in its neighbours. An India that can be trusted to speak up against injustice anywhere in the world.

An India where "work" does not mean back-breaking, mind-numbing toil that still leaves stomachs hungry. Where a "job" does not come wedded to "joblessness." An India where people matter, not profits. An India which will recognise the truth: that all value is created by the labour of workers. When workers—the *mehnatkash*—can demand their rightful share from the world—not a field or a country, but the whole world. When we can put behind us the nightmare India where a tiny few enjoy Antilla-like palaces and the vast majority have no home; and awaken to a new India where every person can be sure of a home to call their own. Where education and health care of the best quality can be availed by every Indian as a right, rather than being a commodity to be bought by the rich.

An India where "justice" won't mean a hangman's noose. Rather, where justice will mean that we as Indian people will have the courage and conscience to face and admit the truths about the violence done in our name, in our country's name. Where the truth about the rapes and murders of Manorama, Neelofer and Asiya, the rapes of Kunan Poshpora, the mass graves of Kashmir, the little adivasi children killed by paramilitary forces during harvest festivals in Bastar, the cries of pain and humiliation arising from the torture chambers that are called "police lock-ups" all over the country, can be acknowledged by all Indians. Where "national pride" or "national security" will not be equated with tolerance of these crimes against humanity. And where the acceptance of the truth can be foundation of dignity and democracy for India.

An India where animals and humans do not need to fear each other and are not thrown into conflict with each other by a short-sighted and greedy economy. An India where the "environment"—land, water, forests, air, flora and fauna—are not seen as "commodities" to be "owned" and "exploited," but as a world we inherit and are duty-bound to enrich and pass on to future generations rather than allow a few greedy men to devour.

Our revolutionary dreams cannot be bounded by the confines of a country. Naturally, those dreams are dreamed for the entire world, not India alone. We dream of a world free of oppression, free of ownership. A world where the many thousands of peoples live in unity, where domination, military occupation and war are things of the past. Where work is not inspired by the fear of hunger, where a "living" does not have to be "earned," where instead, human beings work and play to express their humanity.

As I said before, there is no copyright on the dreams of revolutionaries. Where do the dreams of Bhagat Singh end and ours begin, after all? That is why, when I try to give my dreams the shape of words, I often find the words of poets and dreamers past come to my lips. So I'll end with the immortal words from John Lennon's anthem "Imagine":

> You may say I'm a dreamer
> But I'm not the only one
> I hope someday you'll join us
> And the world will be one.

This book opened in chapter 1 with what was originally the first paragraph to my 2005 essay on John Holloway's *Change the World without Taking Power*:

> In the beginning is the dream, the promise of a society which permits the full development of human potential, a society in which we relate to each other as human beings and where the mere recognition of the need of another is sufficient to induce our deed. In the beginning is the vision of a society where the products of our past activity serve our own need for development and where in working together we develop our capacities, our needs, our human wealth.

Here is the next paragraph in that essay:

> That dream moves us—even as we catch only fleeting glimpses. It underlies our struggles—our struggles for wages (to satisfy the needs of socially developed human beings), our struggles over the length and intensity of the workday (in order to have time and energy for ourselves), our struggles to make the state—controlled and used by others to enforce our exploitation—into our own agency, our struggles to end our oppression (for example, as women, blacks, indigenous people), our struggles for our share of civilization. And in those struggles we ourselves develop. Not only does the dream itself become clearer through our collective activity but we transform ourselves, we grow; through our revolutionary practice, where we

simultaneously change circumstances and ourselves, we make ourselves fit to create a new world, the world that corresponds to the dream.[53]

Imagine the socialist dream, and let us join together to put an end to capitalism with "tomorrow's songs on our lips."

Bibliography

Badiou, Alain. *The Communist Hypothesis* (London: Verso, 2010).

Barclay, David E., and Weitz, Eric D., eds. *German Socialism and Communism from 1840 to 1990* (New York: Berghahn Books, 2009).

Centro Internacional Miranda. "Worker's Control: Theory and Experiences," http://www.socialistproject.ca/leftstreamed/ls26.php).

Chávez, Hugo Frias. *Alo Presidente* #263, #264, and #268, 2007, http://www.alopresidente.gob.ve/.

——. *Golpe de timón* (Caracas: Ediciones Correo del Orinoco, 2012).

Daly, Herman E., and Cobb, John B., Jr. *For the Common Good: Redirecting the Economy toward Community, the Environment and a Sustainable Future* (Boston: Beacon Press, 1989).

Eisenach Programme. http://www.germanhistorydocs.ghi-dc.org/sub_document.cfm?document_id=688 and de.wikipedia.org/wiki/Eisenacher_Programm.

Engels, Friedrich. *The Peasant War in Germany* (Moscow: Foreign Languages Publishing House, 1956).

——. "Introduction" to *The Civil War in France*, in Marx and Engels, *On the Paris Commune* (Moscow: Progress Publishers, 1971).

Erfurt Program. http://www.marxists.org/history/international/social-democracy/1891/erfurt-program.htm.

Filzer, Donald A., ed. *The Crisis of Soviet Industrialization: Selected Essays of E. A. Preobrazhensky* (White Plains, NY: M. E. Sharpe, 1979).

Foster, John Bellamy, and Magdoff, Fred. "What Every Environmentalist Needs to Know about Capitalism," *Monthly Review* 61/10 (March 2010).

Foster, John Bellamy. *Marx's Ecology: Materialism and Nature* (New York: Monthly Review Press, 2000).

———. *The Ecological Revolution: Making Peace with the Planet* (New York: Monthly Review Press, 2009).

García Linera, Álvaro. "A Message to the Left of Europe and the World," *Links International Journal of Socialist Renewal,* at http://links.org.au/node/3712.

Harnecker, Marta. *Rebuilding the Left* (London: Zed Books, 2007).

———. *De los consejos comunales a las comunas. construyendo el socialismo del siglo xxi,* 2009, http://www.rebelion.org.

———."A Decentralised Participatory Planning Proposal Based on the Experiences of Brazil, Venezuela and the State of Kerala, India," *Links International Journal of Socialist Renewal,* 19 December 2014, at http://p.feedblitz.com/t3.asp?/343373/2850429/4870515/links.org.au/node/4208.

Hegel, G. W. F. *Hegel's Science of Logic,* trans. W. H. Johnston and L. G. Struthers, 2 vols. (London: Allen & Unwin, 1961).

High, Holly. "Cooperation as Gift versus Cooperation as Corvee," paper presented at "Regenerations: New Leaders, New Visions in Southeast Asia," Council of Southeast Asian Studies, Yale University, http://www.freebay.net/site/content/view/801/34/.

Holloway, John. *Change the World Without Taking Power* (London: Pluto Press, 2002).

———. "John Holloway: Cracking Capitalism vs. the State Option," interview by Amador Fernandez-Savater in *ROAR Magazine,* 29, September 2014.

Intergovernmental Panel on Climate Change. "Severe, Widespread, and Irreversible Impacts," http://climateandcapitalism.com/2014/11/02/severe-widespred-irreversible-impacts-globally/.

Jun, Li. "Collective Action of Laid-off Workers and Its Implication on Political Stability: Evidences from Northeast China" (PhD diss., City University of Hong Kong, 2008).

Kagarlitsky, Boris. "Interview," *Against the Current,* March 3, 1995.

Kopstein, Jeffrey. "Workers' Resistance and the Demise of East Germany," http://libcom.org/history/workers-resistance-demise-east-germany-jeffrey-kopstein.

Kornai, Janos. *Economics of Shortage* (Amsterdam: North-Holland, 1980).

———. *Growth, Shortage and Efficiency: A Macrodynamic Model of the Socialist Economy* (Berkeley: University of California Press, 1982).

Korsch, Karl. "Introduction to the Critique of the Gotha Programme," 1922, http://www.marxists.org/archive/korsch/1922/gotha.htm.

Krishnan, Kavita. *Outlook,* posted at *Links International Journal of Socialist Renewal,* August 21, 2014, http://links.org.au/node/4014.

Laibman, David. "Quotology, Stages, and the Posthumous Anarchization of Marx," *Science & Society* (July 2014).

Lassalle, Ferdinand. "Open Letter," http://germanhistorydocs.ghi-dc.org/ pdf/eng/6_EL_Socialist%20View_Lasalle.pdf.

———. *The Working Man's Programme* (London: Modern Press, 1884).

Lebowitz, Michael A. "Kornai and Socialist Laws of Motion," *Studies in Political Economy* 18 (Autumn 1985).

———. *Beyond Capital: Marx's Political Economy of the Working Class* (New York: Palgrave Macmillan. 2003).

———. "Holloway's Scream: Full of Sound and Fury," *Historical Materialism* 13/4 (2005).

———. "New Wings for Socialism," *Monthly Review* 58/11 (April 2007).

———. "Building Upon Defects: Theses on the Misinterpretation of Marx's Gotha Critique," *Science & Society* (October 2007).

———. *El Camino al Desarrollo Humano: Capitalismo o Socialismo?* (Caracas: Centro Internacional Miranda, 2008).

———. *La logica del capital versus la logica del desarrollo humano* (Caracas: El Perro y la Rana, 2008).

———. "The Path to Human Development: Capitalism or Socialism?" *Monthly Review* 60/9 (February 2009).

———. *Following Marx: Method, Critique and Crisis* (Chicago: Haymarket Books, 2009).

———. *The Socialist Alternative: Real Human Development* (New York: Monthly Review Press, 2010).

———. "Trapped Inside a Box? Five Questions for Ben Fine," *Historical Materialism* 18/1 (2010).

———. "Socialism for the Twenty-First Century and the Need for Socialist Globalization," *International Critical Thought* 1/3 (September 2011).

———. *Contradictions of "Real Socialism": The Conductor and the Conducted* (New York: Monthly Review Press, 2012).

———. "Understanding the Critique of the Gotha Programme," *Marksist Klasikleri Okuma Kılavuzu* (Istanbul: Yordam Kitap, 2013).

———. "Human Development and Socialist Accounting," paper presented at the annual meeting of the World Association of Political Economy, Hanoi, May 2014.

———. "Build It 'From the Outset': An Infantile Disorder?" *Science & Society* 79/3 (July 2015).

Ledeneva, Alena V. *Russia's Economy of Favours: Blat, Networking and*

Informal Exchange (Cambridge: Cambridge University Press, 1998).

Lenin, V. I. *State and Revolution* (Beijing: Foreign Languages Press, 1965).

Lenin, V. I. *The Right of Nations to Self-Determination, Lenin: Selected Works*, vol. 1 (Moscow: Foreign Languages Publishing, 1961).

Luebbert,Gregory M. *Liberalism, Fascism, or Social Democracy: Social Classes and the Political Origins of Regimes in Interwar Europe* (Oxford: Oxford University Press, 1991).

Marx, Karl, and Engels, Friedrich. *The Communist Manifesto*, in Marx and Engels, *Collected Works*, vol. 6 (New York: International Publishers, 1976).

————. *Collected Works*, vol. 43 (New York: International Publishers, 1988).

————. *Collected Works*, vol. 45 (New York: International Publishers, 1992).

————. *Collected Works*, vol. 24 (New York: International Publishers, 1989).

————. *Collected Works*, vol. 49 (New York: International Publishers, 2002).

Marx, Karl. *Critique of the Gotha Programme*, in Marx and Engels, *Selected Works*, vol. 2 (Moscow: Foreign Languages Publishing House, 1962).

————. *Theories of Surplus Value, Part 2* (Moscow: Progress Publishers, 1968).

————. *Theories of Surplus Value, Part 3* (Moscow: Progress Publishers, 1971).

————. "First Outline of *The Civil War in France*," in Marx and Engels, *On the Paris Commune* (Moscow: Progress Publishers, 1971).

————. *The Civil War in France*, in Marx and Engels, *On the Paris Commune* (Moscow: Progress Publishers, 1971).

————. *Grundrisse* (New York: Vintage, 1973).

————. *On the Jewish Question*, in Marx and Engels, *Collected Works*, vol. 3 (New York: International Publishers, 1975).

————. *Comments on James Mill*, in Marx and Engels, *Collected Works*, vol. 3 (New York: International Publishers, 1975).

————. *Economic and Philosophical Manuscripts of 1844*, in Marx and Engels, *Collected Works*, vol. 3 (New York: International Publishers, 1975).

————. Letter to Ludwig Feuerbach, 11 August 1844, in Marx and Engels, *Collected Works*, vol. 3 (New York: International Publishers, 1975).

————. *Theses on Feuerbach*, in Marx and Engels, *Collected Works*, vol. 5 (New York: International Publishers, 1976).

————. *The Poverty of Philosophy*, in Marx and Engels, *Collected Works*, vol. 6 ((New York: International Publishers, 1976).

————. *Capital*, vol. 1 (New York: Vintage, 1977).

————. *The Eighteenth Brumaire of Louis Bonaparte*, in Marx and Engels, *Collected Works*, vol. 11 (New York: International Publishers, 1979).

————. *New York Daily Tribune*, July 14, 1853, in Marx and Engels, *Collected Works*, vol. 12 (New York: International Publishers, 1979).

————. *Capital*, vol. 3 (New York: Vintage, 1981).

————."Inaugural Address of the Working Men's International Association," in Marx and Engels, *Collected Works*, vol. 20 (New York: International Publishers, 1985).

————. *Value, Price and Profit*, in Marx and Engels, *Collected Works*, vol. 20 (New York: International Publishers, 1985).

————. *Economic Manuscripts of 1861-63*, in Marx-Engels, *Collected Works*, vol. 30 (New York: International Publishers, 1988).

————. "Instructions for the Delegates of the Provisional General Council: The Different Questions," in *Minutes of the General Council of the First International, 1864-66* (Moscow: Foreign Languages Publishing House, 1964).

McNally, David. *Monsters of the Market: Zombies, Vampires and Global Capitalism* (Chicago: Haymarket, 2011).

Mehring, Franz. *Karl Marx: The Story of his Life* (New York: Covici Friede, 1935).

Nail, Thomas. "Zapatism and the Global Origins of Occupy," *Journal for Cultural and Religious Theory* 12/3 (Spring 2013).

Ostrom, Elinor. *Governing the Commons: The Evolution of Institutions for Collective Action* (Cambridge: Cambridge University Press, 1990).

Panebianco, Angelo. *Political Parties: Organization and Power* (Cambridge: Cambridge University Press, 1988).

Preobrazhensky, Evgeny. *The New Economics* (Oxford: Clarendon Press, 1965).

Robinson, J. H., ed. *Readings in European History* (Boston: Ginn, 1906), available at http://history.hanover.edu/texts/gotha.htm; and http://delong.type.pad.com/sdj/2009/10/the-gotha-program-of-1875.html.

Scott, James C. *The Moral Economy of the Peasant: Rebellion and Subsistence in Southeast Asia* (New Haven: Yale University Press, 1976).

Sève, Lucien. *Man in Marxist Theory and the Psychology of Personality* (Sussex: Harvester Press, 1978).

Sitrin, Marina. "Horizontalism," http://marinasitrin.com/?page_id=108.

Sojo, Cleto A. "Venezuela's Chávez Closes WSF with Call to Transcend Capitalism," http://venezuelanalysis.com/news/907, January 31, 2005.

Steenson, Gary P. *After Marx, Before Lenin: Marxism and Socialist Working-Class Parties in Europe, 1884-1914* (Pittsburgh: University of Pittsburgh Press, 1991).

————. *Not One Man! Not One Penny! German Social Democracy, 1863-1914* (Pittsburgh: University of Pittsburgh Press, 1981).

Tablada, Carlos. *Che Guevara: Economics and Politics in the Transition to Socialism* (Sydney: Pathfinder, 1989).

Thompson, E. P. "The Moral Economy of the English Crowd in the Eighteenth Century," *Past and Present* 50 (1971).

Notes

1. The Capitalist Nightmare and the Socialist Dream

1. David McNally, *Monsters of the Market: Zombies, Vampires and Global Capitalism* (Chicago: Haymarket, 2011). See esp. chap. 2, "Marx's Monsters"; Karl Marx, *Capital*, vol. 1 (New York: Vintage, 1977), 416.
2. Marx, *Capital*, vol. 1, 367.
3. Karl Marx, *Grundrisse* (New York: Vintage, 1973), 270.
4. Marx, *Capital*, vol. 1,: 342. Note also Marx's comment that legislation on the workday was "a barrier to the transformation of children's blood into capital" (382).
5. See my discussion of the nature of capital in Michael A. Lebowitz, *Beyond Capital: Marx's Political Economy of the Working Class* (New York: Palgrave Macmillan, 2003).
6. Marx, *Capital*, vol. 1, 270.
7. Ibid., 490–91.The theme in this section and the next of capital's barriers and its transcending of these was explored initially in "Marx's Falling Rate of Profit: A Dialectical View" (1976), reprinted in Michael A. Lebowitz, *Following Marx: Method, Critique and Crisis* (Chicago: Haymarket Books, 2009), chap. 7. See also Lebowitz, "Why Marx? A Story of Capital," in *Beyond Capital*, chap. 1.
8. Marx, *Capital*, vol. 1, 911, 900.
9. Ibid., 504.
10. Ibid., 506.

11. Ibid., 579. These two barriers were explored in "The General and Specific in Marx's Theory of Crisis" (1982), reprinted in Lebowitz, *Following Marx,* chap. 8.

12. Karl Marx, *Capital,* vol. 3 (New York: Vintage, 1981), 213–14.

13. Ibid., 201, 206.

14. Ibid., 214.

15. Marx, *Grundrisse,* 409.

16. Among his many seminal works in this field are John Bellamy Foster, *Marx's Ecology: Materialism and Nature* (New York: Monthly Review Press, 2000); and *The Ecological Revolution: Making Peace with the Planet* (New York: Monthly Review Press. 2009). See also his many articles in *Monthly Review* including (with Fred Magdoff), "What Every Environmentalist Needs to Know about Capitalism," *Monthly Review* 61/10 (March 2010).

17. Marx, *Capital,* vol. 1, 637.

18. Marx, *Capital,* vol. 3, 949.

19. Marx, *Capital,* vol. 1, 348.

20. Ibid.,579–80.

21. Marx, *Capital,* vol. 3, 358.

22. Ibid., 353.

23. Ibid., 365.

24. Marx, *Grundrisse,* 405, 407.

25. Ibid., 408.

26. Ibid., 408–10.

27. Marx, *Grundrisse,* 539.

28. Ibid., 415–16.. Marx planned to explore crises in the sixth of his planned books, the book on the world market.

29. Karl Marx, *Theories of Surplus Value,* Part 2 (Moscow: Progress Publishers, 1968), 528.

30. *Capital,* vol. 3, 357.

31. G. W. F. Hegel, *Hegel's Science of Logic,* trans. W. H. Johnston and L. G. Struthers, 2 vols. (London: Allen & Unwin, 1961) 1:146.

32. Ibid., 1:147.

33. Marx, *Grundrisse,* 334.

34. Ibid., 410, 421.

35. Hegel, *Hegel's Science of Logic,* 1:149.

36. Ibid., 1:142.

37. Karl Marx and Friedrich Engels, *The Communist Manifesto,* in Marx and Engels, *Collected Works,* vol. 6 (New York: International Publishers, 1976), 496.

38. Marx, *Capital*, vol. 1, 450.
39. Ibid., 482–84, 548, 607–8, 614.
40. Ibid., 548, 643, 799.
41. Ibid., 270.
42. Marx, *Grundrisse*, 488.
43. Ibid., 287; Lebowitz, *Beyond Capital*: 32–44.
44. Karl Marx, *Theories of Surplus Value*, Part 3 (Moscow: Progress Publishers, 1971), 78–79.
45. Karl Marx, *Economic Manuscripts of 1861–63*, in Marx and Engels, *Collected Works*, vol. 30 (New York: International Publishers, 1988), 62–63.
46. Hegel, *Hegel's Science of Logic*, 1:147.
47. Marx, *Capital*, vol. 1, 283.
48. Ibid., 290.
49. Marx, *Grundrisse*, 85, 87.
50. Marx, *Capital*, vol. 1, 290, 202.
51. Ibid., 284–85.
52. Marx, *Capital*, vol. 3: 754n.
53. Marx, *Capital*, vol. 1, 638.
54. Marx, *Capital*, vol. 3: 911, 916.
55. Marx, *Grundrisse*, 726.
56. Marx, *Capital*, vol. 1, 635–36.
57. Marx, *Grundrisse*, 726; Marx, *Capital*, vol. 3, 369.
58. Marx, *Capital*, vol. 1, 638.
59. Ibid., 381.
60. Karl Marx, "On the Jewish Question," in Marx and Engels, *Collected Works*, vol. 3 (New York: International Publishers, 1975), 162.
61. See the discussion in Lebowitz, *Beyond Capital*, 157–58.
62. Ibid., 156-60.
63. Michael A. Lebowitz, *The Socialist Alternative: Real Human Development* (New York: Monthly Review Press, 2010), 66–68.
64. Karl Marx, "Instructions for the Delegates of the Provisional General Council: The Different Questions," in *Minutes of the General Council of the First International, 1864–66* (Moscow: Foreign Languages Publishing House, n.d.), 146, 344–45; Lebowitz, *Beyond Capital*, 96–98, 189–90. See also "Situating the Capitalist State," in Lebowitz, *Following Marx*, chap. 18, 327–37.
65. Marx, *Capital*, vol. 1, 680, 733; Lebowitz, *Beyond Capital*, 172–74.
66. See chapter 9 in this volume for a discussion of "Fairness.
67. Marx, *Capital*, vol. 1, 730–33, 675, 680; Lebowitz, *Beyond Capital*, 172–76.

68. Marx, *Grundrisse*, 694; Marx, *Capital*, vol. 1, 1058; Lebowitz, *Beyond Capital*, 156–57.
69. Marx, *Capital*, vol. 1, 899.
70. Ibid., 899. 935.
71. Ibid., 772.
72. Ibid., 988, 548.
73. Ibid., 425.
74. Ibid., 799.
75. Marx, *Grundrisse*, 325.
76. Marx, *Capital*, vol. 1, 450.
77. Marx, *Capital*, vol. 3, 178.
78. Marx, *Capital*, vol. 1, 447.
79. Ibid., 284, 448–49, 489–90, 549; Marx, *Capital*, vol. 3, 510.
80. Marx, *Capital*, vol. 3, 571; Marx and Engels, *Collected Works*, vol. 20 (New York: International Publishers, 1985), 190.
81. Marx, *Capital*, vol. 1, 284, 643.
82. Karl Marx, *Critique of the Gotha Programme*, in Marx and Engels, *Selected Works*, vol. 2 (Moscow: Foreign Languages Publishing House, 1962), 24.
83. Marx, *Capital*, vol. 1, 619.
84. Ibid., 614, 618.
85. Lucien Sève, *Man in Marxist Theory and the Psychology of Personality* (Sussex: Harvester Press, 1978), 304, 313.
86. Lebowitz, *Beyond Capital*, 42–4.
87. Marx, *Critique of the Gotha Programme*, 24.
88. Marx, , *Capital*, vol. 3, 911, 916.
89. Ibid., 949; Marx, *Capital*, vol. 1 635–36.
90. Marx, *Capital*, vol. 3, 754–55n.
91. See, for example, Foster (2009), chapter 9, "Marx's Theory of Metabolic Rift," esp. 171–82.
92. Marx, *Capital*, vol. 1, 635–6.
93. Marx, *Capital*, vol. 3, 754n.
94. Ibid., 911.
95. Ibid., 949.
96. Karl Marx, "On the Jewish Question," in Marx and Engels, *Collected Works*, vol. 3 (New York: International Publishers, 1975), 64.
97. Lebowitz, *The Socialist Alternative*, 61, 68–69.
98. See chapter 4 in this volume; and Lebowitz, *The Socialist Alternative*, chap. 3.
99. See Elinor Ostrom, *Governing the Commons: The Evolution of*

Institutions for Collective Action (Cambridge: Cambridge University Press, 1990); Lebowitz, *The Socialist Alternative*, in particular, "Expanding the Commons," 146–48.

100. Marx and Engels, *The Communist Manifesto*, 506; Karl Marx, *Economic Manuscripts of 1861–63*, in Marx and Engels; *Collected Works*, vol. 30 (New York: International Publishers, 1988), 190–92.

101. Holly High, "Cooperation as Gift versus Cooperation as Corvee," paper presented at "Regenerations: New Leaders, New Visions in Southeast Asia" seminar, Council of Southeast Asian Studies, Yale University. Available at http://www.freebay.net/site/content/view/801/34/.

102. Karl Marx, "Comments on James Mill," in Marx and Engels, *Collected Works*, vol. 3, 225–28; Lebowitz, "The Solidarian Society," in *The Socialist Alternative*, 65–81.

103. Marx, *Grundrisse*, 172.

104. Ibid., 171–72.

105. Herman E. Daly and John B. Cobb, Jr., *For the Common Good: Redirecting the Economy toward Community, the Environment and a Sustainable Future* (Boston: Beacon Press, 1989), 172.

106. Marx, *Grundrisse*, 172.

107. Marx, *Capital*, vol. 1, 171.

108. Marx, *Grundrisse*, 158, 171.

109. This point is developed in Lebowitz, *The Socialist Alternative* and in chapters 5 and 6 in this volume. Note that in his last reflection (expressed during the televised cabinet meeting on 20 October 2012), Chávez stressed the importance of building the communes, "*comuna o nada*," argued the necessity of replacing capitalist workplaces with their built-in hierarchical social division of labor with one that involves the full participation of the associated producers and an appropriate means of coordination—and thus "radically different" from the organization of both the capitalist economy and the post-capitalist variety "presented deceivingly as 'planning'"—and indicated that, although working along with small producers, social property and the socialist spirit should be instilled throughout the whole production and distribution chain. In this talk marked by self-criticism, Chávez understood the importance of rectifying problems (in particular, the gap between passing new laws and making them real): "If we don't realize this, we are liquidated and we are not only liquidated, we would be the liquidators of this project." Hugo Chávez Frias, *Golpe de timón* (Caracas: Ediciones Correo del Orinoco, 2012).

110. Marx, *Grundrisse*, 158–59, 171–72; Lebowitz, *The Socialist Alternative*, 78–81.

111. Karl Marx, *The Eighteenth Brumaire of Louis Bonaparte*, in Marx and Engels, *Collected Works*, vol. 11 (New York: International Publishers, 1979), 106–7.

2. Understanding the *Critique of the Gotha Programme*

1. Michael A. Lebowitz, "Understanding the Critique of the Gotha Programme," *Marksist Klasikleri Okuma Kılavuzu* (Istanbul: Yordam Kitap, 2013). Unless otherwise attributed, quotations are from Marx's *Critique*.

2. This section draws upon the following works: Hermann Beck, "Working-Class Politics at the Crossroads of Conservatism, Liberalism and Socialism," and Toni Offerman, "The Lassallean Labor Movement in Germany," both in *German Socialism and Communism from 1840 to 1990*, ed. David E. Barclay and Eric D. Weitz (New York: Berghahn Books, 2009); Gregory M. Luebbert, *Liberalism, Fascism, or Social Democracy: Social Classes and the Political Origins of Regimes in Interwar Europe* (Oxford: Oxford University Press, 1991); Angelo Panebianco. *Political Parties: Organization and Power* (Cambridge: Cambridge University Press, 1988); Gary P. Steenson, *Not One Man! Not One Penny! German Social Democracy, 1863–1914* (Pittsburgh: University of Pittsburgh Press, 1981); and Gary P. Steenson, *After Marx, Before Lenin: Marxism and Socialist Working-Class Parties in Europe, 1884–1914* (Pittsburgh: University of Pittsburgh Press, 1991).

3. Marx to W. Bracke, 5 May 1875, in Marx and Engels, *Collected Works*, vol. 24, 77–78 (New York: International Publishers, 1989).

4. Engels to A. Bebel, 18–28 March 1875, in ibid., 67–73.

5. Engels to A. Bebel, 1–2 May 1891, in Marx and Engels, *Collected Works*, vol. 49 (New York: International Publishers, 2001), 175–84.

6. Engels to A. Bebel, 18–28 March 1875, in Marx and Engels, *Collected Works*, vol. 24, 77–78.

7. Engels to W. Bracke, 11 October 1875, in Marx and Engels, *Collected Works*, vol. 45 (New York: International Publishers, 1991), 94–96.

8. Engels to A. Bebel, 18–28 March 1875, in ibid.

9. Marx to Bracke, 5 May 1875, in ibid.

10. Engels to Bebel, 12 October 1875, in ibid., 97–98.

11. Steenson, *After Marx, Before Lenin*, 279.

12. August Bebel, *My Life* (London 1912), quoted in Karl Korsch,

"Introduction to the Critique of the Gotha Programme" (1922), available at http://www.marxists.org/archive/korsch/1922/gotha.htm.

13. Lenin, *The Right of Nations to Self-Determination, in Lenin: Selected Works*, vol. 1 (Moscow: Foreign Languages Publishing), 556.

14. Engels to Bebel, 18–28 March 1875, in Marx and Engels, *Collected Works*, vol. 45.

15. The Eisenach Program can be found at http://www.germanhistory-docs.ghi-dc.org/sub_document.cfm?document_id=688 and de.wiki pedia.org/wiki/Eisenacher_Program.

16. The Erfurt Program can be found at http://www.marxists.org/history/international/social-democracy/1891/erfurtprogramme.htm.

17. See, for example, the discussion of this period in Franz Mehring, *Karl Marx: The Story of His Life* (New York: Covici Friede, 1935).

18. Friedrich Engels, *The Peasant War in Germany* (Moscow: Foreign Languages Publishing House, 1956), 32–33.

19. Ferdinand Lassalle, "Open Letter," available at http://germanhist-orydocs.ghi-dc.org/pdf/eng/6_EL_Socialist%20View_Lasalle.pdf.

20. Ferdinand Lassalle, *The Working Man's Programme* (London: Modern Press, 1884), 55.

21. Engels to Bebel, 18–28 March 1875, in Marx and Engels, *Collected Works*, vol. 45.

22. Karl Marx, "Inaugural Address of the Working Men's International Association" (1864), in Marx and Engels, *Collected Works*, vol. 20 (New York: International Publishers, 1985), 10–11; Karl Marx, "Instructions for the Delegates of the Provisional General Council. The Different Questions," in *Minutes of the General Council of the First International, 1864–66* (Moscow: Foreign Languages Publishing House, n.d.), 346. See chap. 5, "The Political Economy of Wage-Labour," in Michael A. Lebowitz, *Beyond Capital: Marx's Political Economy of the Working Class* (New York: Palgrave Macmillan, 2003).

23. Karl Marx, *Theses on Feuerbach*, in Marx and Engels, *Collected Works*, vol. 5 (New York: International Publishers, 1976), 4.

24. Engels to Bebel, 18–28 March 1875, in Marx and Engels, *Collected Works*, vol. 45.

25. Certainly, one important contribution of the *Critique* was the clarity with which Marx insisted that "Labour is *not the source* of all wealth. *Nature* is just as much the source of use values (and it is surely of such that material wealth consists!) as is labour, which

itself is only the manifestation of a natural force, human labour power." Nature as an original source of wealth is a point that Marx had earlier stressed in *Capital* but his forceful statement here demonstrates how central to his perspective was Marx's view of nature (see chapter 1 in this volume for the discussion there). My original chapter for the Turkish collection did not stress this point here, and I am indebted to John Bellamy Foster for encouraging me to underline this point for this volume.

26. Karl Marx, *Grundrisse* (New York: Vintage, 1973), 278.

27. Karl Marx, *Capital*, vol. 1 (New York: Vintage, 1977), 711.

28. Ibid., 772.

29. Marx, *Grundrisse*, 325, 488, 541, 708.

30. See chap. 4, "The Being and Becoming of an Organic System," in Michael A. Lebowitz, *The Socialist Alternative: Real Human Development* (New York: Monthly Review Press, 2010).

31. Marx, *Grundrisse*, 459–60, 278.

32. Ibid., 172.

33. Ibid., 158.

34. Karl Marx, *Capital*, vol. 3 (New York: Vintage, 1981), 178–79.

35. Karl Marx, *Economic and Philosophical Manuscripts of 1844*, in Marx and Engels, *Collected Works*, vol. 3 (New York: International Publishers, 1975), 241; Lebowitz, *The Socialist Alternative*, 70–72.

36. See the discussion of self-interest as an infection in socialism, "The Solidarian Society," in Lebowitz, *The Socialist Alternative*, chap. 3.

37. Interestingly, Marx did not suggest any tendency associated with these.

38. Karl Marx, *The Civil War in France*, in Marx and Engels, *On the Paris Commune* (Moscow: Progress Publishers, 1971), 68–73.

39. Karl Marx, "First Outline of *The Civil War in France*," in Marx and Engels, ibid., 155–56.

40. Ibid., 154–55.

41. Marx, *Civil War in France*, 75.

42. Friedrich Engels, "Introduction" to *The Civil War in France* (1891), in Marx and Engels, *On the Paris Commune*, 34.

43. Marx, *Grundrisse*, 171–72.

44. Ibid., 172–73.

45. See Lebowitz, *The Socialist Alternative*, in particular chap. 6, "Making a Path to Socialism."

46. Marx, "First Outline," 152–53.

47. See my earlier critique of the idea of "building upon defects" in "Building Upon Defects: Theses on the Misinterpretation of Marx's

Gotha Critique," *Science & Society* (October 2007), based on my presentation at the Third International Conference on "Karl Marx and the Challenges of the 21st Century," in Havana, 3–6 May 2006. For his recognition of this point, see Hugo Chávez Frias, *Alo Presidente* #268, http://www.alopresidente.gob.ve/.

48. See, for example, the discussion in Lenin, *State and Revolution* (Beijing: Foreign Languages Press, 1965), 114.

49. Michael A. Lebowitz, *Contradictions of "Real Socialism": The Conductor and the Conducted* (New York: Monthly Review Press, 2012), 138. Note the discussion in chapters 6 and 8 respectively of the attack on the moral economy of the working class in "real socialism" and the examination of the characteristics of "Vanguard Marxism."

50. Carlos Tablada, *Che Guevara: Economics and Politics in the Transition to Socialism* (Sydney: Pathfinder, 1989), 92.

3. Transcending the Crisis of Socialist Economy

1. See, in particular, the discussion in *Contradictions of "Real Socialism"* about how the capacities of the working class were limited by the nature of productive relations.

2. See Michael A. Lebowitz, "Kornai and Socialist Laws of Motion," *Studies in Political Economy* 18 (Autumn 1985); and Lebowitz, *Contradictions of "Real Socialism."*

3. As I noted subsequently in *Contradictions of "Real Socialism"* with respect to the Soviet Union, "Labor shortages were by no means universal" (109). Population growth rates in Central Asian republics were twice the Soviet average and, given the location of new investment, there was substantial long-term unemployment in parts of the Soviet Union.

4. Interestingly, even where new machines have been introduced within a particular enterprise, the old and often obsolete machines often continue in use.

5. Lebowitz, "Kornai and Socialist Laws of Motion."

6. Since we have avoided any discussion of commodity production as such in our argument, we cannot look simply to the problem of commodity production, markets, etc., but must look deeper.

4. Contested Reproduction and the Contradictions of Socialism

1. As I argue in my Foreword to Gal Kirn, *Partizanski prelom in pro-tislovja trznega socializma v Jugoslaviji* (Partisan break and the

contradictions of market socialism in Yugoslavia) (Lubljana: Sophia, 2014), the Yugoslav experience with market-self-management in many respects is a lost history. Lost because placed on the Index of Forbidden Experience in the countries once within the Soviet sphere, lost because surgically severed through the lobotomies performed in the countries of the former Yugoslavia, and lost elsewhere because its ultimate result was failure. At this time when many who are turned off by capitalism (but reject as well the "real socialism" of the Soviet Union and its copies) look to production cooperatives as the answer to capitalism, knowledge of the history of Yugoslav market-self-management may reveal much about tendencies in a system-wide society based upon individual cooperatives.

2. Various websites including Russian-language ones cite the Northstar Compass (Toronto) for February 2000 as their source but the "confession" disappeared from there.

3. See the discussion in Lebowitz, *Contradictions of "Real Socialism,"* 135–37.

4. Branko Horvat, "Yugoslav Economic Policy in the Post-War Period: Problems, Ideas, Institutional Developments," *Surveys of National Economic Policy Issues and Policy Research, Supplement, American Economic Review* (June 1971): 76.

5. Charles Bettelheim, *Economic Calculation and Forms of Property: An Essay on the Transition between Capitalism and Socialism* (New York: Monthly Review Press, 1975), 74; Lebowitz, *Contradictions,* 102–6.

6. Karl Marx, *The Eighteenth Brumaire of Louis Bonaparte,* in Marx and Engels, *Collected Works,* vol. 11 (New York: International Publishers, 1979), 130–31.

7. Lebowitz, *Contradictions,* 127–28.

8. For references, see "Seven Difficult Questions," chap. 6 in Michael A. Lebowitz, *Build It Now: Socialism for the 21st Century* (New York: Monthly Review Press, 2006), 73–84.

9. See "Goodbye to Vanguard Marxism," chap. 8 in Lebowitz, *Contradictions.*

10. Carlos Tablada, *Che Guevara: Economics and Politics in the Transition to Socialism* (Sydney: Pathfinder, 1989), 92.

5. Proposing a Path to Socialism

1. An additional paper I prepared, "Year of Total Education," stressing, for example, education within worker-managed enterprises,

education through practice, and an educational television station, was expanded upon by El Troudi (subsequently Minister of Planning and currently Minister of Transport) to add political and ethical education, and this was an inspiration for the program *Moral y Luces* announced in 2007 by Chávez.

2. In the period before Chávez, managers of PDVSA, the state-owned oil company, succeeded in performing the magical feat of ensuring that revenues of the firm disappeared from Venezuela, and thus as state revenues, and appeared instead on the books of offshore refining, etc., subsidiaries.

3. In Venezuela, PDVSA was the obvious example of such a "statist" firm. Its revenue was critical for supporting, among other things, state programs such as the social missions.

4. I subsequently explored the incoherence and dysfunction characteristic of "real socialism" in *Contradictions of "Real Socialism": The Conductor and the Conducted* (Monthly Review Press: 2012). See also chapter 4 in this volume.

5. I confess that I had in mind particular ministers.

6. In 2006, Communal Councils, based upon 200–400 families in existing urban neighborhoods and 20–50 in the rural areas, became a major focus in the effort to build socialism for the twenty-first century in Venezuela. Their size permitted the general assembly rather than elected representatives to be the supreme decision-making body. This was important, I pointed out in 2007, because "those councils were envisioned as a basis not only for the transformation of people in the course of changing circumstances but also for productive activity which really is based upon communal needs and communal purposes. With Chávez's re-election in December 2006 on the explicit theme of building a new socialism, these new councils have been identified as the fundamental cell of Bolivarian socialism and the basis for a new state." Leaving no doubt as to his conception, Chávez proclaimed in 2007, "All power to the communal councils!" Michael A. Lebowitz, "Venezuela: A Good Example of the Bad Left of Latin America," *Monthly Review* (July–August 2007). See an initial discussion of the councils in Lebowitz, *Build It Now: Socialism for the 21st Century* (Monthly Review Press: 2006); a later consideration of the links of communal councils to workplaces and communes may be found in chapter 6, "Making a Path to Socialism," in Lebowitz, *The Socialist Alternative*, and in the discussion of the new state in chapter 10 in this volume. For the

place of Communal Councils in the concept of socialism for the twenty-first century, see Marta Harnecker, *A World to Build: New Paths toward Twenty-first Century Socialism* (New York: Monthly Review Press, 2015), chapter 7.

7. See the discussion of "socialist conditionality" and its tendency to generate capital strikes with the result (noted in the *Communist Manifesto*) that "the proletariat will see itself compelled to go always further" in Lebowitz, *The Socialist Alternative*, 135–37.

8. István Mészáros, *Beyond Capital: Toward a Theory of Transition* (New York: Monthly Review Press, 1995), 832.

9. Mészáros, 974–75, 837.

10. In *The Socialist Alternative*, I explore capitalism and socialism as organic systems, drawing upon this quotation from Marx in *The Poverty of Philosophy*,

11. Article 62 of the Bolivarian Constitution, discussed in Lebowitz, *Build It Now* and *The Socialist Alternative*, chap. 2, "The Production of People."

12. The idea of "profiles" and of the step-by-step emergence of full worker management was developed in the course of meetings in 2005 between the managers of CADAFE (the major state electrical firm at the time) and FETRAELEC (the electrical workers federation) where Marta Harnecker and I played the role of marriage counselors after a breakdown in the process of "co-management" within the firm. Both sides agreed to this proposal but after management consulted with the Ministry of Oil and Energy, all such discussions of worker management were ended, presumably because they were contrary to the policy of the ministry, whose minister, Rafael Ramirez, was also the president of PDVSA.

13. A few days earlier, I had incorporated much of the above discussion of socialism as an organic system into a talk (subsequently published in the April 2007 issue of *Monthly Review* as "New Wings for Socialism") at the launch of the Venezuelan edition of my *Build It Now*. But there was no mention of a socialist triangle there because that graphic image had yet to be invented by Chávez. Subsequently, I drew explicitly upon his concept of the socialist triangle as a way to represent socialism as an organic system, beginning with two books published in Venezuela in 2008: *El Camino al Desarrollo Humano: Capitalismo o Socialismo?* and *La logica del capital versus la logica del desarrollo humano*; and in "The Path to Human Development: Capitalism or Socialism?," *Monthly Review*

(February 2009). This was followed by *The Socialist Alternative: Real Human Development*, in which the socialist triangle served as the organizing theme, and by the discussion in chapter 6 in this volume.

14. Some examples of Chávez's discussion of the socialist triangle were incorporated in the video *Worker's Control: Theory and Experiences*, which was based on a conference on 26–27 October 2007 organized by the Program on Human Development and Practice of Centro Internacional Miranda. It is available online at http://www.socialistproject.ca/leftstreamed/ls26.php.

6. Socialism: The Goal, the Paths, and the Compass
1. I am indebted to comrades at the Socialist Project for this diagram.

7. What Makes the Working Class a Revolutionary Subject?
1. Karl Marx and Frederick Engels, *The German Ideology*, in Marx and Engels, *Collected Works*, vol. 5 (New York: International Publishers, 1976), 323. See also Lebowitz, *Beyond Capital*, "Class Struggle as Production," 179–84.

8. Three Perspectives on Democracy
1. Karl Marx, *Grundrisse* (New York: Vintage, 1973), 156–58. See also the discussion of capitalist society in chapter 1 in this volume.
2. Karl Marx, *Grundrisse*, 159.
3. Marx, *Capital*, vol. 1, 449.
4. See the "Overture: The Conductor and the Conducted," in Lebowitz, *Contradictions*, 21–27.
5. Ibid., 62–63.
6. See the discussion of the socialist dream in chapter 1 of this volume.
7. On the Bolivarian Constitution, see Lebowitz, *Build It Now: Socialism for the 21st Century*, 72, 89–90.
8. Álvaro García Linera, "A Message to the Left of Europe and the World," speech delivered to Fourth Congress of the Party of the European Left, December 14, 2013, Madrid, translated by Marie-Rose Ardiaca in *Transform!* Available at *Links International Journal of Socialist Renewal*, http://links.org.au/node/3712.

9. The Concept of "Fairness": Possibilities, Limitations, Possibilities
1. Karl Marx, *Capital*, vol. 1 (New York: Vintage, 1977), 772.
2. Michael A Lebowitz, *Build It Now: Socialism for the 21st Century*

(New York: Monthly Review Press, 2006), 109; Cleto A. Sojo, "Venezuela's Chávez Closes WSF with Call to Transcend Capitalism," Venezuelanalysis.com, January 31, 2005.

3. E. P. Thompson, "The Moral Economy of the English Crowd in the Eighteenth Century," *Past and Present* 50 (1971).

4. Li Jun, "Collective Action of Laid-off Workers and Its Implication on Political Stability: Evidences from Northeast China" (PhD diss., City University of Hong Kong, 2008), 34.

5. James C. Scott, *The Moral Economy of the Peasant: Rebellion and Subsistence in Southeast Asia* (New Haven: Yale University Press, 1976), 4–5, 7.

6. Jeffrey Kopstein, "Workers Resistance and the Demise of East Germany," http://libcom.org/history/workers-resistance-demise-east-germay-jeffrey-kopstein.

7. Thompson, "The Moral Economy of the English Crowd in the Eighteenth Century," 129.

8. Boris Kagarlitsky, "Interview," *Against the Current*, March 3, 1995. See "The Social Contract," chap. 2 in Lebowitz, *Contradictions*.

9. Kopstein, "Workers' Resistance and the Demise of East Germany."

10. Jun, "Collective Action of Laid-off Workers," 64.

11. Janos Kornai, *Growth, Shortage and Efficiency: A Macrodynamic Model of the Socialist Economy* (Berkeley: University of California Press, 1982), 4–5, 24–33, 47–48, 76; Janos Kornai, *Economics of Shortage* (Amsterdam: North Holland, 1980), chap. 21, 382. See also the discussion in Michael A. Lebowitz, "Kornai and Socialist Laws of Motion," *Studies in Political Economy* 18 (Autumn 1985).

12. Kornai, *Economics of Shortage*, 383, 509–10.

13. Ibid., 212.

14. Karl Marx, *New York Daily Tribune*, July 14, 1853, in Marx and Engels, *Collected Works*, vol. 12 (New York: International Publishers, 1979), 169; Karl Marx, *Value, Price and Profit*, in Marx and Engels, *Collected Works*, vol. 20 (New York: International Publishers, 1985), 148.

15. Lebowitz, *Contradictions*, chapter 5.

16. Thompson, "The Moral Economy of the English Crowd in the Eighteenth Century," 131.

17. Marx, *Value, Price and Profit*, 143–45.

18. Ibid., 148–49.

19. Marx, *Capital*, vol. 1, 675.

20. Ibid., 680.

21. Ibid., 680–82.
22. Karl Marx, *Capital*, vol. 3 (New York: Vintage, 1981), 983; Marx, *Capital*, vol. 1, 711, 713, 717, 732. See also "The Fallacy of Everyday Notions," in Michael A. Lebowitz, *Following Marx: Method, Critique and Crisis* (Chicago: Haymarket, 2009), esp. 12–15.
23. See "The Missing Book on Wage-Labor," in Michael A. Lebowitz, *Beyond Capital: Marx's Political Economy of the Working Class* (New York: Palgrave Macmillan, 2003), 27–50.
24. Marx, *Capital*, vol. 1, 729–30, 1064; Lebowitz, *Beyond Capital*, 172–74.
25. Lebowitz, *Beyond Capital*, 170–77.
26. See the summary and deepening of this discussion in Michael A. Lebowitz, "Trapped Inside a Box? Five Questions for Ben Fine," *Historical Materialism* 18/1 (2010).
27. Lebowitz, *Beyond Capital*, 87.
28. Marx to S. Meyer and A. Vogt, 9 April 1870, in Marx and Engels, *Collected Works*, vol. 43 (New York: International Publishers, 1988), 475.
29. Lebowitz, *Beyond Capital*, 99, 86–87.
30. Marx, *Capital*, vol. 1, 772.
31. Ibid., 284.
32. See Lebowitz, "Toward a Society of Associated Conductors," in *Contradictions*, 153–71.
33. Alena V. Ledeneva, *Russia's Economy of Favours: Blat, Networking and Informal Exchange* (Cambridge: Cambridge University Press, 1998), 140–42, 147.
34. See, in particular, chap. 5, "The Conductor and the Battle of Ideas in the Soviet Union," in Lebowitz, *Contradictions*.
35. Michael A. Lebowitz, *The Socialist Alternative: Real Human Development* (New York: Monthly Review Press, 2010). As indicated in chapter 5 of this volume, the initial discussion of these three elements occurred in a paper written for Chávez in December 2006 when I was directing a program on "Transformative Practice and Human Development" at Centro Internacional Miranda in Venezuela. See *Alo Presidente* # 263 and #264, http://www.alopresidente.gob.ve/.
36. The following discussion draws directly upon "Introduction: New Wings for Socialism," in Lebowitz, *Contradictions*, 17–19. See also Lebowitz, *The Socialist Alternative*.
37. See Lebowitz, *The Socialist Alternative*, chap. 1.
38. Karl Marx, "Theses on Feuerbach," in Marx and Engels, *Collected Works*, vol. 6 (New York: International Publishers, 1976), 4.

39. Lebowitz, *The Socialist Alternative*, 50–55, 154–59.
40. Ibid., 131.

10. The State and the Future of Socialism

1. Karl Marx and Frederick Engels, *Collected Works*, vol. 12 (New York: International Publishers, 1979), 169. See the discussion in Michael A. Lebowitz, *Beyond Capital: Marx's Political Economy of the Working Class*, 181–83.
2. Alain Badiou, *The Communist Hypothesis* (London: Verso, 2010), 21, 27.
3. Ibid., 17.
4. Karl Marx, *New York Daily Tribune*, 14 July 1853, in *Collected Works*, vol. 12, 169; Lebowitz, *Beyond Capital*, 182–83.
5. Michael A. Lebowitz, "Holloway's Scream," *Historical Materialism*, 13/4 (2005).
6. Karl Marx, *Capital*, vol. 1, 899.
7. Ibid., 899, emphasis added.
8. Ibid., 284.
9. Karl Marx and Frederick Engels, *The Communist Manifesto*, in Marx and Engels, *Collected Works*, vol. 6 (New York: International Publishers, 1976), 510.
10. Cleto A. Sojo, "Venezuela's Chávez Closes WSF with Call to Transcend Capitalism," Venezuelanalysis.com, January 31, 2005; Lebowitz, *Build It Now: Socialism for the 21st Century*, 109.
11. Marx, *Capital*, vol. 1, 772.
12. Marx, *Grundrisse*, 488, 541, 708. See the discussion of Marx's concept of the "rich human being" and the concept of human wealth in Lebowitz, *Beyond Capital*, 131; and in Lebowitz, *The Socialist Alternative*, 42–44.
13. Lebowitz, *Build It Now*, 53–60.
14. Karl Marx, *Theses on Feuerbach*, in Marx and Engels, *Collected Works*, vol. 6, 4.
15. Lebowitz, *Beyond Capital*, 180–83.
16. Marx, *Grundrisse*, 494.
17. Marx, *Capital*, vol. 1, 799.
18. Lebowitz, *The Socialist Alternative*, 50–55, 154–59.
19. Lebowitz, *Beyond Capital*, 192–96.
20. See the presence of this key link in the Bolivarian Constitution of Venezuela, which indicates that "the participation of the people in forming, carrying out and controlling the management of public affairs is the necessary way of achieving the involvement to ensure their complete development, both individual and collective." See

Lebowitz, *Build It Now*, 72, 89–90; and Lebowitz, *The Socialist Alternative*, 14–15.

21. Marx, *Capital*, vol. 1, 617–18.
22. Karl Marx, *Critique of the Gotha Programme*, in Marx and Engels, *Selected Works*, vol. 11 (Moscow: Foreign Languages Publishing House, 1962), 24.
23. Marx, *Capital*, vol. 1, 643, 614.
24. Marx, *Critique of the Gotha Programme*, 24.
25. Lebowitz, *Build It Now*, 66.
26. Marx, *Capital*, vol. 1, 447.
27. Lebowitz, *The Socialist Alternative*, 24–25.
28. Karl Marx, *The Poverty of Philosophy*, in Marx and Engels, *Collected Works*, vol. 6, 167; Marx, *Grundrisse*, 99–100.
29. I owe much to Marta Harnecker's work on participatory diagnosis and planning for my ideas on this process. See Marta Harnecker, "A Decentralised Participatory Planning Proposal Based on the Experiences of Brazil, Venezuela and the State of Kerala, India," *Links International Journal of Socialist Renewal*, 19 December 2014, available at http://p.feedblitz.com/t3.asp?/343373/2850429/4870515/links.org.au/node/4208; and Marta Harnecker, *De los consejos comunales a las comunas. construyendo el socialismo del siglo xxi*, 2009, available at http://www.rebelion.org.
30. As an example of the size of such units, in Venezuela communal councils represent 200 to 400 families in urban areas. See Lebowitz, *Build It Now*, 112.
31. It is assumed that workers in units of production within the commune live in different neighborhoods and thus direct representation of workers' councils begins at the commune level. While those who discuss these questions in the workplace are members of the communities and presumably have been involved in community discussions, in the workers' councils they explore the question as collective producers.
32. Part of that imbalance may be able to be resolved by going outside the national level, that is, by imports and exports—but we don't need to explore this here.
33. Marx, *Grundrisse*, 158, 171–72.
34. Karl Marx, "First Outline of *The Civil War in France*," in Karl Marx and Frederick Engels, *On the Paris Commune* (Moscow: Progress Publishers, 1971), 152–53; Marx, *Critique of the Gotha Programme*, 30. See the discussion of the "workers' state" in Lebowitz, *Beyond Capital*, 189–96.

35. John Holloway, *Change the World Without Taking Power* (London: Pluto Press, 2002), 12.
36. A slight paraphrase of Marx in the *Grundrisse*, 278.
37. Marx, *Critique of the Gotha Programme*, 23.
38. Marx, *Grundrisse*, 278.
39. Evgeny Preobrazhensky, *The New Economics* (Oxford: Clarendon Press, 1965), 77.
40. Lebowitz, *The Socialist Alternative*, 70–72, 78–81, 108–9.
41. Marx, *Capital*, vol. 1, 900, 931.
42. Marx, *Capital*, vol. 1, 874, 1083.
43. Donald A Filzer, ed., *The Crisis of Soviet Industrialization: Selected Essays of E. A. Preobrazhensky* (White Plains, NY: M. E. Sharpe, 1979), 173.
44. Preobrazhensky, *The New Economics*, 62–65. Note the analysis of interpenetration and deformation in "real socialism" in Lebowitz, *Contradictions*.
45. Marx, *Capital*, vol. 1, 899, 904, 905.
46. Lebowitz, *The Socialist Alternative*, 96–99.
47. Marx, *Capital*, vol. 1, 382, 899.
48. Marx and Engels, *The Communist Manifesto*, 504; Lebowitz, *Beyond Capital*, 189–93.
49. Karl Marx, *The Civil War in France* in *On the Paris Commune*, 68–69.
50. Lebowitz, *Beyond Capital*, 189–96.
51. Marx, *The Civil War in France*, 75.
52. Marx, "First Outline of *The Civil War in France*," 152–53; Marx, *Critique of the Gotha Programme*, 32.
53. Karl Marx, "Instructions for the Delegates of the Provisional General Council: The Different Questions," in *Minutes of the General Council of the First International, 1864–66* (Moscow: Foreign Languages Publishing House, n.d.), 346.
54. Marx, "First Outline of *The Civil War in France*," 152–54; Marx, *The Civil War in France*, 72–73.
55. Lebowitz, *The Socialist Alternative*, 154–59.
56. Holloway, *Change the World Without Taking Power*, 12–13, 17, 72–73, 91–94, 214.
57. Ibid., 76, 88–89.
58. Marta Harnecker, *Rebuilding the Left* (London: Zed Books, 2007), 86–88. See also Lebowitz, *The Socialist Alternative*, 60–63.
59. Holloway, *Change the World Without Taking Power*, 17.
60. Harnecker, *Rebuilding the Left*, 70–71, 83–91.
61. See the discussion of the interaction between state and party in Lebowitz, *Contradictions of "Real Socialism."*

62. Harnecker, *Rebuilding the Left*, 99.

11. End the System

1. Herman E. Daly and John B. Cobb Jr., *For the Common Good*, 21.
2. John Bellamy Foster and Fred Magdoff, "What Every Environmentalist Needs to Know about Capitalism," *Monthly Review* 61/10 (March 2010).
3. Intergovernmental Panel on Climate Change, "Severe, widespread, and irreversible impacts," http://climateandcapitalism.com/2014/11/02/severe-widespred-irreversible-impacts-globally/.
4. Daly and Cobb, *For the Common Good*, 59–60.
5. Ibid., 143, 145. In private correspondence, John Bellamy Foster has pointed out that, given there are numerous ecosystems within the biosphere, it is more accurate to speak of the latter as the total system and, even more so, to conceive of the total system as the ecological system (which I do in the text that follows).
6. Karl Marx, *Grundrisse*, 270.
7. Ibid., 408–10.
8. Marx, *Capital*, vol. 3, 754n.
9. See chapter 1.
10. Karl Marx, *Theories of Surplus Value, Part 2* (Moscow: Progress Publishers, 1968), 524–28.
11. Marx, *Capital*, vol. 3, 367.
12. See my critique of John Holloway in Lebowitz, "Holloway's Scream: Full of Sound and Fury," *Historical Materialism* 13/4 (2005).
13. Marx, *Capital*, vol. 1, 899. 935
14. See the extended discussion of this one-sidedness in Lebowitz (2003).
15. Lucien Sève, *Man in Marxist Theory and the Psychology of Personality* (Sussex: Harvester Press, 1978), 304.
16. Ibid., 313.
17. In Michael A. Lebowitz, "Human Development and Socialist Accounting," paper presented at the annual meeting of the World Association of Political Economy in Hanoi (May 2014), I pointed out that "a high capacity, that is a high potential for carrying out acts, doesn't mean that all of that capacity is necessarily utilised. There is the potential of unutilised capacity. And if particular capacities are unutilised, they tend to *atrophy*—even if they have been built up in the past."
18. Karl Marx, *New York Daily Tribune*, July 14, 1853, in Marx and Engels, *Collected Works*, vol. 12 (New York: International Publishers, 1979), 169; Karl Marx, *Value, Price and Profit*, in Marx and Engels,

Collected Works, vol. 20 (New York: International Publishers, 1985), 148.

19. See the discussion of "class struggle as production" in Lebowitz, *Beyond Capital*, 179–84.
20. Marx, *Grundrisse*, 285–87.
21. Marx, *Capital*, vol. 1, 1068.
22. Marx to S. Meyer and A. Vogt, 9 April 1870, in Marx and Engels, *Collected Works*, vol. 43 (New York: International Publishers, 1988), 475; Lebowitz (2003), 156–60.
23. Marx, *Capital*, vol. 1, 899, 904, 905.
24. Karl Marx and Friedrich Engels, *The Communist Manifesto*, in Marx and Engels, *Collected Works*, vol. 6 (New York: International Publishers, 1976), 504; see Lebowitz, *Beyond Capital*, chap. 10.
25. Lebowitz, *The Socialist Alternative*, 61–62.
26. Marina Sitrin, "Horizontalism," available at http://marinasitrin.com/?page_id=108.
27. See the discussion on distinction between common property and open-access property in chapter 1. Note that the size of such assemblies may make the reaching of consensus difficult, and this provides the space for decisive actions initiated by subgroups.
28. Thomas Nail, "Zapatism and the Global Origins of Occupy," *Journal for Cultural and Religious Theory* 12/3 (Spring 2013): 24–25.
29. John Holloway, *Change the World Without Taking Power* (London: Pluto Press, 2002), 20–21, 150, 157, 193.
30. Ibid., 158–59.
31. "John Holloway: Cracking Capitalism vs. the State Option," interview by Amador Fernandez-Savater in *ROAR Magazine*, 29 September 2014, http:/roarmag.org/2014/09/john-holloway.
32. Holloway, *Change the World Without Taking Power*, 199, 202–3.
33. Ibid., 12–13, 214.
34. Ibid., 20–21, 16–17.
35. Ibid., 155; Lebowitz, "Holloway's Scream."
36. Lebowitz, ibid.
37. Ibid.; Holloway, *Change the World Without Taking Power*, 215.
38. Lebowitz, *The Socialist Alternative*, 160–62.
39. Ibid., 131.
40. Karl Marx, *Economic Manuscripts of 1861-63*, in Marx and Engels, *Collected Works*, vol. 30 (New York: International Publishers, 1988), 191.
41. For a more extended discussion, see Michael A. Lebowitz, "Socialism for the Twenty-First Century and the Need for Socialist Globalization," in *International Critical Thought* 1/3 (September 2011).

42. Marx, *Capital*, vol. 1, 911, 949.
43. Lebowitz, *The Socialist Alternative*, 165.
44. See in particular the section "The Germs of Socialism," in Lebowitz, *Contradictions*, 155–60.
45. Marx, *Grundrisse*, 171–72.
46. Marx, *Capital*, vol. 1, 171.
47. See the discussion of Marx's *Critique of the Gotha Program* in chapter 2.
48. Karl Marx to Ludwig Feuerbach, 11 August 1844, in Marx and Engels, *Collected Works*, vol. 3, 354.
49. Lebowitz, *The Socialist Alternative*, 131.
50. Marx, *Grundrisse*, 158–59, 171–72; Lebowitz, *The Socialist Alternative*, 78–81.
51. Marx, *Capital*, vol. 1, 284.
52. Kavita Krishnan, *Outlook* (August 21, 2014), posted at *Links International Journal of Socialist Renewal*.
53. Lebowitz, "Holloway's Scream."

Index